# The Great Crusade

This is an original example of the D-Day message from General Eisenhower, supreme commander of the Allied forces in Europe, which was issued on June 5 and 6, 1944, to every single soldier, sailor and airmen of the Allied Expeditionary Force who would be participating in the D-Day landings and the supporting operations. The letter was presented on SHAEF headed paper and bore the plain signature of Dwight D Eisenhower with no rank indicated. Courtesy Tony Cooper (D-Day Spitfire pilot with 64 Sqn) from whose logbook this was copied.

Soldiers, Sailors and Airmen of the Allied Expeditionary Force!

You are about to embark upon the Great Crusade, toward which we have striven these many months. The eyes of the world are upon you. The hopes and prayers of liberty-loving people everywhere march with you. In company with our brave Allies and brothers-in-arms on other Fronts, you will bring about the destruction of the German war machine, the elimination of Nazi tyranny over the oppressed peoples of Europe, and security for ourselves in a free world.

Your task will not be an easy one. Your enemy is well trained, well equipped and battle-hardened. He will fight savagely.

But this is the year 1944 ! Much has happened since the Nazi triumphs of 1940-41. The United Nations have inflicted upon the Germans great defeats, in open battle, man-to-man. Our air offensive has seriously reduced their strength in the air and their capacity to wage war on the ground. Our Home Fronts have given us an overwhelming superiority in weapons and munitions of war, and placed at our disposal great reserves of trained fighting men. The tide has turned ! The free men of the world are marching together to Victory !

I have full confidence in your courage, devotion to duty and skill in battle. We will accept nothing less than full Victory !

Good Luck ! And let us all beseech the blessing of Almighty God upon this great and noble undertaking.

Dwight D Eisenhower

'Over the beaches of Normandy on D-Day'. In the early evening of D-Day, June 6, 1944, Operation Mallard took place to tow gliders carrying the remainder of the British 6th Airborne Division into Normandy. The glider-tugs and gliders were escorted on this daylight operation by fighter aircraft. The nearest Spitfire Mk.IXb, code letters 'AGM', is the personal aircraft of Group Captain AG 'Sailor' Malan, the commanding officer of No 145 (Free French) Wing, who flew his Spitfire as a section leader with 340 ('Ile de France') Squadron on D-Day, escorting the glider-towing 'heavies'. The Spitfire Mk.Vs, in the centre of the picture, are from 345 (Free French) Squadron. Short Stirling of 196 and 299 Squadrons can be seen below the fighter escort, plodding towards enemy territory towing their Horsa gliders. The North American Mustang IIIs (top right) are from 315 (Polish) Squadron which was also on Mallard escort. The Hawker Typhoons (lower right) are 'Bomphoons' of 197 Squadron on armed reconnaissance. Artwork: Gary Eason

# Contents

Author:
Clive Rowley MBE RAF (Retd)

Design:
Craig Lamb
Kriele Ltd
design_lamb@btinternet.com

Leanne Lawrence

Publishing director:
Dan Savage

Publisher:
Steve O'Hara

Production editor:
Dan Sharp

Marketing manager:
Charlotte Park

Commercial director:
Nigel Hole

Published by:
Mortons Media Group Ltd,
Media Centre,
Morton Way,
Horncastle,
Lincolnshire LN9 6JR.
Tel. 01507 529529

Printed by:
William Gibbons and Sons,
Wolverhampton

Credits:
Special thanks to the following for
their help and generosity in providng
assistance, artwork or images for this
publication:
RAF Battle of Britain Memorial Flight
Jon Bleasdale
Tim Callaway
Tony Cooper
John Dibbs
Gary Eason
Martin Johnston
Len Krenzler
Wiek Luijken
Robert Taylor
Adam Tooby
Spencer Trickett

ISBN: 978-1-911703-41-9

# Introduction

## From the author:
## Squadron Leader Clive Rowley MBE RAF (Retd)

I have been fascinated by the D-Day story since my father took me to see the film The Longest Day at the cinema when I was 11 years old. At that age I was at once enthralled and shocked by the events portrayed on the big screen and totally in awe of the courage and heroism of those who carried the fight to the enemy.

Having subsequently served for 36 years as a fighter pilot in the Royal Air Force, my interest, perhaps not surprisingly, became orientated towards the RAF's involvement in the war and in the D-Day invasion. I have never lost sight, though, of the fact that where D-Day was concerned, the air element was only a part of an all-arms campaign of almost unbelievable scale that was undoubtedly one of the greatest military feats of all time.

My 11 years flying with the RAF Battle of Britain Memorial Flight (BBMF), including my time as the officer commanding the flight, gave me the privileged opportunity to fly two actual D-Day veteran Spitfires, the

story of one of which is included in these pages. In 2004, for the 60th anniversary commemorations of D-Day, I was privileged to fly that Spitfire as part of the BBMF formation which conducted a number of flypasts over commemorative ceremonies in Normandy, including the main one on June 6, with no fewer than 17 heads of state and assorted members of European royalty, including our own Queen, watching on the ground. This was an occasion I will never forget and heightened my interest in the D-Day events of 1944.

Since joining the BBMF in 1996 I have also had the privilege of meeting many wartime veterans, some of whom were involved in the operations surrounding D-Day, of hearing their stories first hand and in some cases getting to know them well.

Their understated accounts and innate modesty serve only to highlight the sheer courage and outright heroism of those who took part, without which the war would not have been won. To my knowledge there has never been a publication which focusses

specifically on the RAF involvement in the build-up to D-Day, the invasion and the subsequent Battle of Normandy. Although the D-Day story has been well covered in the past, most accounts centre, not surprisingly, on the ground elements

RAF BBMF D-Day 60th commemorative flypast in 2004 over the Normandy beaches – the author was flying one of the Spitfires.
Crown copyright

A RAF BBMF formation consisting of the C-47 Dakota, Lancaster and two D-Day Spitfires overflies Arromanches for the D-Day 60th anniversary commemorations on June 6, 2004 – the author was flying one of the Spitfires. Crown copyright

(which, of course, were fundamental to the whole thing). The few air power related D-Day narratives, which have been published, have covered the subject as an Allied campaign, which is exactly what it was. However, the natural bias towards the surface elements and also towards the American forces participating in the Allied effort can lead to the vital and not insignificant part played by the RAF being somewhat overlooked.

I can't help wondering, whether the real D-Day story has been done a disservice by some books and films which have focussed too much on the American part and rather downplayed the British, Commonwealth and other occupied nations' involvement in the great event. Would I be wrong to suggest that some might be surprised to learn of the scale and importance of the involvement of the other Allies and of the RAF in the success of the D-Day operations?

With all this in mind, I have set out to provide, in the space available, an overview of the RAF's operations in the build-up to D-Day (roughly from the beginning of April 1944), the invasion operations from June 6, and the subsequent Battle of Normandy up to the end of August, accepting that the RAF part is a relatively 'small cog in a much larger machine'. The scale of even just the RAF operations in this period was immense and there simply is not the space to cover it all. I have not been able, for example, to cover the RAF Air Sea Rescue organisation's

part (it rescued 163 aircrew and 60 other personnel on D-Day alone and during June 1944 a total of 355 people were saved by the RAF ASR aircraft and boats). Neither could I include the part played by RAF personnel on the surface during the invasion, such as the RAF beach and balloon squadrons, the fighter control radar operators on landing craft off the beaches, the RAF Servicing Commandos and the RAF Regiment gunners. The first of these RAF men landed on the Normandy invasion beaches on the afternoon of D-Day, some of them on Omaha beach with the Americans.

The content of this publication is not set out chronologically. Rather, it is divided by the different roles of the RAF aircraft and crews, such as fighters and fighter-bombers, heavy bombers, medium bombers, and so on. Each section has a short 'documentary' introduction, with the essential details, to set a framework for what follows and to introduce the aircraft types involved. There are then separate accounts of individual actions or operations by pilots and crews flying in that role, some of them in the individuals' own words.

There is a tendency for the D-Day story to be narrated with a strategic orientation, focusing on the parts played by the great military men who planned and commanded the operations. But the success of the endeavour, and the ultimate liberation of Europe, is just as much the story of the many individuals who fought their own

small battles, in many cases without official recognition or without becoming household names. By telling some of their stories I hope to paint a picture of what it was like to be involved in this stage of the war with the RAF, and to commemorate the courage of those who did so.

For them, it seems, this was an event not to be missed, despite the obvious risks to life and limb. It is difficult for us, today, to put ourselves in their shoes, with four long years of war and Nazi domination of Europe behind them, with their sense of duty, their patriotism, their acceptance of risks and losses that would seem intolerable today and, frankly, with little alternative.

Now was the chance to strike back, to liberate Europe from the tyranny of the Nazis. To quote Tony Cooper, a D-Day Spitfire pilot whose story features in this publication and who I was proud to call my friend: "We had become used to hearing and accepting bad news, setbacks and sometimes personal losses, but now, at last, we were fighting back and this time we knew that we were going to win!"

I hope that readers may find this publication a thought-provoking and fitting commemoration of the 80th anniversary of D-Day and the RAF's part in it. Most importantly, I hope that it may serve as a tribute to the men and women of the RAF who flew and fought in these operations and to their courage, tenacity and sheer heroism. ■

# D-Day

## The greatest military operation of all time

On Tuesday, June 6, 1944, a date known to most as D-Day, a mighty armada crossed the sea from England to France and cracked the Nazi's four year long grip on Western Europe. On this day in history the greatest amphibious operation displayed its awesome power in a feat of arms that led to the liberation of Northern France by August 1944 and to the defeat of Nazi Germany the following spring. The Normandy landings were the beginning of the end of the war in Europe.

In military terminology 'D-Day' is the code word used for the day that an attack or operation is initiated, with H-Hour being the start time. It had been used in connection with other operations before the Normandy invasion and has been used since; the landings at San Carlos during the Falklands

War in 1982 being an example. For most people though, the codeword D-Day is synonymous with the Allied invasion of Normandy on June 6, 1944.

Operation Overlord, as it was named, was the largest air, land, and sea operation ever undertaken. Overlord was the name assigned to the establishment of a large-scale force on the Continent, an operation that began on June 6, 1944, and continued until the Allied forces crossed the River Seine on August 19. The assault phase of the operation – the seaborne invasion, the landings and the gaining of a secure foothold – which began on D-Day and ended on June 30, was codenamed Operation Neptune. Numerous other operations were part of the overall plan, such as Operations Tonga, Detroit and Chicago for the landing of the British 6th Airborne and the American 82nd and 101st Airborne Divisions.

Years of meticulous planning and preparation, the painstaking build-up of forces and their intensive training came to fruition on June 6, 1944. The assault had been planned to take place on June 5, but due to poor weather General Dwight Eisenhower, the Supreme Allied Commander, decided at the last moment to delay the invasion by 24 hours.

In the months leading up to D-Day the Allied forces conducted an extensive deception operation aimed at misleading the Germans with respect to the exact date and place of the invasion. This was so successful that the invasion actually took the German military high command completely by surprise, even though they knew it was coming, that it was only a question of time and was bound to happen soon. Low tides and bad weather – combined with the Allied deception plans – had convinced the Germans that an attack was unlikely at this time and they had not been able to second-guess the planned location for the landings either.

As British bombers began to pummel Normandy's coastal defences on the night of June 5-6, and the invasion armada was making its way slowly across the English Channel, Generalfeldmarschall Erwin Rommel, the German general responsible for the defence of the French coast against the long anticipated Allied invasion, was taking a break in Germany, celebrating his wife's birthday. He was convinced that there was no better time to be absent from his duties.

It is hard to conceive the epic scope of this decisive battle that foreshadowed the end of Hitler's plan for Nazi domination. Quite apart from the military combat elements of the operation, Overlord required a logistics plan that could ensure that a vast amount of men and equipment could be landed by the end of D-Day.

On the eve of the landings more than 1000 Allied bombers pounded the German coastal artillery positions and a sophisticated RAF operation jammed and deceived the enemy radars. As the naval armada neared the coast, the beach defences in Normandy were pulverised by naval gunfire from 200 warships. Before the bombers made their presence felt, some 23,000 Allied airborne troops were dropped into the area behind the beach head by almost 2000 transport aircraft and the gliders they towed, with the task of disrupting the organisation of German land forces and seizing a variety of tactical targets such as bridges and crossroads, thereby

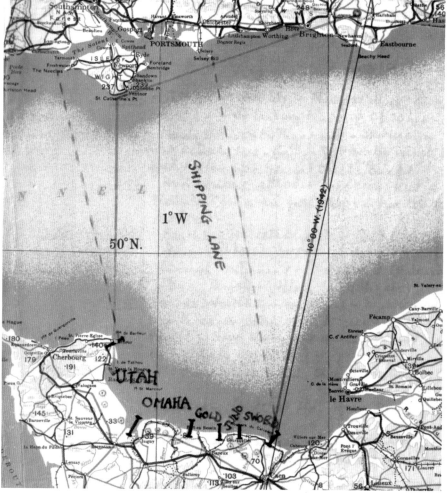

Map from the logbook of D-Day RAF Spitfire pilot Tony Cooper, showing the invasion beaches with their code names in his own writing. Courtesy Tony Cooper

Allied troops wading ashore in Normandy on D-Day.

protecting the flanks of the invasion. During D-Day itself, between the first landings at 6.30am British Double Summer Time (GMT +2) and midnight, another 132,000 American, British and Canadian troops were landed by sea on five beaches, code named (from west to east) Utah, Omaha, Gold, Juno and Sword, along a 50 mile stretch of the heavily fortified Normandy coast.

The Americans landed 59,000 men on the beaches at Utah and Omaha, while 73,000 British and Canadian troops landed on Sword, Juno and Gold beaches. These men were transported and supported by more than 5000 ships, crewed by almost 196,000 sailors from the Allied and Merchant Navies.

When D-Day was over, thousands of men had died. British Prime Minister Winston Churchill had said to his wife, Clementine: "Do you realise that by the time you wake up in the morning 20,000 men may have been killed?" He was not far wrong if the casualties on both sides are taken into account.

Although sources vary somewhat, the Allies lost around 10,500 men killed, wounded, missing in action or taken prisoner on June 6, 1944, and the Germans had a similar number of casualties. Yet somehow, partly due to the extensive planning and preparation and mostly to the sheer courage, fighting spirit and sacrifice of the Allied forces, 'Fortress Europe' had been breached. The Allies had gained a foothold in France, the Germans were forced back from the beaches and the advance across Europe to defeat Hitler had begun.

By June 11, D-Day +5, 326,547 troops, 54,186 vehicles and 104,428 tons of supplies had been landed on the beaches to support the advance inland with yet more continuing to arrive.

The sheer valour of those men who landed in enemy territory and into the unknown on D-Day, June 6, 1944, should never be belittled. Many of them feared the worst, but willingly did their duty anyway and, in many cases, especially among those in the first waves, they did not survive the slaughter on the invasion beaches.

Many more of those who somehow made it ashore unscathed were to pay the ultimate price in the battles that followed. ■

D-Day: the Allied armada photographed from an RAF aircraft on June 6, 1944.

*"For four long years, much of Europe had been under a terrible shadow. Free nations had fallen... Europe was enslaved, and the world prayed for its rescue. Here in Normandy the rescue began. Here the Allies stood and fought against tyranny in a giant undertaking unparalleled in human history."*

(President Ronald Reagan during a speech on the 40th anniversary of D-Day in 1984).

# D-Day air power
## And the RAF's contribution

**M**ost D-Day accounts rightly and understandably focus on the landings and the action on the ground. However, it is widely accepted that the invasion and the subsequent Battle of Normandy would not have been successful without the air supremacy fought for and achieved by the Allied air armada that ruled the skies over northern France. In fact, the part played by air power in the success of the operation was crucial, as the senior Allied commanders, including General Bernard Montgomery, recognised.

This publication aims to separate and to focus on the specific involvement of the Royal Air Force in this greatest-ever military operation, while accepting and acknowledging the fact that it was, indeed, only a part of a combined effort.

Essential to maintaining this perspective is an understanding of the background, the context and framework within which these RAF operations occurred. It is also important to state at the outset that this 'air power won the day' focus is not intended in any way to detract from the courage, resilience and capabilities of the Allied soldiers and sailors on the surface, without which victory could not have been achieved.

## COMBINED OPERATIONS

By 1944, in the European theatre of war, all operations were 'combined'. Firstly, there was the combination of the Allies. The extent of integration and co-operation

General Bernard Montgomery, Land Forces Commander, Operation Overlord.

between the British and Americans at all significant command levels was remarkable, beginning at the top, the Supreme Headquarters Allied Expeditionary Forces (SHAEF). Air operations at lower levels also displayed this combined quality and the Tactical Air Forces in particular mingled their efforts, adopted each other's methods and jargon and shared each other's targets.

The RAF of 1944 included the air forces of several other commonwealth and enemy-occupied nations, subsumed within it. On D-Day the Allied nations represented in the air included: Australia, which provided 11,000 participating aircrew; Belgium, with two Spitfire squadrons; Canada, which committed 39 strategic and tactical squadrons; Czechoslovakia with three squadrons of Spitfires plus a Coastal Command Liberator squadron.

French aircrew operated four Spitfire squadrons and two squadrons of Boston medium bombers; the Netherlands had a squadron of Spitfires and one of Mitchells; New Zealand, which had 11,000 men serving with the RAF and provided four tactical squadrons plus two Coastal Command squadrons; Norway with two Spitfire squadrons and Poland with nine tactical squadrons of fighters and Mosquitos. Individual airmen from several other countries also flew with the RAF on D-Day (the full RAF order of battle on D-Day can be found on pages 15-18).

Combined between Allies, the Overlord enterprise was also, of course, combined between the services; it was in fact the most spectacular of all examples of the inter-service co-operation which some had been preaching ardently for years. Air Chief Marshal Sir Arthur Tedder, the Commander-in-Chief Air and Deputy Supreme Allied Commander SHAEF, was one of the great exponents of combined operations, saying: "I do not myself believe that any modern war can be won either at sea or on the land alone or in the air alone... in other words, war has changed to three dimensional."

There are very many examples of this inter-service 'jointery' in the operations before, during and after D-Day. For example, RAF pilots spotted for naval artillery; Army pilots flew Taylorcraft Auster Air Observation Posts (AOP) in nominally RAF squadrons to provide artillery spotting for the land forces; gliders flown by Army glider pilots were towed and released by RAF transports, which also, of course, dropped Army paratroopers; and Royal Observer Corps aircraft recognition

Air Chief Marshal Sir Arthur Tedder. Commander-in-Chief Air and Deputy Supreme Commander SHAEF.

experts were drafted on to Merchant Navy vessels to help in avoiding incidents of friendly fire.

As well as being inter-allies and inter-services, the RAF operations were also inter-command. It was, quite simply, no longer possible for RAF commands to operate as independently or with such defined roles as they had done earlier in the war. By 1944 it was clear that bombing could be carried out not only by dedicated bombers but by fighter aircraft too.

Fighters could carry bombs and could use cannons and rockets against ground targets, and they could carry out reconnaissance as well as being employed in air combat.

The most startling evidence of the new crossover of roles between and within commands was the scarcely credible disappearance of the name Fighter Command in November 1943. It had become apparent that Fighter Command would have to provide both air cover and tactical support for Overlord, while still remaining responsible for defending the homeland.

It was therefore decided to split Fighter Command into the old (pre-1936) Air Defence of Great Britain (ADGB) and the new Second Tactical Air Force (2 TAF). This was a relatively short-lived experiment and the name Fighter Command returned to life in October 1944 as the war entered its final phase.

Officers of the RAF, the Royal Navy and the British Army discuss plans on the bridge of a Landing Craft Tank (LCT) en route to Normandy, demonstrating the combined nature of Operation Overlord.

## THE ALLIED TACTICAL AIR FORCES

As Operation Overlord embarked upon its preparatory phase, tactical air power increasingly came into play. Two great tactical air forces were formed to support the ground forces in the invasion, the USAAF's Ninth Air Force and the RAF's Second Tactical Air Force. Both were under the overall command of RAF Air Chief Marshal Sir Trafford Leigh-Mallory.

The RAF's Second Tactical Air Force (2 TAF) had grown out of initiatives in mid-1943 to structure a composite group to support the invasion of Europe. In January 1944, Air Marshal Sir Arthur Coningham took command of 2 TAF, and two months later he assumed the additional duties of commander of the Advanced Allied Expeditionary Air Force (AAEAF).

By D-Day 2 TAF consisted of four RAF Groups: 2 Group, 83 Group, 84 Group and 85 Group. Of these, 2, 83 and 84 Groups were readily available for the air-land battle in Normandy, while 85 Group was under the temporary operational control of 11 Group. ADGB. 2 Group consisted of four wings of Boston, Mitchell and Mosquito light and medium bombers. 83 Group consisted of a reconnaissance wing and some light aircraft used for artillery spotting, one Mustang wing, four Spitfire wings and four Typhoon wings. 84 Group consisted of one Mustang wing, five Spitfire wings and three Typhoon wings as well as recce and spotting aircraft.

As the campaign progressed, 2 TAF's subordinate units directly supported units of the 21st Army Group. The British Second Army relied upon 83 Group while 84 Group supported the First Canadian Army. In total, including the USAAF elements, the tactical air forces had 2434 fighters and fighter-bombers, together with around 700 light and medium bombers, available for the Normandy campaign.

## ALLIED AIR EFFORT IN THE BUILD-UP TO D-DAY

These forces were used to strike against the Germans from the air during the preparatory campaign from the end of 1943 up to D-Day. The immense scope and the resounding effects of this air battle are less well known than some other Second World War campaigns; but its success, at significant human cost, and its importance to the outcome of the invasion, cannot be overstated.

Air Chief Marshal Sir Trafford Leigh-Mallory stated: "If it had not been for the air attacks by bombers, fighter-bombers and fighters, delivered before D-Day and immediately afterwards, it is my view that the Army would have had double, if not three times the amount of resistance which they have in fact encountered. As it is, the Germans in front of them are short of petrol and ammunition and are in a generally poor state. This is due to air attack."

Spitfire Mk.IX of 443 Squadron (RCAF) 2 TAF.

This series of attacks began during December 1943 with the steady destruction of German 'V'-weapon storage and launching sites to prevent the weapons being used against the Allied forces massing in the south of England. There followed an expansion in specific types of operations over France, including a very large number of sorties to drop supplies to the Resistance. The aim of this concerted effort was to build up the fighting effectiveness of the Resistance forces in all occupied territories and to thereby cause the maximum disruption to the German command and communications structure.

The Allied air campaign for the invasion of Europe consisted of three phases. First, Allied fighters would attempt to destroy the Luftwaffe. The second phase called for isolating the battlefield by interdicting road and rail networks. Once the invasion began, Allied air forces would concentrate on battlefield interdiction and close air support.

USAAF A-20 Havocs (known as Bostons in RAF service) bombing a target in Normandy.

## AIR SUPREMACY

The outstanding feature of D-Day and the whole of the remainder of the war in the West, the value of which cannot be overstated, was the Allied air supremacy which existed, at least by day.

Allied air superiority happened suddenly and rather unexpectedly in the early months of 1944 and the German Luftwaffe was effectively destroyed between January and June 1944. According to German sources, 2262 German fighter pilots died during that time including some of the most experienced and best commanders.

During the so-called 'Big Week' in February 1944, the American air forces targeted the German aircraft industry for special treatment and, while production continued, the Luftwaffe fighter force took staggering losses. In March 1944, fully 56%

of the available German fighters were lost, 43% were lost in April (as the bomber effort switched to Germany's petroleum production) and 50% in May, a month in which no less than 25% of Germany's total fighter pilot force (which averaged 2283 at any one time during this period) perished. This Allied air campaign was staggeringly successful and devastating to the Germans.

By June 1944, the months of concentrated air warfare had given the Allies not only air superiority but air supremacy as well. This meant that Allied fighters, fighter-bombers and medium and heavy bombers could operate in daylight virtually without interference from the Luftwaffe and had only to contend with anti-aircraft flak, which could still, however, be intense and extremely dangerous. The fighters and fighter-bombers were able to roam over the occupied territories bombing, strafing and rocketing anything that moved

and that could be deemed hostile. It is a relatively well-known fact that only a single flight of two Luftwaffe fighters made an appearance over the invasion beaches on D-Day itself – proof indeed of the success of the air superiority campaign undertaken prior to the landings.

## AIR INTERDICTION

At D-Day minus 60 days, the Allied air forces began their interdiction attacks against rail targets and marshalling yards; these attacks increased in ferocity and tempo up to the eve of the invasion itself and were accompanied by strategic bomber raids against the same targets.

Raids against bridges, railway marshalling yards and major crossroads were carried out by medium bomber forces; and, later, the strategic heavy bombers of both the USAAF and RAF were tasked to continue these attacks to isolate the Normandy area. As part of the transportation plan fighter-bombers attacked pinpoint targets, such as locomotives, rolling stock and bridges, as well as military vehicles on the roads.

The bridge campaign, which aimed at isolating the battlefield by destroying bridges on the River Seine below Paris and bridges on the Loire below Orleans, began on D-Day minus 46. Here, fighter-bombers proved more efficient than medium or heavy bombers. Their agility enabled them to make pinpoint dive-bombing attacks in a way that the larger bombers, committed to horizontal bombing runs, could not. The fighter-bombers also had the speed, firepower, and manoeuvrability to evade and even to dominate the Luftwaffe, although enemy anti-aircraft fire and, occasionally, enemy fighters did cause losses against the attacking Allied fighter-bombers.

By D-Day minus 21, the Allied air forces medium bombers and fighter-bombers were attacking German airfields within a radius of 130 miles of the battle area and these operations continued up to the assault on the beachhead.

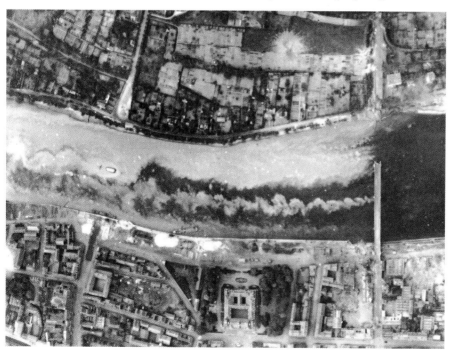

Aerial reconnaissance photograph of destroyed road bridges across the Seine at Elbeuf taken on June 8, 1944

RAF airfield engineers constructing an advanced landing ground airfield in Normandy, laying metal wire mesh matting.

Next on the list of priorities was the interdiction of rail and road traffic and these communications targets were followed by attacks against radar and coastal defence sites. Individual buildings housing military and Gestapo headquarters were attacked and radar stations were destroyed or put out of use. All six of the long range radar stations south of Boulogne were destroyed before D-Day and 15 others rendered unserviceable.

The requirement to keep the planned invasion sites secret and to encourage the Germans to devote their attention to the region of the Pas-de-Calais complicated the air campaign. To maintain the element of surprise a greater number of targets were attacked north and east of the Seine, and for every mission flown over Normandy two were flown over the Pas-de-Calais. Rocket-armed Royal Air Force Hawker Typhoon fighter-bombers of the Second Tactical Air Force (2 TAF) attacked two radar installations outside the planned assault area for every one they attacked within it.

Finally, in the build-up to the invasion itself, two more elements of air power came into play. Fighter sweeps and standing air patrols were flown to prevent any German air activity over the channel ports and invasion area, creating an impenetrable air superiority 'bubble'.

## THE HUMAN COST OF THE PRE-INVASION AIR CAMPAIGN

From the beginning of April 1944, in the lead-up to D-Day, 195,200 sorties were flown by Allied aircraft, of which the RAF flew 71,800, excluding the work of Coastal Command. During this period the RAF dropped 94,200 tons of bombs to the USAAF's 101,200 tons. The Allies lost a total

of 1953 aircraft in just over nine weeks, of which 1251 were USAAF and 702 were RAF.

In human terms the total loss was some 12,000 officers and men and this was before the great Allied armada ever sighted the shores of Normandy. This was an immense effort and a great human cost, which has to be weighed into the total cost of the D-Day invasion. Without the efforts and sacrifices of these airmen, Operation Overlord may not have succeeded and certainly there would have been many more casualties on the ground both during the landings and the subsequent Battle of Normandy.

## ALLIED AIR OPERATIONS ON D-DAY

The air plan for D-Day was the most complex ever devised, involving thousands of Allied aircraft, all with specific tasks, each unit needing to be de-conflicted with the others.

On the night of June 5-6, 1944, the eve of D-Day, a huge airborne armada of some 1900 transport aircraft and converted heavy bombers towed and released gliders and dropped paratroopers behind and on the flanks of the invasion beaches. By midnight on June 5, some 1333 heavy bombers had dropped 5316 tons of bombs on radar stations and the 10 most important German gun batteries in the assault area. Meanwhile sophisticated jamming and spoof operations by RAF heavy bombers continued to sow confusion as to where the invasion fleet was heading.

During the D-Day assault itself a total of 171 squadrons of USAAF and RAF fighters undertook a variety of tasks in support of the invasion. Fifteen squadrons provided shipping cover, 54 provided beach cover, 33

undertook bomber escort and offensive fighter sweeps, 33 struck at targets inland from the landing area and 36 provided direct air support to invading forces.

Although the commanders at SHAEF knew they had air supremacy (otherwise the invasion would not have gone ahead) they expected a major German air reaction similar to that encountered over Dieppe during Operation Jubilee in 1942. The directive issued to Allied fighter forces by SHAEF stated that: "The intention of the British and American fighter forces is to attain and maintain an air situation which will assure freedom of action for our forces without effective interference by the German air force, and to render maximum air protection to the land and naval forces in the common object of assaulting, securing and developing the bridgehead."

The scale of Allied air operations on D-Day was so vast that sources vary considerably over the exact details, numbers and statistics. The Allied air forces had at their disposal over 11,500 aircraft of all types, of which some 5500 belonged to the RAF and its associated air forces.

Despite poor flying weather on June 6, 1944, with a cloud base of around 2000ft over the invasion beaches in the morning, the Allies flew an astonishing 14,674 sorties during the 24 hours of D-Day itself; the RAF's contribution to this staggering total was 5656 sorties. In comparison, the depleted German Luftwaffe flew a paltry 319 sorties that day. An operation of this scale was bound to suffer losses and 113 Allied aircraft failed to return from their missions, mostly the victims of flak, not all of it fired by the Germans.

# THE BATTLE OF NORMANDY

D-Day was only the beginning of the end. The fiercely fought Battle of Normandy followed immediately on from the landings, lasting officially until September 1, 1944. Enemy air activity continued to be limited in the days immediately after D-Day, but it gradually increased and more reports of air combat came in from the battle areas.

After June 10, Allied fighter squadrons were able to land at Advanced Landing Grounds (ALGs) in Normandy to re-arm and refuel. Six days later squadrons began operating permanently from these hastily constructed forward airfields, which endowed the fighter aircraft with much quicker reaction times and longer time on task.

However, the forward strips were often perilously close to enemy positions and came under frequent shelling. In one case, RAF Hawker Typhoons operating from a forward strip attacked German tanks and fortifications a mere 1000 yards away from the runway. In addition, the peculiar thick dust of Normandy played havoc with the engines of the Spitfires and Typhoons until special air filters were fitted to the aircraft. Meanwhile, the engineers had to water down the runway surfaces.

Ground attack and close air support now became the norm for the fighter squadrons in Normandy, although they retained their air-to-air capabilities. Between D-Day and the end of June 1944 the Allied air forces carried out 99,000 sorties over France. The total number of Allied aircraft lost during this month, including the heavy bombers of the USAAF 8th Air Force and RAF Bomber Command (which alone lost 300 bombers in June 1944, many of them over France) was around 1200. During the same period the Luftwaffe flew 13,315 sorties and lost 646 fighters, fighter-bombers and medium bombers in France. The Allies lost about 10% of their strength in aircraft in the month, while the Luftwaffe lost 50%.

As the Battle of Normandy raged, the concepts, practice and effectiveness of Allied close air support evolved into a triumphant fusion of air power with ground assaults by infantry, tanks and artillery.

A battalion commander in a tank regiment reported: "Our air cover has been excellent and has helped us out of many tight spots. … they knocked out eight German Mark V Panther and Mark VI Tiger tanks that were giving us a great deal of trouble … they are on call by any unit down to a platoon, requested through company and battalion, and given the location of the target. Then the ASPO (Air Support Party Officer) contacts the air cover and gets a strike within a matter of minutes. I have seen the air strike within three minutes after the call was made. We like to know the air is there. We want it all the time."

By the end of the Normandy campaign, all the elements, procedures and relationships for the remainder of the war in Western Europe were in place, with forward air controllers (occasionally airborne controllers), radar direction of strikes, 'on-call' or 'cab rank' fighter-bombers and true close air support, to name just a few facets.

Normandy was neither the victory of a single branch of arms, nor the victory of a single nation. Instead, it was and still is the classic example of complex combined arms, multi-service and coalition warfare. It was a true air-land battle.

## THE RAF CONTRIBUTION

During the whole period of the Battle of Normandy, between June 6 and August 31, 1944, the RAF flew 224,889 sorties in Europe and lost 2036 aircraft (983 of which were from Bomber Command and 224 from Coastal Command). In the same period 2 TAF lost 1035 aircrew killed or missing in action. Clearly, this was an extremely dangerous time to be flying with the RAF. In the pages that follow, the lead-up to D-Day, the invasion and the subsequent Battle of Normandy are explored in detail from the RAF perspective. Individual accounts and stories of particular parts of the action aim to give the reader a feel for what it was actually like to be involved in this great campaign with the RAF in 1944.

Sherman tanks moving up to Tilly-sue-Seulles on June 17 pass a crashed Spitfire of 412 Squadron 'bellied in' by the road. Pilot Officer D R Jamieson's MJ316 'VZ-S' suffered a glycol leak and engine overheating on June 10 and he put the aircraft down in Allied-held territory. Many losses, such as this one, had nothing to do with enemy action.

# D-Day RAF units and aircraft (the air order of battle)

## RAF 2ND TACTICAL AIR FORCE

**2 Group**
**137 Wing:**
88, 342(Fr) Sqns, Hartford Bridge, Hants, Boston IIIA
226 Sqn, Hartford Bridge, Hants, Mitchell II

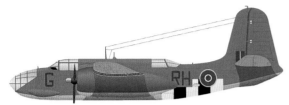

**138 Wing:**
107, 305(Pol), 613 Sqns Lasham, Hants, Mosquito VI

**139 Wing:**
98, 180, 320(Dutch), Sqns Dunsfold, Surrey, Mitchell II

**140 Wing:**
21, 464(RAAF), 487(RNZAF) Sqns, Gravesend, Kent, Mosquito VI

**83 Group**

**39 (RCAF) Reconnaissance Wing:**
400(RCAF) Sqn, Odiham, Hants, Spitfire XI
168, 414(RCAF), 430(RCAF) Sqns, Odiham, Hants, Mustang I

**121 Wing:**
174, 175, 245 Sqns, Holmsley South, Hants, Typhoon IB

**122 Wing:**
19, 65, 122 Sqns, Funtington, Sussex, Mustang III

**124 Wing:**
181, 182, 247 Sqns, Hurn, Hants, Typhoon IB

**125 Wing:**
132, 453(RAAF), 602 Sqns, Ford, Sussex, Spitfire IX

**126 Wing:**
401(RCAF), 411(RCAF), 412(RCAF) Sqns, Tangmere, Sussex, Spitfire IX

**127 Wing:**
403(RCAF), 416(RCAF), 421(RCAF) Sqns, Tangmere, Sussex, Spitfire IX

**129 Wing:**
184 Sqn, West Hampnett, Sussex, Typhoon IB

**143 Wing:**
438(RCAF), 439(RCAF), 440(RCAF) Sqns, Hurn, Hants, Typhoon IB

**144 Wing:**
441(RCAF), 442(RCAF), 443(RCAF) Sqns, Ford, Sussex, Spitfire IX

**Air Observation Posts:**
652 Sqn, Cobham, Surrey Auster IV
653 Sqn, Penshurst, Kent Auster IV
658 Sqn, Collyweston, Northants Auster IV
659 Sqn, East Grinstead, Sussex Auster IV
662 Sqn, Westley, Suffolk Auster IV

**84 Group**

**35 Reconnaissance Wing:**
2, 268 Sqns, Gatwick, Sussex, Mustang IA
4 Sqn, Gatwick, Surrey, Spitfire XI

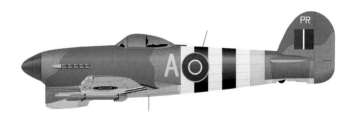

**123 Wing:**
198, 609 Sqns, Thorney Island, Sussex, Typhoon IB

**131 Wing:**
302(Pol), 308(Pol), 317(Pol) Sqns, Chailey, Sussex, Spitfire IX

**132 Wing:**
66, 331(Nor), 332(Nor) Sqns, Bognor, Sussex, Spitfire IX

**133 Wing:**
129, 306(Pol), 315(Pol) Sqns, Coolham, Sussex, Mustang III

**134 Wing:**
310(Cz), 312(Cz), 313(Cz) Sqns, Appledram, Sussex, Spitfire IX

**135 Wing:**
222, 349(Belg), 485(RNZAF) Sqns, Selsey, Sussex, Spitfire IX

**136 Wing:**
164, 183 Sqns, Thorney Island, Sussex, Typhoon IB

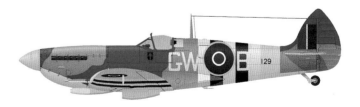

**145 Wing:**
329(Fr), 340(Fr), 341(Fr) Sqns, Merston, Sussex, Spitfire IX

**146 Wing:**
193, 197, 257, 266 Sqns, Needs Oar Point, Hants, Typhoon IB

**Air Observation Posts:**
660 Sqn, Westhanger, Kent, (Advanced Landing Ground) Auster IV

661 Sqn, Fairchilds, Kent, (Advanced Landing Ground) Auster IV
No 85(Base) Group

**141 Wing**
91 Sqn, West Malling, Kent, Spitfire XIV
124 Sqn, Bradwell Bay, Essex, Spitfire VII
322(Dutch) Sqn, Hartford Bridge, Hants, Spitfire XIV

**142 Wing**
264 Sqn, Hartford Bridge, Hants, Mosquito XIII
604 Sqn, Hurn, Hants, Mosquito XIII

**147 Wing**
29 Sqn, West Malling, Kent, Mosquito XIII

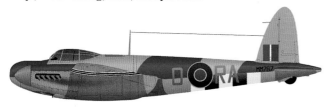

**148 Wing**
409(RCAF) Sqn, West Malling, Kent, Mosquito XIII

**149 Wing**
410(RCAF) Sqn, Hunsden, Herts, Mosquito XIII
488(RNZAF) Sqn, Zeal, Wilts, Mosquito XIII

**150 Wing**
56 Sqn, Newchurch, Kent, Spitfire IX
3, 486(RNZAF) Sqn, Newchurch, Kent, Tempest V

**34 Reconnaissance Wing**
16 Sqn Northolt, Middlesex, Spitfire XI
140 Sqn Northolt, Middlesex, Mosquito IX/XVI
69 Sqn Northolt, Middlesex, Wellington XIII

**Air Spotting Pool**
26, 63 Sqn, Lee on Solent, Hants, Spitfire V
808(FAA), 897(FAA) Sqns, Lee on Solent, Hants, Seafire III
885(FAA), 886(FAA) Sqns, Lee on Solent, Hants, Seafire III
1320 Special Duty Flight, Lee on Solent, Hants, Typhoon

---

# AIRBORNE AND TRANSPORT FORCES

### 38 Group

295, 570 Sqns, Harwell, Berks, Albemarle/Horsa
296, 297 Sqns, Brize Norton, Oxford, Albemarle/Horsa
190, 620 Sqns, Fairford, Glos, Stirling IV/Horsa
196, 299 Sqns, Keevil, Wilts, Stirling IV/Horsa
298, 644 Sqns, Tarrant Rushton, Dorset, Halifax V/Horsa/Hamilcar

### 46 Group

48, 271 Sqns, Down Ampney, Glos, Dakota/Horsa
233 Sqn, Blakehill Farm, Wilts, Dakota/Horsa
512, 575 Sqns, Broadwell, Glos, Dakota/Horsa

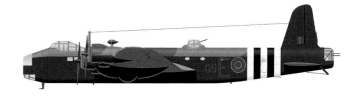

---

# RAF AIR DEFENCE OF GREAT BRITAIN

### 10 Group
1, 165 Sqns, Predannack, Cornwall, Spitfire IX

151 Sqn, Predannack, Cornwall, Mosquito XIII
41 Sqn 'B' Flight, 276 Sqn(A/SR), Bolt Head, Devon Spitfire,
Warwick, Walrus
126 Sqn, Culmhead, Somerset, Spitfire IX
131, 616 Sqns, Culmhead, Somerset, Spitfire VII
263 Sqn, Harrowbeer, Devon, Typhoon IB
610 Sqn, Harrowbeer, Devon, Spitfire XIV
68 Sqn, Fairwood Common, Glos Beaufighter VIF
406(RCAF) Sqn, Winkleigh, Devon, Beaufighter VIF, Mosquito XII
1449 Flight, St Mary's, Scillies, Hurricane IIB

### 11 Group

33, 74, 127 Sqns, Lympne, Kent, Spitfire IX
64, 234, 611 Sqns, Deanland, Sussex, Spitfire VB
80, 229, 274 Sqns, Detling, Ken,t Spitfire IX
130, 303(Pol), 402(RCAF) Sqns, Horne, Surrey, Spitfire VB
345(Fr) Sqn, Shoreham, Sussex, Spitfire VB
'A' Flight 277 Sqn, Shoreham, Sussex Spitfire, Sea Otter, Walrus
350(Belg) Sqn, Friston, Sussex, Spitfire VB
501 Sqn, Friston, Sussex, Spitfire IX
137 Sqn, Manston, Kent, Typhoon IB
605 Sqn, Manston, Kent, Mosquito VI
96 Sqn, West Malling, Kent, Mosquito XIII
125(Newfoundland) Sqn, Hurn, Hants, Mosquito XVII
219 Sqn, Bradwell Bay, Essex, Mosquito XVIII
'A' Flight 278 Sqn, Bradwell Bay, Essex, Warwick
456(RAAF) Sqn, Ford, Sussex, Mosquito XVII
418(RCAF) Sqn, Holmsley South, Hants, Mosquito VI
275 Sqn, Warmwell, Dorset, Spitfire, Walrus
'B' Flight 277 Sqn, Hawkinge, Kent, Walrus, Spitfire
'B' Flight 278 Sqn, Martlesham Heath, Suffolk, Walrus, Spitfire

## 12 Group

'A' Flight 504 Sqn, Digby, Lincs, Spitfire VB

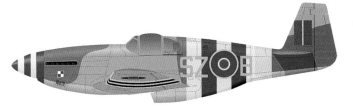

316(Pol) Sqn, Coltishall, Norfolk, Mustang III
'B' Flight 504 Sqn, Coltishall, Norfolk, Spitfire VB
25 Sqn, Coltishall, Norfolk Mosquito XVII
307(Pol) Sqn, Church Fenton, Yorks, Mosquito XII
Fighter Interception Unit, Wittering, Northants Beaufighter,
Tempest, Mosquito, Mustang

### No 13 Group

'A' Flight 118 Sqn, Sumburgh, Shetlands, Spitfire VB
'B' Flight 118 Sqn, Skeabrae, Orkneys, Spitfire VB
309(Pol) Sqn, Drem, East Lothian, Hurricane IIC

# RAF BOMBER COMMAND

## 1 Group

12, 626 Sqns, Wickenby, Lincs, Lancaster I/III
100 Sqn, Grimsby, Lincs, Lancaster I/III
101 Sqn, Ludford Magna, Lincs, Lancaster I/III
103, 576 Sqns, Elsham Wolds, Lincs, Lancaster I/III
166 Sqn Kirmington, Lincs, Lancaster I/III
300(Pol) Sqn, Faldingworth, Lincs, Lancaster I/III
460(RAAF) Sqn, Binbrook, Lincs, Lancaster I/III
550 Sqn, N Killingholme, Lincs, Lancaster I/III
625 Sqn, Kelstern, Lincs, Lancaster I/III

## 3 Group

15, 622 Sqns, Mildenhall, Suffolk, Lancaster I/III
75(RNZAF) Sqn, Mepal, Cambs, Lancaster I/III
115 Sqn, Witchford, Cambs, Lancaster I/III
514 Sqn, Waterbeach, Cambs, Lancaster II
90 Sqn, Tuddenham, Suffolk, Stirling III, Lancaster I/III
149 Sqn, Methwold, Norfolk, Stirling III
218 Sqn, Woolfox Lodge, Rutland, Stirling III
138(Special Duty) Sqn, Tempsford, Beds, Halifax, Stirling
161(Special Duty) Sqn, Tempsford, Beds, Hudson, Lysander, Halifax

## 4 Group

10 Sqn, Melbourne, Yorks, Halifax III
51 Sqn, Snaith, Yorks, Halifax III
76 Sqn, Holme-on-Spalding-Moor, Yorks, Halifax III
78 Sqn, Breighton, Yorks, Halifax III
102 Sqn, Pocklington, Yorks, Halifax III
158 Sqn, Lissett, Yorks, Halifax III

346(Fr) Sqn, Elvington, Yorks, Halifax V/III
466(RAAF) Sqn, Driffield, Yorks, Halifax III
578 Sqn, Burn, Yorks, Halifax III
640 Sqn, Leconfield, Yorks, Halifax III

## 5 Group

9 Sqn, Bardney, Lincs, Lancaster I/III
44(Rhodesian), 691 Sqns, Dunholme Lodge, Lincs, Lancaster I/III
49 Sqn, Fiskerton, Lincs, Lancaster I/III
50, 61 Sqns, Skellingthorpe, Lincs, Lancaster I/III
57, 630 Sqns, East Kirkby, Lincs, Lancaster I/III
106 Sqn, Metheringham, Lincs, Lancaster I/III
207 Sqn, Spilsby, Lincs, Lancaster I/III
463(RAAF), 467(RAAF) Sqns, Waddington, Lincs, Lancaster I/III
97, 83 Sqns, Coningsby, Lincs, Lancaster I/III
617 Sqn, Woodhall Spa, Lincs, Lancaster I/III, Mosquito IV
627 Sqn, Woodhall Spa, Lincs, Mosquito IV

## 6 Group

408(RCAF) Sqn, Linton-on-Ouse, Yorks, Lancaster II
419(RCAF) Sqn, Middleton St George, Durham, Lancaster X
428(RCAF) Sqn, Middleton St George, Durham, Halifax II,
Lancaster X
420(RCAF), 425(RCAF) Sqns, Tholthorpe, Yorks, Halifax III
424(RCAF), 433(RCAF) Sqns, Skipton-on-Swale, Yorks, Halifax III
426(RCAF) Sqn, Linton-on-Ouse, Yorks, Halifax III
427(RCAF), 429(RCAF) Sqns, Leeming, Yorks, Halifax III
431(RCAF), 434(RCAF) Sqns, East Moor, Yorks, Halifax III/VII

## 8 Pathfinder Group

7 Sqn, Oakington, Cambs, Lancaster I/III
35 Sqn, Graveley, Hunts, Lancaster I/III
156 Sqn, Upwood, Hunts, Lancaster I/III
405(RCAF) Sqn, Gransden Lodge, Hunts, Lancaster I/III
582 Sqn, Little Staughton, Hunts, Lancaster I/III
635 Sqn, Downham Market, Norfolk, Lancaster I/III
105 Sqn, Bourn, Cambs Mosquito, IX
109 Sqn, Little Staughton, Hunts, Mosquito IX/XVI
139 Sqn, Upwood, Hunts, Mosquito
571 Sqn, Oakington, Cambs, Mosquito XVI
692 Sqn, Graveley, Hunts, Mosquito IV/XVI

## 100(BS) Group

85(BS) Sqn, Swannington, Norfolk, Mosquito XIX
141(BS) 239(BS) Sqns, West Raynham, Norfolk, Mosquito VI
157(BS) Sqn, Swannington, Norfolk, Mosquito XVII
169(BS) Sqn, Gt Massingham, Norfolk, Mosquito II
23(BS), 515(BS) Sqns, Little Snoring, Norfolk, Mosquito VI
214(BS) Sqn, Oulton, Norfolk, Fortress II, III
192(BS) Sqn, Foulsham, Norfolk, Wellington X, Halifax III,
Mosquito VI
199 Sqn, North Creake, Norfolk, Stirling III

# RAF COASTAL COMMAND

## 15 Group

59, 120 Sqns, Ballykelly, Londonderry, Liberator V
422(RCAF), 423(RCAF) Sqns, Castle Archdale, Fermanagh, Sunderland III
811(RCAF) Sqn, Limavady, Swordfish, Wildcat

## 16 Group

143 Sqn, Manston, Kent, Beaufighter X
848(FAA) Sqn, Manston, Kent, Avenger
819(FAA) Sqn, Manston, Kent, Swordfish
236, 254 Sqns, North Coates, Lincs, Beaufighter X
455(RAAF), 489(RNZAF) Sqns, Langham, Norfolk, Beaufighter X
Part 415(RCAF) Sqn, Bircham Newton, Norfolk, Wellington XIII
854(FAA), 855(FAA) Sqns, Hawkinge, Kent, Avenger

## 18 Group

86 Sqn, Tain, Ross and Cromarty, Liberator
210 Sqn, Sullom Voe, Shetlands, Catalina IV
330(Nor) Sqn, Sullom Voe, Shetlands, Sunderland III
Part 333(Nor) Sqn, Sumburgh, Shetlands, Mosquito
Part 333(Nor) Sqn, Leuchars, Fifeshire, Mosquito VI
Part 333(Nor) Sqn, Woodhaven, Fifeshire, Catalina IB
1693 Flight, Skitten, Caithness, Anson

## 19 Group

144, 404(RCAF) Sqns, Davidstowe Moor, Cornwall, Beaufighter X

235 Sqn, Portreath, Cornwall, Beaufighter X
248 Sqn, Portreath, Cornwall, Mosquito VI
58, 502 Sqns, St David's, Pembs, Halifax II
53, 224, 547 Sqns, St Eval, Cornwall, Liberator V
206 Sqn, St Eval, Cornwall, Liberator VI
311(Cz) Sqn, Predannack, Cornwall, Liberator V
179 Sqn, Predannack, Cornwall, Wellington XIV
10(RAAF) Sqn, Mount Batten, Devon, Sunderland III
201, 228, 461(RAAF) Sqns, Pembroke Dock, Pembs, Sunderland III
172, 304(Pol), 407(RCAF), 612 Sqns, Chivenor, Devon, Wellington XIV
524 Sqn, Davidstowe Moor, Cornwall, Wellington XIII
816(FAA) Sqn, Perranporth, Cornwall, Swordfish II
849(FAA), 850(FAA) Sqns, Perranporth, Cornwall, Avenger I
838(FAA) Sqn, Harrowbeer, Devon, Swordfish

## 106 (Photo Reconnaissance) Group

541, 542 Benson, Oxfordshire, Spitfire XI
540, 544 Benson, Oxfordshire, Mosquito IX / XIV ∎

C-47 Dakota ZA947 of the RAF Battle of Britain Memorial Flight (BBMF) painted with invasion stripes. Crown copyright

A Spitfire Mk.IX of 411 Squadron (RCAF) being painted with invasion stripes at Tangmere, Sussex, by LACs Ken Applesby (working on the fuselage) and Stan Rivers (on the wing).

# D-Day invasion stripes

The need for special recognition or identification markings on Allied aircraft involved in Operation Overlord was conceived in a study conducted by SHAEF some weeks before D-Day.

The invasion of Sicily in 1943 had taught the Allies a salutary lesson when 23 of 144 troop-carrying C-47 Dakotas were shot down by gunners of the Allied invasion fleet as they passed over it on their way to the drop zone. Another 37 C-47s were badly damaged and 1400 of the 5300 paratroopers on board the transport aircraft were killed or missing – one of the worst so-called 'friendly fire' incidents in modern warfare.

It was obvious that the sheer number of combatant units involved in Overlord, coupled with the Allied and inter-service nature of the operation, could lead to misidentifications occurring. Similar or worse losses to 'friendly fire' might occur if no action was taken to minimize them.

The scheme for marking aircraft with identification stripes was approved by Air Chief Marshal Sir Trafford Leigh-Mallory, commander of the Allied Expeditionary Air Force, on May 17, 1944. One British paint company, Walpamur of Blackburn, Lancashire, received an order to deliver 90,000 gallons of white water paint in a very short timescale for the painting of the stripes.

A small scale test exercise was flown over the invasion fleet on June 1 to familiarise ships' crews with the markings.

However, for security reasons, orders to units to paint the identification stripes on Allied aircraft were not issued until June 3 to the troop carrier squadrons, and June 4 to other units.

In most cases the stripes were painted by the ground crews with only a few hours' notice, few of the stripes were 'masked' and, as a result, depending on the abilities of those applying them, the stripes were often far from neat.

In the Official Record Book of 64 Squadron, which was equipped with Spitfire Mk.VBs at Deanland, in Sussex, the entry for June 4, 1944, recorded: "In the evening the business of distempering distinctive markings on the aircraft began. This job was spoiled by heavy rain which removed the distemper with an enthusiasm equal to that of the ground crew who were putting it on. Work was discontinued until early next morning when the weather cleared."

The identification stripes were five alternating black and white bands (three white and two black) painted on the wings and rear fuselage. On single-engine aircraft each stripe was to be 18in (46cm) wide, placed 6in (15cm) inboard of the roundels on the wings and 18in (46cm) forward of the leading edge of the tailplane on the fuselage.

National markings and serial number were not to be obliterated. On twin-engine aircraft the stripes were 24in (61cm) wide, placed 24in (61cm) outboard of the engine

nacelles on the wings, and 18in (46cm) forward of the leading edge of the tailplane around the fuselage.

Whether the width of these stripes was intended to be the same width as the heads on standard-issue Air Ministry barrack room brooms is another thing entirely, but it makes a good story.

For some unknown reason some fighter aircraft units of 10 Group, ADGB, such as 131 Squadron (Spitfire Mk.VII) and 126 Squadron (Spitfire Mk.IX) painted narrower stripes on their aircraft. At 9in wide, they were exactly half the width specified in the official directive.

Most of the Allied aircraft involved in the D-Day operations were marked up with these 'invasion stripes', although some low-flying tactical reconnaissance aircraft, such as those used for artillery spotting, received a dispensation allowing them to paint the stripes only on the under surfaces of their aircraft.

The heavy four-engine bombers of both the USAAF 8th Air Force and RAF Bomber Command were exempted from wearing the stripes altogether as they would mostly be operating at night and, in any case, the Germans had very few aircraft with which they could be confused.

To avoid aircraft being compromised while on the ground at forward airfields in France, orders were received a month after D-Day to remove the stripes from the upper surfaces of aircraft. They were completely removed by the end of 1944. ■

# Fighters and fighter-bombers

**R**AF single-seat fighter and fighter-bomber aircraft played an enormous part in the build-up to D-Day, during the invasion itself and in the subsequent Battle of Normandy.

## PRIOR TO D-DAY

Prior to the invasion, operating in the pure air-to-air fighter role on 'Ranger' and 'Rodeo' fighter sweeps, they helped to clear the Luftwaffe from the skies over the continent. The RAF fighters also escorted heavy and medium bombers on daylight bombing raids as they targeted bridges, marshalling yards, coastal artillery and military facilities. Meanwhile, the fighter-bombers strafed, bombed and rocketed tactical targets with great accuracy.

## D-DAY – ADGB AND 2 TAF

During the D-Day assault itself, fighter and fighter-bomber squadrons provided shipping cover, beach cover, and bomber escort, they flew offensive fighter sweeps, provided direct air support to invading forces and struck at targets inland from the landing area.

The fighter squadrons of Air Defence of Great Britain (ADGB) were tasked with suppressing enemy air and sea activity in the areas from Brittany to Pas-de-Calais. Operating in conjunction with 2nd Tactical Air Force (2 TAF) fighter Squadrons, ADGB Spitfire squadrons flew 363 'Low Cover' sorties over the landing area and they also assisted in escorting the glider and tug combinations during Operation Mallard on the evening of D-Day.

In total, ADGB aircraft flew 169 defensive patrol sorties, 134 offensive patrol sorties, 203 convoy patrol sorties, 152 naval spotting patrol sorties and 57 anti-shipping recce and strike sorties during D-Day.

Pilot Officer Sid Bergman with his 441 Squadron Spitfire Mk.IX, Normandy, August 2, 1944.

Meanwhile, the 2 TAF fighter squadrons flew more than 1300 'Low Cover' patrol sorties over the beachheads, as well as 90 escort and convoy protection sorties, all encountering negligible resistance. In addition, the fighter-bomber squadrons of 2 TAF flew 400 close air support and armed reconnaissance sorties in support of the landings.

## BATTLE OF NORMANDY

Following the invasion and during the Battle of Normandy, Allied fighter sweeps continued to maintain the hard-won and vital air supremacy by engaging any Luftwaffe aircraft they came across in the skies over France, permitting increasing use of fighter aircraft as supplementary ground attack assets and as fighter-bombers.

Roaming freely over the areas to the rear of the battlefronts, seeking targets of opportunity and bombing or strafing any military vehicles or personnel caught in the open in daylight, they became the bane of the lives of German ground troops. The German soldiers became extremely fearful of these Allied fighter-bombers, which they nicknamed 'jabos', from the German 'jäger bomber' or 'hunter-bomber'. One veteran Wehrmacht soldier, Helmut Hesse, said later that "the jabos were a burden on our soul".

Without doubt, the 'jabos' had a decisive effect on the Battle of Normandy. Their presence and effectiveness prevented the Germans from moving reinforcements forward during daylight hours and much increased the time it took to do so.

## FORWARD AIR CONTROL AND BATTLEFIELD RADAR

The part played in the effectiveness and success of the fighter and fighter-bomber operations over the continent after D-Day by forward-based ground radar units and control centres cannot go unmentioned.

The Allied air forces had radar available to them from the very first day of Normandy operations, and it was soon incorporated into tactical air control as well as for early warning and air defence purposes. Radar had, of course, been used by the RAF from the Battle of Britain onwards and it had first been used by the Allies for tactical air control during the Italian campaign.

Now, in Normandy and during the subsequent breakout, the radar and tactical control systems reached new levels of refinement. Each tactical air command had a radar control group built around a tactical control centre (also called a fighter control centre), with a microwave early warning (MEW) radar

Mobile fighter controllers Major D Gray (British Army) and Sqn Ldr R A Sutherland (RAF).

Stills from a Typhoon gun camera film of a strafe attack on a locomotive.

Hawker Typhoon 1B MN293 'TP-D' of 198 Squadron takes off from Thorney Island, armed with 3-inch rockets, flown by Flt Sgt J S Fraser-Petherbridge.

located within 10 to 30 miles of the front, three forward director posts, three or four close control radar units and, finally, four direction finding stations.

Originally developed for air defence purposes, this radar network now took on added importance for the control of tactical air strikes. When an air-ground coordination party sent in a request for immediate air support the request went directly to a combined operations centre where it was evaluated. If it was considered legitimate and was approved by both army and air commanders the request was relayed to the Tactical Control Centre (TCC).

Typically, the TCC would relay the request to airborne fighter-bombers, and a geographically appropriate forward director post would furnish precise radar guidance and navigation information to the fighter-bomber formation from the MEW and close control radars, vectoring them to the target area.

Once in the target area, the flight leader would communicate with the air-ground coordination party which had sent in the original request, via a forward air controller, for final details. If possible the air-ground coordination party would arrange for artillery to mark the target with coloured smoke and also, if possible, to undertake suppressive artillery fire against known enemy anti-aircraft defences.

Operation Overlord saw many important developments in tactical air operations, but one of the most significant was the use of forward air controllers on the ground to direct waiting fighter-bomber aircraft, such as rocket-equipped Typhoons or bomb-carrying Spitfires, to attack enemy targets; a system which had originated in the Italian theatre of operations. Today, forward air control is an integral part of close air support operations for many of the world's air forces, including the RAF.

## RAF FIGHTER AND FIGHTER-BOMBER AIRCRAFT TYPES

For the operations in support of the D-Day landings and the subsequent Battle of Normandy the RAF had three principal types of fighter/fighter-bomber available to its commanders. The Supermarine Spitfire and the Hawker Typhoon together made up the vast majority of the RAF's fighter assets, while the North American Mustang III was operated in smaller numbers. These types are covered in more detail in the following pages, with individual stories to give a 'flavour' of what it was like to fly them at this stage of the war.

One other fighter type, the Hawker Tempest Mk.V (the aircraft intended to replace the Typhoon), was operated by just two squadrons on D-Day. 3 and 486 (RNZAF) Squadrons, based at Newchurch in Kent, were equipped with the Tempest, as part of 150 Wing. A third Tempest squadron, 56 Squadron, joined 150 Wing in June 1944, after D-Day. Most of the operations carried out by 150 Wing comprised high altitude fighter sweeps, offensive operations known as 'Rangers' (long-range sorties inside enemy territory, specifically to attack ground vehicles) and anti-shipping reconnaissance.

On June 13, 1944, the first German V-1 flying bombs were launched against London. The Tempest's excellent performance at low-altitude made it one of the preferred tools for dealing with these small fast-flying unmanned missiles. 150 Wing was transferred back to the ADGB where the Tempest squadrons racked up a considerable percentage of the total RAF kills over the flying bombs (638 of a total of 1846 destroyed by aircraft). ■

Hawker Tempest of 486 (RNZAF) Squadron.

# Supermarine Spitfire

On D-Day, the RAF's order of battle included 61 squadrons of the RAF's ubiquitous Second World War fighter, the Supermarine Spitfire.

The original versions of this famous aircraft had entered service in August 1938. Continuous updates and improvements, allowed the later versions of Spitfire to keep up with the rapid evolution of aircraft design and capabilities during the war.

As a result, the Spitfire was still in front-line service in considerable numbers at the time of D-Day and indeed to the end of the war in Europe and beyond. The last operational sortie of an RAF Spitfire took place on April 1, 1954, in Singapore.

On June 6, 1944, 57 squadrons of Spitfires were available to ADGB and 2 TAF for offensive operations in support of the D-Day landings, including two squadrons which were used for naval artillery spotting duties. Another four squadrons of Spitfire Mk.XIs were employed in the 'recce' role and, in addition, a further four air sea rescue squadrons had a few Spitfires on their strength.

## SPITFIRES OVER NORMANDY

Nine Spitfire squadrons gave initial air cover to the first troops ashore on D-Day, while others patrolled the convoys with the vital task of preventing enemy air reconnaissance. One Spitfire pilot had a grandstand view of the invasion – he was shot down into the channel on June 5, quite likely by 'friendly fire', and was not picked up from his dinghy until June 7.

The Spitfire Mk.IXs of 144 Canadian Wing led by Wing Commander J E 'Johnnie' Johnson (who eventually became the RAF's official highest-scoring fighter pilot of the war) gained the distinction of being the first RAF aircraft to operate from French mainland soil since the fall of France in 1940 when they landed at Advanced Landing Ground (ALG) B3, at St Croix-Sur-Mer, on D-Day +4, June 10, 1944. This, the first temporary airstrip in Normandy to come into operation, had been constructed in just three days.

The Spitfires were refuelled and re-armed by RAF Servicing Commandos and were ready for take-off in 20 minutes. 144 Wing deployed en masse from the UK to B2 ALG, at Bazenville, France, on June 16, the first of

many RAF units to do so. Subsequently, the bulk of the 2 TAF Spitfire squadrons were progressively moved across the Channel to operate from newly constructed forward airfields, close behind the front lines, to provide rapid tactical support and to extend their range and time on task.

## SPITFIRE VERSIONS

The vast majority of the Spitfire squadrons at the time of D-Day were equipped with the Mk.IX version, although 11 squadrons under the command of ADGB were still operating the older Mk.V. Three squadrons were equipped with Mk.VII Spitfires, intended for high-altitude operations, but, in practice, often used at lower levels.

Two units, 91 Squadron and 322 (Dutch) Squadron, were equipped with the new Griffon-engine Spitfire Mk.XIVs. They were involved in pre-invasion fighter sweeps and armed-reconnaissance missions up to D-Day itself, but were then withdrawn back to England where their high speed capabilities could be used on 'anti-diver' patrols against the V-1 'doodlebugs' when attacks on them began in June 1944.

Wing Commander Geoffrey Page, OC 125 Wing, taxies his Spitfire Mk.IX, coded 'AGP', loaded with a 500lb bomb under the fuselage and two 500lb bombs under the wings, at Longues, Normandy. Later the same day, Page was to shoot down his 14th enemy aircraft, a Messerschmitt Bf 109, returning to Longues wounded in the leg and his aircraft damaged by anti-aircraft fire.

TOP: Spitfire Mk.IXs of 66 Squadron on the way to Normandy for a beachhead cover patrol, carrying 90 gallon drop tanks, on June 13, 1944.

## FIGHTERS AND FIGHTER-BOMBERS

The Spitfires could operate as classic fighter aircraft or in the ground-attack, strafing role and they were also used as fighter-bombers, carrying a 250lb (113kg) bomb under each wing or a 500lb (226kg) bomb under the centre fuselage. To extend the rather limited range of the Spitfire this centre 'station' was sometimes taken up with a 90 gallon drop tank, which provided a useful sortie duration of around three hours.

The gun armament of the Spitfires in use in 1944 – usually two 20mm cannons and either four .303 machine guns, or two .50 heavy machine guns – provided the aircraft with a valuable air-to-ground strafe capability. With the increasing use of the Spitfire in the ground attack role, the vulnerability of its Merlin engine's water and glycol cooling system to hits from small arms fire and light flak proved to be a concern for its pilots and the main cause of losses. There may not have been too much danger from German fighter aircraft, but there certainly was from flak. As one Spitfire pilot put it: "By this stage of the war the German anti-aircraft gunners were not short of practice!" A loss of engine coolant would quickly cause the engine to seize or catch fire and the low altitude inherent in ground attack missions meant that there were few options and only limited gliding range.

Of 152 Spitfires destroyed or damaged from all causes during the month of June 1944 all except 21, which fell to German fighters, were lost to light flak (up to 30mm calibre). However, considering that attacks against ground targets were far from everyone's thoughts when the Spitfire was originally conceived, it is a testament to the brilliance of the original design and to the subsequent modifications that the aircraft was able to fulfil this role so successfully. ■

Spitfires operating from Advanced Landing Ground (ALG) B3 St Croix-sur-Mer, Normandy, June 1944.

# Flight Lieutenant Tony Cooper
## (64 Squadron Spitfire pilot)

Tony Cooper had wanted to be a pilot ever since the time when he had a 'joyride' in an aircraft of Alan Cobham's Flying Circus, sitting on his sister's lap at the age of five.

His dreams were almost shattered when he was later refused entry to the RAF twice because the medical showed up a badly damaged eardrum. Then in late 1937, aged 21, Cooper was accepted for pilot training with the RAF Volunteer Reserve at Luton. It seemed that the RAFVR was less particular and, as he says: "There was a war coming."

### INSTRUCTOR

After completing his flying training on Miles Magisters and Hawker Harts, he was sent to the Central Flying School (CFS) at Upavon in July 1940 on a flying instructor's course. There he flew the Avro Tutor biplane and the North American Harvard –

the first aircraft he had experienced with a retractable undercarriage – and within the month he had qualified as a flying instructor.

Cooper spent some time instructing at 7 Service Flying Training School (SFTS), Peterborough, on the Fairey Battle, and was then posted, in November 1940, as an instructor on 31 FTS at Kingston, Ontario, Canada. There he flew the Fairey Battle, the North American BT-9 Yale training aircraft and, from July 1941, the Harvard. By June 1942, he had over 1300 hours total flying and was assessed as an above average flying instructor.

### BACK TO THE UK AND TO THE SPITFIRE

While in Kingston, Cooper met and married a Canadian girl, but this did not stop him from continually pestering the authorities to be allowed to return to the UK on 'ops'.

Eventually, his wish was granted and he returned to England with his wife, who was moving from a land of plenty to a strange war-torn country with all its restrictions, shortages and dangers, where she knew no one.

Cooper's parents took her in while he attended a Spitfire conversion course at 61 Operational Training Unit (OTU) at Rednal (and its 'satellite' airfield at Montford Bridge) in Shropshire, initially flying the Harvard, with which he was by now very familiar, and then Mk.I and Mk.II Spitfires. He completed the OTU course at the end of June 1943 and, although he had less than 60 hours on the Spitfire, he was assessed as an above average Spitfire pilot.

### 64 SQUADRON SPITFIRES

In July 1943, Tony Cooper joined 64 Squadron, which was undergoing a period of rest and training, and was temporarily

Flt Lt Tony Cooper chats to his ground crew as he straps into his Spitfire. Tony Cooper

based at Ayr in Scotland with its Mk.Vb Spitfires. He was to serve with the squadron for the next 16 months. Although he had yet to acquire any operational experience, he was now a very experienced pilot with some 2000 hours of flying under his belt as he entered the fray.

His truly operational flying began when 64 Squadron moved from Ayr to Friston in August 1943 and, a few days later, on to Gravesend in Kent. Many of the operations conducted by the squadron were over occupied Europe. The pilots flew on fighter sweeps and escort missions to daylight bombing raids carried out by medium bombers, such as Martin Marauders or Lockheed Venturas.

They also escorted Coastal Command Bristol Beaufighters on anti-shipping strikes off the coast of Holland. On these sorties enemy anti-aircraft fire, flak, was, if anything, more dangerous than encounters with Luftwaffe fighters and, in his comments in his logbook, Cooper frequently wrote "heavy flak". The escorting Spitfires were often hit by enemy ground fire and on many occasions Cooper witnessed one or more of the bombers they were escorting being shot down. Sometimes Cooper led a section of Spitfires down low over the Continent to strafe targets such as bridges. On April 18, 1944, while 64 Squadron was flying from Coltishall,

Norfolk, Cooper's logbook records a "dinghy search" and his notes give the story: "Junior baled out 70 miles off the coast whilst on a 'Jim Crow' mission – Patrols lost sight of him after three hours – we found him again after an hour and directed launch to pick him up – safe and sound!" 'Junior' was John Harder, an American pilot serving in the RAF with 64 Squadron. He was one of Cooper's best friends and he was obviously relieved that he had been picked up.

## DEANLAND ('TENTLAND')

At the end of April 1944, in preparation for the impending invasion of France, 64 Squadron moved to the advanced landing ground at Deanland, near Lewes in Sussex, where conditions were primitive. Unlike permanent stations there was no accommodation for personnel, everyone was expected to live under canvas and only four blister hangars were provided for aircraft maintenance work.

For many of the personnel, Deanland (or 'Tentland' as it was sometimes known) took some getting used to. Tony Cooper later recalled: "Deanland was a bit of a comedown; luckily it was summer time when we suddenly found ourselves on this hump in the middle of the Downs. We were in tents and I found myself using the same equipment my father had used in the First

World War: a truckle bed made of wood and canvas and the same materials for a bath and washstand. At night it was very cold, but when D-Day came along we didn't get much sleep as we were doing up to four shows a day and were kept very busy."

An entry in Cooper's logbook against May 5, 1944 – a day when he flew a dawn patrol for one hour and 55 minutes – proudly notes the birth of his son, Peter John. On May 22, he records that he took over a new personal aircraft, Spitfire Mk.Vb BM327, coded 'SH-F', which he named PeterJohn 1 after his newly-born son, who he was not able to see until his christening some weeks later.

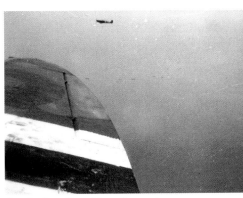

One for the album! Tony Cooper's photograph taken from his Spitfire over the Channel on D-Day. Tony Cooper

## D-DAY

On D-Day, June 6, 1944, Cooper's logbook records that he flew twice. 64 Squadron was tasked with providing "low beach cover" over the American assault. The Squadron ORB records that Cooper was allocated his personal Spitfire BM327, 'SH-F', for both sorties. He took off at 4.30am (before dawn) for his first sortie of the day, as part of a 13-aircraft formation, providing "fighter cover for Utah beach" and landed back after a total of two hours and 40 minutes airborne (the first hour recorded as night flying). The naval barrage was so intense that it was not safe to be over the coast and the Wing Leader withdrew the formation to a safer distance.

Cooper's remarks in his logbook give an interesting picture of the confusion that reigned and suggest that the invasion stripes, so painstakingly painted on by the ground crew, were not entirely effective: "Navy shelling coast defences – first landing (by the invading troops) made at 6.20am. Nearly shot down by a Thunderbolt – Spitfire in front actually was – another Spit hit by naval shell and blew up – General Brock's benefit!"

Remarkably, Tony Cooper took his camera with him and took a photograph over the striped wing of his Spitfire just after dawn broke on D-Day, looking towards another of the squadron's Spitfires in tactical formation. He remembered, he said,

'PeterJohn 1' inscription on Tony Cooper's Spitfire Mk.Vb BM327. Tony Cooper

"a huge cloud of smoke and dust totally covering the beaches," caused by the bombing of the night before and the naval barrage. "From our transit height of 12,000ft," he said, "it appeared that the sea was full of a multitude of ships."

In the evening of June 6, Cooper flew his aircraft on another sortie over the invasion beaches, taking off at 10pm, this time tasked with "fighter cover for Omaha Beach". His comments in his logbook against this sortie read: "Hun bombers attacked invasion fleet – tremendous return fire from ships – one bomber destroyed." He landed back at 10 minutes past midnight – almost 18 hours after his first take-off that day – logging two hours and five minutes of night flying. When later asked about night landings in the Spitfire on the short runways of Deanland, Tony said: "I remember them well with reasonably controlled terror, especially in the rain!"

## D-DAY +1

On June 7 (D-Day +1) Tony Cooper flew three fighter cover patrols over the Utah and Omaha beaches; two of them in his personal aircraft PeterJohn 1. In all, Cooper was airborne for a total of seven hours 25 minutes that day. The Spitfires' freedom of movement was severely restricted by the low cloud base and the many anti-aircraft balloons being flown from the Allied ships involved in supporting the landings; this led to a much increased risk of collision.

The last operation of the day took place in the late evening, with Cooper leading a section of four Spitfires, flying in formation on him in the dark with no lights showing. This sortie provided ample evidence that it was possible to be nearly as frightened by your own side as by the enemy, as Cooper recorded in his logbook: "Very bad visibility – no attacks – sent 40 miles out to sea on return owing to reciprocal homing vectors – very shaky experience – brought in eventually by rockets". By the time Cooper's section landed, it was completely dark and one pilot ran out of fuel as he was taxiing

back to dispersal. Cooper recorded two hours and 35 minutes of night flying in his logbook for the sortie.

## JUNE 1944

The intense flying rate continued; on June 10, Cooper flew three times, then once on the 11th, twice on the 12th and three times on the 13th. As was typical of many other units during June 1944, 64 Squadron had its busiest month of the war; its total flying hours amounted to a staggering 1150 hours – the bulk of which were flown in the two-week period after D-Day.

Everyone was stretched to the limit, especially the ground crews who had to work long hours to keep the squadron's Spitfires in the air. Meanwhile, the pilots had to endure the strain of continuous operations. Cooper's experience was typical and his personal flying total for the month was 75 hours, of which 71 were operational and 25 hours were flown in the dark.

## SPITFIRE MK.IXS

On June 23, Tony Cooper was appointed as flight commander of 'A' Flight, just as 64 Squadron was moved to Harrowbeer, in Devon to be part of a Spitfire wing with 129 Squadron. A few days later the squadron was re-equipped with Mk.IXb Spitfires, and Cooper flew one of the new, more powerful Spitfires for the first time on July 3, 1944.

Once again the squadron was involved in fighter sweeps out over France and it continued to take losses. Sometimes pilots were able to bring a flak-damaged aircraft safely home to base, sometimes they force-landed, sometimes they had to bale out and all too frequently a pilot was killed. On July 7, Flying Officer Dryburgh died ("His machine dived straight in," reported Cooper), and the next day Flight Lieutenant Collis baled out, but was picked up.

Many sorties now involved strage attacks against ground targets such as locomotives, vehicles and barges; inevitably there was enemy flak to contend with and on almost every sortie at least one of the Spitfires was hit. It was, therefore, an event worthy of note when Cooper wrote in his logbook against one bomber escort sortie: "No aircraft hit! All returned."

On July 27, the other flight commander and Cooper's good friend, John Harder was hit and forced to bale out over the sea for the second time, which he did successfully.

## BOMBING AND STRAFING

On July 29, 1944, the Harrowbeer Wing Spitfires, with Tony Cooper leading 64 Squadron, carried out an unusual pre-planned low-level bombing raid against a German army headquarters and garrison in the small Brittany village of Scrignac.

The raid was led by Wing Commander 'Birdy' Bird-Wilson, the wing leader. Each Spitfire carried a 500lb bomb under the centre of the fuselage. Intelligence indicated that all of the French civilian inhabitants of the village had been evacuated and only the

"Out of the darkness..." Artist Spencer Trickett captures Tony Cooper's 64 Squadron Spitfire Mk.Vb 'SH-F', with his wingman in 'SH-L', lifting off from Deanland at dusk for his evening sortie on D-Day – recorded in his logbook as "fighter cover for Omaha Beach".

German garrison remained. The raid appeared to be a total success, with the German HQ and much of the village destroyed and only the church left standing among the rubble. This apparent success was reported in the British newspapers and on the BBC radio nine o'clock news (years later, after the war, amid rumours regarding double agents, it came to light that there had been some misinformation and, in fact, the local population had not been evacuated from Scrignac. Tragically, 23 civilians including women and children had been killed in the raid).

On August 1, with Wing Commander 'Birdie' Bird-Wilson leading the squadron and Cooper leading a section, the Spitfires strafed enemy gun positions at a target in France, before the bombers went at it. They then saw and chased a German Bf 109, "at deck level, flat out for five minutes".

Cooper's logbook records: "Birdie got in front of me and got strikes on him – I got in a burst from 500 yards – Birdie finished him off – German pilot baled out."

Four days later, on August 5, after escorting 15 Lancasters of 617 Squadron, which dropped 12,000lb Tallboy bombs on the U-boat pens at Brest, Cooper led his section of four Spitfires in a strafe attack on flak positions. He said that as they dived on their target: "It was the worst flak I've ever seen in my life."

Unbeknown to them, since planning the attack, two German flak ships had moved into the harbour during the previous night and they put up an intense barrage. One of Cooper's section was killed during the attack; another was hit and forced to bale out only two miles off the enemy coastline. The pilot climbed into his dinghy and was picked up by an Air-Sea-Rescue Walrus seaplane, in a courageous rescue, and he was back at base within three hours.

On August 26, during a sortie to strafe enemy transports and railway trucks, Flying Officer Blake Smiley, who had been lucky so far having been hit by flak several times but always getting home, was hit by flak and baled out five miles off Manston. He spent the night on a buoy and was picked up at 10.30am the next day. Another 64 Squadron pilot, Flying Officer Schmitz, did not pull out of his attack dive and was killed.

## OFF 'OPS'

In November 1944 Tony Cooper was posted off 'ops' and back to instructing. In his 16 months with 64 Squadron he had flown some 600 hours, the vast majority of it operational flying and had twice been 'mentioned in dispatches'. He had seen much action, including being involved in the D-Day operations; he had made a significant contribution and he was very lucky to be alive. Many of his fellow pilots on the Squadron – his friends and colleagues – had not been so fortunate.

Tony was awarded the Legion d'Honneur by France in 2015. He died in January 2017, 11 days before his 101st birthday. ∎

64 Squadron Spitfire Mk.Vb 'SH-L' taxies out for a beachhead cover patrol sortie from Deanland. Tony Cooper

*Lineshoot for home – To show how the dear boy earns his money!*

Tony Cooper with his 64 Squadron Spitfire and his own caption from his photo album.

# Spitfire Mk.IX MK356

## (443 Squadron (RCAF) and Flying Officer Gordon Ockenden DFC)

Gordon Ockenden in 1944, aged 21.

In the early evening of June 4, 1944, 12 Spitfires Mk.IXs of 443 ('Hornet') Squadron (RCAF), led by the squadron commander, 15 victory ace Squadron Leader Henry Wallace 'Wally' McLeod DFC and Bar, flew the last of their pre-invasion ground attack missions, the type of operation they had been involved in since mid-April.

This was a dive bombing mission against a German radar site on the coast 10 miles south east of Fécamp, part of the carefully orchestrated plan to blind the enemy. One of the Spitfires was forced to return early to

Spitfire Mk.IX MK356 – a true D-Day survivor – now flies with the RAF BBMF. (Rachel Warnes Crown Copyright)

A 443 Squadron Spitfire Mk.IX taxies at B2 ALG, Bazenville, Normandy, while French farmers gather in their crop.

With a ground crewman laying on the wing to guide the pilot, a 443 Squadron Spitfire Mk.IX (with a 45 gallon 'slipper' tank) taxies past a Hawker Typhoon at B2 ALG, Bazenville, Normandy, creating the usual cloud of dust.

the squadron's base at Ford, in Sussex, due to engine trouble, but the other 11 bombed the target successfully and four direct hits were observed as well as some near misses within damaging distance. Despite intense light flak from nearby batteries, none of the Spitfires were hit.

One of the pilots flying on this mission was 21-year-old Flying Officer Gordon 'Ockie' Ockenden from Alberta, a founder member of 443 Squadron, who was flying his favourite aircraft, Spitfire Mk.IX LF, MK356, coded '2I-V' (the 'LF' designation indicating that the Spitfire was fitted with a Rolls-Royce Merlin 66 engine optimised for lower levels). This aircraft is still flying today with the RAF's Battle of Britain Memorial Flight (BBMF) and the author has had the privilege of flying this Spitfire himself on many occasions during his 11 years as a display pilot with the flight.

## 443 SQUADRON IN THE BUILD-UP TO D-DAY

Formed in February 1944, 443 Squadron was part of 144 (Canadian) Wing, under the command of RAF fighter ace and renowned fighter leader Wing Commander J E 'Johnnie' Johnson DSO and Bar DFC and Bar (who eventually became (officially) the highest scoring RAF fighter ace with 34 confirmed kills).

In the build-up to D-Day, between April 13 and June 5, 1944, 443 Squadron flew 487 operational Spitfire sorties on 43 offensive operations.

The squadron's victory 'score card' was started by Squadron Leader McLeod on April 19 when he destroyed a Dornier 217 bomber near Louvain. On April 25, a 144 Wing formation led by 'Johnnie' Johnson 'bounced' six Luftwaffe Fw 190s and destroyed them all. Two of the 190s were shot down by Johnson

himself and two of the others were claimed by 443 Squadron's Flight Lieutenants Don Walz and Hugh Russel, both of whom will feature in this story again.

On May 5, Wally McLeod shot down another Fw 190, his 15th confirmed victory. Combats with the enemy were the exception rather than the rule, however, in this pre-D-Day period. On most of the fighter sweeps and bomber escorts the main opposition encountered was German flak.

443 Squadron carried out its first dive-bombing mission on April 26, against a V-1 flying-bomb site south of Dieppe. In the next six weeks there were many such fighter-bomber operations against 'Noballs' (the V-l sites), bridges, rail junctions and yards, and radar posts. On most of these attacks the pilots had to run a gauntlet of intense flak and many of the Spitfires returned peppered with holes.

## D-DAY FOR 443 SQUADRON

On June 5, there was no operational flying by 443 Squadron as the Allies 'paused for breath' prior to D-Day and 'invasion stripes' were applied to the aircraft. The next day – D-Day itself – 12 of 443 Squadron's Spitfire Mk.IXs took off from Ford at 0620, carrying 90 gallon drop tanks, led by Wally McLeod and tasked with a beachhead cover patrol between Courseulles and Le Havre.

The squadron penetrated up to five miles inland, no enemy aircraft were seen, but the pilots saw plenty of intense and accurate flak being thrown up from five flak ships in Le Havre harbour and they also reported seeing naval shells passing close to their aircraft! The Spitfires landed back at their base at 8.25am, two hours and five minutes after they had taken off.

Gordon Ockenden had to sit out this first mission of D-Day, but he flew Spitfire MK356, '2I-V', on the next two beachhead-cover patrols that day, taking off at 11.25am and 3.40pm respectively, each mission lasting about two hours and both being relatively uneventful with no enemy aircraft seen. Spitfire MK356 was also flown on a third mission on D-Day, taking off at 7.45pm, in the hands of Flying Officer Arthur Horrell. By the end of D-Day, 443 Squadron had flown a total of 48 sorties and 95 hours.

## D-DAY +1

On D-Day +1, 443 Squadron was again tasked with four beachhead cover patrols. Spitfire MK356 was flown on the second of these by Flight Sergeant G E Urquhart.

On this mission, Flight Lieutenant I R Maclennan, who was flying MH850 '2I-H', was forced to crash-land just beyond the beach head, his engine having failed due to a glycol leak. Unfortunately, he landed in an area which was not controlled by Allied troops. His aircraft was considerably damaged by prepared 'anti-invasion' obstacles in the field, but he was seen to climb from the cockpit and run away, before

flak forced his wingman to retire. Maclennan was captured and became a prisoner of war.

On the third mission of the day, Ockenden flew MK356 again, taking off at 3.40pm for another patrol over the invasion beaches, as one of 12 Spitfires of 443 Squadron. Under heavy cloud cover, the patrol was uneventful until nearing the time to leave, when Flight Lieutenant Prest, leading the four Spitfires of 'B' Flight which included Ockenden, spotted four Luftwaffe Bf 109s which they 'bounced' east of Caen.

Prest chased one of the 109s south, but one of his cannons jammed and, although the 109 appeared to give off some smoke, it escaped. The two Spitfires flown by Flight Lieutenant Hugh Russel and Ockenden chased another of the 109s out over the sea, both firing at it. They were rewarded with the sight of the German fighter exploding in midair under the onslaught of their combined cannon and machine gun fire. Unsure which of them had delivered the coup de grace, they claimed half a kill each. This was the first of an eventual total of four combat kills, plus one 'damaged', for Ockenden, who was also later credited with destroying at least 35 enemy vehicles (Ockenden was awarded the Distinguished Flying Cross (DFC) in December 1944).

## SPITFIRE MK356'S WAR

The Spitfire that Ockenden was flying when he claimed his first (shared) kill was his favourite, MK356 '2I-V'.

This Spitfire had a typically short but intensive war. It flew 60 operational sorties in a period of 61 days between April 14, 1944 (when it was flown on a 'Rodeo' fighter sweep between Compiègne, Paris and Rouen, encountering light flak) and its last wartime sortie on June 14. On 19 of these sorties Ockenden was at the controls.

MK356 was hit by ground fire on at least three occasions and neatly-repaired bullet holes can still be seen in its rear fuselage. On June 14, 1944, as Flying Officer Gordon

Munro lifted MK356 off the runway at Ford for another beachhead cover patrol over Normandy, one of its main wheels fell off. Munro continued the sortie, completed the patrol and then executed a successful 'belly landing' back at Ford on his return.

When 443 Squadron was deployed forward to France two days later, before MK356 had been repaired, the aircraft was left behind to be collected by a maintenance unit. It subsequently spent 53 years on the ground, always in RAF hands, until eventually being returned to airworthy condition. It took to the skies again in November 1997 and then joined the RAF BBMF collection – a true D-Day survivor.

## 443 SQUADRON IN NORMANDY

443 Squadron moved with 144 Wing from Ford to the newly completed B2 ALG at Bazenville, Normandy, on June 16 to continue the war from forward bases on the continent, the first of many RAF units to do so. By day the field was blanketed with clouds of dust; at night the incessant din of the Allied artillery barrage and anti-aircraft fire, along with enemy bombing, made sleep almost impossible.

The Spitfires continued to be used for strafing and dive-bombing missions as well as for fighter sweeps and patrols. Luftwaffe fighters were appearing in greater numbers over Normandy and the Spitfire pilots of 141 Wing found themselves in more frequent combats with some success.

However, tragedy struck on June 16, a day which started well with Spitfires of 443 Squadron being scrambled from cockpit readiness at 5am to intercept 20-plus Bf 109s over the beachhead. The Spitfires broke up the enemy formation and chased the 109s away; Flight Lieutenant Don Walz claimed a Bf 109 destroyed. The day ended badly, though, with the deaths of three of the 443 Squadron pilots, including Hugh Russel who had shared the kill with 'Ockie' Ockenden only nine days earlier on June 7.

Spitfires of 144 Wing, including '2I-N' of 443 Squadron, some equipped with 90 gallon drop tanks, at ALG B3 St Croix-sur-Mer on June 10, 1944 for refuel and re-arm. The first time that Spitfires had landed in France since 1940.

Spitfire Mk.IX MK356 in its original colour scheme as 443 Squadron's '2I-V' – it now flies with the RAF BBMF. (Chris Elcock – Crown Copyright)

Eighteen Spitfires of the wing, under the leadership of Wing Commander Johnson, were on a late evening fighter sweep of the Argentan area. They ran into large numbers of Bf 109s and Fw 190s near Caen. The Spitfires tore into the German raiders, which initially stayed to fight and then turned and ran. Wing Commander Johnson shot down an Fw 190, which was running away at very low level; Wally McLeod claimed a Bf 109.

One of the sections of four Spitfires was last seen climbing into thick cloud near Caen amid a barrage of flak. It is believed that the section of four engaged some Fw 190s above the cloud near Caen, not realising in the fading light that they were considerably outnumbered by the Germans. It seems that the Fw 190 pilots took advantage of their superior situation, stayed to fight and shot down all four Spitfires. Squadron Leader J D Hall, Flight Lieutenant Hugh Russel and Flying Officer Luis Perez-Gomez (from Mexico) were all killed.

Flight Lieutenant Walz, the only survivor of the four-aircraft section, was forced to take to his parachute. He managed to evade capture with help from the French Resistance and eventually returned to the squadron.

Hugh Russel's loss was especially painful for his older brother, Squadron Leader Dal Russel DFC and Bar (later DSO, DFC and Bar), who was the squadron commander of 442 Squadron, a sister squadron on 144 Wing.

By the middle of July the number of blazing, smoking or damaged vehicles attacked by 443 Squadron Spitfires had risen to 99, plus four locomotives or trains, a barge, and a railroad signal house. On July 14, when the fighter wings in Normandy were reorganised, 144 Wing was broken up and Squadron Leader McLeod's 443 Squadron joined 127 Wing at Crépon.

## 'WALLY' MCLEOD'S DEATH

Ockenden's decorated and highly successful squadron commander, Squadron Leader Wally Mcleod DSO DFC and Bar, eventually achieved a total score of 21 enemy aircraft destroyed, three probably destroyed and 11 damaged (13 of his kills had been achieved while flying from Malta in 1942).

On September 27, 1944, McLeod led the squadron as part of a patrol by 141 Wing, but he failed to return after the Spitfires became involved in a mass combat on the banks of the Rhine. One of the squadron's pilots last saw him fighting a lone Bf 109 in a 'dogfight' above the clouds. It seems that he fell victim to the 109's pilot, who was probably the Luftwaffe 'experten' Major Siegfried Freytag of JG 77, who claimed a Spitfire in the Duisburg area near Wesel that day for his 101st victory.

After the war McLeod's body was discovered in the wreckage of his Spitfire IX on the outskirts of Wesel; he was buried in the Commonwealth War Graves cemetery at Rheinberg.

## THE ODDS

It is a sad fact, and an indication of the risks willingly accepted by these men, that of the pilots who had formed 443 Squadron at Digby, Lincolnshire, in February 1944, half of them were dead by the time that the war in Europe ended in May 1945.

Ockenden was one of the lucky ones, he survived, to serve in the postwar RCAF and to rise to the rank of Major General (Air Vice Marshal).

After the war he freely admitted that he had joined the RCAF in 1942 just to fly. "I never thought of going to war," he said, "but flying operations you suddenly realised, hey, this isn't just fun flying this is a serious business. I was pretty scared at times."

Gordon Ockenden passed away in 2000, aged 77. ∎

Gordon Ockenden at the end of the war in Europe.

'Spitfire v Bf 109 combat scene'. On June 7, 1944, D-Day +1, the Spitfires of 443 Squadron RCAF were tasked with four beachhead cover patrols. On the third mission of the day, Spitfire Mk.IX MK356, '2I-V' was flown by its regular pilot, Flying Officer Gordon Ockenden RCAF. The patrol was uneventful until nearing the time to leave, when the Spitfire pilots spotted four Luftwaffe Bf 109s east of Caen. Ockenden in MK356, in company with the Spitfire of Flight Lieutenant Hugh Russell, chased one of the Bf 109s out over the sea. The German fighter exploded in mid-air under the onslaught of their combined cannon and machine gun fire. Unsure which of them had delivered the coup de grace, they claimed half a kill each. This was the first of an eventual total of four combat kills plus one 'damaged' for Ockenden, who was awarded the Distinguished Flying Cross (DFC) in December 1944. Spitfire MK356 today flies with the RAF Battle of Britain Memorial Flight. Artwork: Adam Tooby adamtooby.artstation.com

German 88mm anti-aircraft flak gun of III Flakkorps in Normandy in 1944.

# Shot down by flak

## Flight Lieutenant Walter 'Johnny' Johnston (234 Squadron Spitfire Mk.VB pilot)

On June 14, 1944, 12 Mk.VB Spitfires of 234 Squadron took off at 2pm from their advanced landing ground airfield at Deanland, situated five miles to the north east of Lewes in Sussex, for a beachhead cover patrol between Bayeux and Caen. Flight Lieutenant Walter 'Johnny' Johnston was one of the pilots taking part, flying Spitfire Mk.VB BL415 'AZ-B'. He takes up the story:

"We started our patrol along a line roughly between Bayeux and Caen, just north of the main road, at a height of about 1500ft. We thought we were over our own

lines at the time and according to the map and with the marker of the road, we should have been... the next thing there was a hell of a bang and a great big flash. I assume it was a very near miss from a German 88mm anti-aircraft battery because you don't get hit directly by one of those and stay airborne.

"The shell burst just underneath my starboard wingtip and blew the aircraft some 200ft upwards and upside down. I was flying a clipped-wing Mk.VB and the explosion took another 2ft off the starboard wingtip, opening up the end of the wing like blowing up a paper bag and leaving the aileron dangling by a piece of cable. While I was on

my back I caught a split-second glimpse of the extent of the damage, but then almost immediately another explosion caught me directly beneath the port wing root, loosening the studs on the port and top engine cowlings and smashing the cockpit hood. The cockpit side door was forced open at the front runner, the acrylic glass of the hood was all smashed and the windscreen was starred. Something had grazed the right side of my flying helmet above the earpiece, luckily without injuring me.

"By this time my prop had stopped and I was coming round in the roll to the right way up. Then yet another burst took out the

Twenty-two-year-old Dennis Simms of 234 Squadron was killed on D-Day.

radiator under the port wing, along with a huge square of the skin above the wing. I couldn't get out of the cockpit because the hood had jammed closed and I could only fly the aircraft with both hands and the stick right over to port as far as it would go. It took all my strength to stop the aircraft turning over and at one point I even cocked my leg over the stick to get the aircraft into the turn and keep it there. I was now coming down in a screaming flat turn. Funnily enough my pitot head was still working and I saw that I had about 200mph on the clock."

## CRASH LANDING

At that moment Johnston saw a small flat strip of ground in front of him. He had made a mental note of this flattish line on the ground from previous passes over the area and now he tried to put his crippled Spitfire down on it. As he thumped on to the ground at about 180mph he thought to himself: "Please don't let me burn." The Spitfire hit the ground "with a hell of a smack", broke its back and spun round and round.

The impact snapped the right-hand shoulder strap and Johnston was flung forward on to the gunsight. Fortunately he had his oxygen mask on and goggles down, which prevented any facial injuries; he did not even get a black eye. The next thing that Johnston remembered was that he had stopped and was surrounded by men in khaki who, it transpired, were from the British unit building the airfield. One of them shoved a rifle into the hood and tore it off to get him out of the cockpit. Johnston was himself a 'Geordie' from the Newcastle area and was surprised to hear one of his rescuers say in a broad Geordie accent, as they hauled him out of the cockpit, "By Christ man, ye haven't half been hit".

As he was led away he suddenly realised that he had lost his gold watch, so he staggered back to the wreck to find it. The impact of hitting the ground had been so great that it had removed his watch from his wrist and over his hand; he found it lying neatly over the throttle, not that there was an engine to throttle.

## 'JOHNNY' JOHNSTON'S WAR UP TO NOVEMBER 1943

By this stage of the war Johnston was a very experienced pilot with over 1100 hours' flying in his logbook, having started flying training as a volunteer reservist in 1939, before war was declared. His first operational flying was as a sergeant pilot on Spitfires with 152 Squadron from February 1941 and then with 92 Squadron from July of that year. With them he flew on many fighter sweeps over enemy-occupied France, he claimed three Bf 109s probably destroyed and one as damaged; he was commissioned in November 1941.

He flew with many of the most famous fighter pilots of the time, no doubt learned much from them and also lost many friends and colleagues. Each of those is recorded in his logbook by name, perhaps with another comment such as "Nice chap"; one page alone records the loss of six fellow Spitfire pilots in a matter of days. In all he recorded the loss of 13 friends during those early years of the war and another seven while with 234 Squadron. In December 1941, Johnson started a long stint as an instructor at a Spitfire Operational Training Unit and then at the Central Gunnery School.

## 234 SQUADRON

In November 1943 Johnston was posted back on to operational duties as a flight commander with 234 Squadron with its Spitfire Mk.VBs. During the spring of 1944 he was involved in the squadron's operations in the build up to D-Day, including, for example, a train busting strafe sortie on May 21, 1944, in the Antwerp area. His logbook records: "Good day! Eleven trains by Wing, two by our section".

## D-DAY

On D-Day Johnston flew twice on beachhead cover patrols; the first taking off from Deanland at 4.30am. On this mission the squadron lost 22-year-old Flight Sergeant Dennis Simms "missing presumed killed"; one of the first British fighter pilots to be killed on D-Day. His aircraft simply disintegrated over the sea after being hit, possibly by enemy flak, but most likely by an Allied naval shell or by anti-aircraft fire from a 'friendly' naval vessel. Sims has no known grave and his name is commemorated on the Commonwealth Air Forces Memorial at Runnymede, Surrey.

## ON THE GROUND IN NORMANDY

On June 14, Johnston's was not the only 234 Squadron Spitfire to be hit by the salvo of flak over Normandy. He was soon joined by two other pilots from his squadron, Flying Officer Bill Painter and Flight Sergeant 'Joe' Fargher, who had also been hit by the barrage of anti-aircraft fire and were forced to land at the same partially completed airstrip, which was in fact B6 Coulombs.

Pilots of 'A' Flight 234 Squadron with a Spitfire Mk.VB at Coltishall in February 1944 (Johnston is fourth from left on the wing). Five of these pilots were destined to die on future operations.

Fargher had been unfortunate because, having landed with his wheels down, his Spitfire had tipped up on landing and he had a badly gashed forehead as a result of hitting the gunsight. Apart from that, all three pilots were uninjured.

The British engineers who were building the airfield had gone to the trouble of bringing to Normandy with them a crate of beer to share with the first pilots to land at their brand new airfield. They reckoned that this had now happened, so the pilots enjoyed a bottle of beer with the engineers while Johnston contemplated his very sad looking Spitfire.

The commanding officer of the Airfield Construction Unit fixed them up with a staff car, complete with a Bren gun on the roof and an Army driver and they set off along the main road from Caen towards Bayeux. They were stopped several times by British soldiers, but eventually reached a British Army HQ. There was a battery of 4.5s "firing away like hell"

nearby and they went inside the HQ to find the officer in charge.

The Spitfire pilots probably looked like a bunch of desperados with their gun belts slung around their waists and knives sticking out of their flying boots. The Army officer who met them was somewhat taken aback and exclaimed, "Good God, what happened to you lot?"

After they had explained their situation and the need to get back to England and to operations as soon as possible, he wrote them a note to flying control at the B2 Bazenville ALG, asking them to provide any assistance possible. The pilots had ideas of their own though; they sent the Army driver away to get some dinner and then stole his vehicle.

## VIP TRANSPORT HOME

After some more driving, they found the airfield at Bazenville, which happened to have a Dakota transport parked on it. Seeing this as a potential lift home, they drove the staff car, with its Bren gun on top, right up to the 'Dak' and to within a few feet of a group of people standing near it.

Johnston's heart sank when, on closer inspection, he recognised two of the group as Air Chief Marshal Sir Trafford Leigh-Mallory (Commander-in-Chief AAEAF) and Air Vice Marshal Harry Broadhurst (AOC 83 Group, 2 TAF).

The air marshals appeared unimpressed with this unscheduled interruption to their business by these scruffy hooligans and demanded an explanation. Johnson obliged and handed over the piece of paper. Leigh-Mallory chuckled and offered the three pilots a VIP lift home.

First though, the air chief marshal milked the situation for the public relations opportunity it provided by getting the accompanying press photographers to take several photographs of the pilots standing by the Dakota.

Eventually they all piled into the 'Dak' and were fed chocolate and drinks on the way back to Thorney Island, where they stopped the night in the officers' mess (with Joe Fargher masquerading as a pilot officer).

'Johnny' Johnston as a Sergeant Pilot in a 92 Squadron Spitfire Mk.VB at Biggin Hill in July 1941.

The three 234 Squadron Spitfire pilots photographed in front of ACM Sir Trafford Leigh-Mallory's C-47 Dakota at B2 Bazenville, Normandy, on June 14, 1944. They are, from left, Flt Sgt 'Joe' Fargher, Fg Off Bill Painter and Flt Lt 'Johnny' Johnston.

## LUCK – GOOD AND BAD

All three pilots were operational again the next day, June 15, having featured prominently in the morning edition of a national daily newspaper. Johnston's logbook entry for his next flight records another beachhead cover patrol with the remark: "Not bad going – back home and over again in less than 24 hours".

Bill Painter's luck ran out on June 17, just three days after their adventures, when returning in the dark from another beachhead cover patrol his section was fired on by the anti-aircraft batteries situated on the English south coast near Brighton. As the Spitfires took evasive action two collided; Bill Painter was killed in the mid-air collision although the other pilot, Flying Officer George Sparrow, managed to land his Spitfire safely at Deanland.

Joe Fargher's good luck continued to hold – just. He was shot down by flak again on July 11, on this occasion over enemy-occupied France. He evaded capture with the help of the Maquis and escaped back to England in a Navy motor gunboat, returning to rejoin the squadron on July 31.

## SEQUEL

Johnston remained with 234 Squadron and converted to Mustang IIIs when the squadron was re-equipped at the end of September 1944. He was promoted to acting squadron leader in November 1944 and survived the war, remaining in the RAF for some years afterwards. Walter 'Johnny' Johnston died in 2009, aged 88. ∎

Thanks to 'Johnny' Johnston's son, Martin Johnston, for his help in providing information for this article.

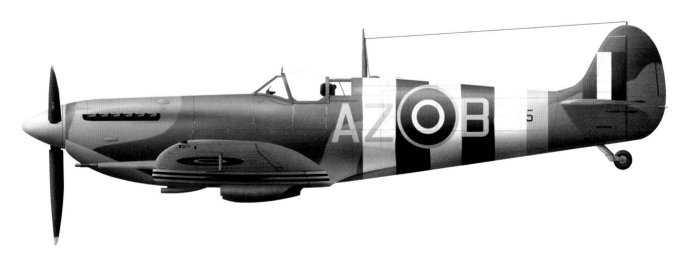

'Johnny' Johnston's Spitfire Mk.VB BL415 'AZ-B'. (Illustration by Chris Sandham-Bailey © INKWORM.com)

# Who got Rommel?

**ABOVE:** Generalfeldmarschall Erwin Rommel.
**BELOW:** Flt Lt Charlie Fox with his 412 Squadron Spitfire Mk.IX.

Generalfeldmarschall Erwin Rommel, the 53-year-old commander of the German forces defending the so-called 'Atlantic Wall' in 1944, was much respected by both sides as a soldier and brilliant military tactician and strategist.

At the time of D-Day, Rommel was in command of the important Army Group B. After the Allied invasion of Normandy he regularly travelled many kilometres every day, meeting with his battle commanders, personal contact being very much part of his leadership style.

## JULY 17, 1944

In the late afternoon of July 17, 1944, Rommel had just left the command post of the I Panzer Corps after a meeting with Generaloberst Josef 'Sepp' Dietrich of the Waffen SS, to drive back to his headquarters at La Roche-Guyon.

With Allied fighter-bombers roaming freely over Normandy the risk of attacks on vehicles moving in daylight was very high. Dietrich suggested that Rommel and his party should not take the main road and might perhaps use a small Volkswagen Type 82 Kübelwagen – a Jeep-like vehicle based on the VW Beetle – in order to be less conspicuous.

Rommel waved off the suggestion and set off as usual in his personal staff car, a large open-topped Horch 830BL, sitting in the front, as was his habit, alongside his regular driver, Unterfeldwebel Karl Daniel. In the back of the car were staff officers Hauptmann Lang, Major Neuhaus and Feldwebel Hoike, who were briefed to act as lookouts for Allied aircraft.

On the N179, between Livarot and Vimoutiers, travelling at high speed, the car came under attack from Spitfires. The officers in the rear of the car spotted the 'Jabos' and shouted their warnings too late.

Shells from the Spitfire hit the vehicle, seriously wounding the driver, who lost control of the speeding car, which hurtled on for several hundred metres before leaving the road and crashing into a ditch. Rommel was thrown against the windshield post, sustaining serious head injuries; the driver died soon afterwards and Major Neuhaus also suffered minor injuries.

Rommel riding in the front seat of a staff car in Normandy.

A Horch car similar to Rommel's staff car.

## A SAD END

In the days after the crash, Rommel's survival was in doubt, but slowly he began to recover. However, he was then implicated in the July 1944 bomb plot against Hitler, not directly, but because he was deemed to have defeatist views and Hitler was now convinced that treachery was everywhere.

In order to save his family and himself from disgrace Rommel was given no option but to commit suicide by taking a cyanide pill on October 14, 1944. Subsequently, he was given a state funeral, officially having died of his wounds. The Germans had lost one of their greatest military commanders, partly as a result of the attack by the Spitfire, but mainly because of Hitler's paranoia. The effect of Rommel's absence from command for the remainder of the war can only be guessed at.

## CLAIMANTS

This much is fact, but who the pilot was who fired the shots that may have changed the course of history on the Normandy front has long been contested. Over the years there have been many claimants to the attack on Rommel's staff car: American, South African, Australian and Canadian pilots have all claimed responsibility.

One of the first to claim credit for the attack on Rommel was American P-47 pilot Lieutenant Ralph Jenkins. According to Jenkins, he strafed a German staff car in the St-Lô area. The car was flying command flags and when Jenkins came around for another pass he saw the car in a ditch with bodies scattered around it. However, the

German accounts clearly indicate that it was Spitfires that attacked Rommel's car, so this claim can easily be discounted.

Australian Spitfire pilot Fred Cowlph of 453 Squadron also claimed responsibility for the strafing attack, asserting that his gun camera verified this, but there are other more credible possibilities.

Squadron Leader Chris le Roux DFC and Bar, a South African Spitfire pilot with 602 Squadron RAF has been widely credited over the years as being the pilot involved in the attack on Rommel's staff car. Le Roux claimed that on July 17, he attacked a German staff car near the village of Sainte-Foy-de-Montgommery, causing it to overturn in a ditch. One of the causes of confusion over these various claims has been the difficulty in resolving exact times between those used by the Allies and the Germans.

Recent research has shown that although Le Roux was in the right area on July 17, it was at the wrong time. In addition, the car carrying Rommel did not overturn; it ran into a ditch and hit a tree stump. Le Roux did not survive the war; he was killed in an aircraft accident on September 19, 1944.

## CHARLIE FOX

In recent years, historians have compared flight logs, consulted German reports (which specifically said that the car was attacked by four Spitfires, two flying high and two flying low), accounted for the time differences between European clocks and British Double Summer time and confirmed the time, location and, therefore, the aircraft and pilot involved.

This research has led to it now being widely accepted that the most likely candidate as the pilot of the Spitfire which attacked Rommel's car is Canadian Flight Lieutenant (later Squadron Leader) Charles W Fox of 412 Squadron (RCAF).

Charlie Fox was in exactly the right place at the right time. His logbook entry for the day records that he was flying his usual aircraft on armed recce duty. Time in the air was one hour and 15 minutes. Under the "results and remarks" column is the seemingly routine entry "1 staff car destroyed". A question mark, added later, precedes the word "Rommel", and then… the word "Yes".

## THE ATTACK

In the late afternoon of July 17, 1944, 12 Spitfires of 412 Squadron took off from B4 Bény-sur-Mer on an armed recce mission. The squadron split into three sections of four aircraft, one of these led by Fox. During the sortie Fox and his wingman, Steve Randall, spotted a large black car travelling at high speed along a road with trees on either side. It was coming towards Fox's section from about his 11 o'clock position. Fox recalled: "I saw this staff car coming along between lines of trees on a main road.

"I did a diving, curving attack and I probably started firing at about 300 yards. I timed the shots so that I was able to fire and get him as the car came through a small opening in the trees. I got him on that pass.

"We were moving pretty fast, but I knew I got him. I saw hits on the car and I saw it start to curve and go off the road. At the time, I had no idea who it was… just a large black open car… gleaming in the sun without any camouflage, which was unusual."

## AFTER THE WAR

Charlie Fox suspected that he had hit Rommel but did not pursue the matter. After the war he did not talk about it for many years, "but it's always been sitting in my logbook," he said.

It is most likely that it was Charlie Fox who put Rommel out of the war. Fox ended the war with a Distinguished Flying Cross and Bar. He lived to the age of 88, passing away in October 2008. ∎

Mk.IX Spitfires of 412 Squadron on B4 ALG at Bény-sur-Mer, Normandy, July 1944.

# Rodeo 194
## 131 Squadron Spitfire Mk.VIIs
### (Squadron Leader R W F 'Sammy' Sampson)

Spitfire HF Mk.VII, showing the extended, pointed wingtips of this mark, which also had a pressurised cockpit.

In August 1944 Squadron Leader 'Sammy' Sampson DFC, an experienced Spitfire pilot and ex-flight commander with 131 Squadron, was a staff officer in the 'ops' section at the 10 Group headquarters at Rudloe Manor, Box, near Bath. His job included planning fighter sweeps for the Culmhead and Harrowbeer Wings' Spitfires.

There were, it appears, certain attractions to the job, as the Group HQ was "well known for its very good-looking WAAF Officers," Sampson said.

As the Germans pulled back from Brittany, the fighter sweeps became longer and longer, stretching the Spitfires' range and endurance to its limits, even with drop tanks fitted. Inevitably, there was some banter from the squadrons against the staff

officers planning these long-range operations. So when Sampson planned the deepest penetration yet – Rodeo 194 – which 131 Squadron was tasked to execute on August 7, 1944, he suggested that to show there was no ill-feeling he should fly on the mission with the squadron. The SASO of 10 Group approved his request.

## SPITFIRE MK.VII

131 Squadron, based at Culmhead on the Blackdown Hills a few miles east of Taunton in Somerset, happened to be Sampson's old unit and it was chosen by the planners for this operation despite the fact that it was, at that time, equipped with Spitfire Mk.VIIs.

This mark of Spitfire was optimised for high altitude duties, being fitted with a pressurised cockpit and extended wing tips.

However, with little call for its high-altitude capability at this stage of the war, the three RAF squadrons equipped with the Mk.VII (including 131 Squadron) found themselves being tasked for low-level operations just like other Spitfire units.

Rodeo 194 was to be a classic example of that. This was to be a low-level fighter sweep, covering an estimated 760 miles, coasting into France at Cherbourg, then heading towards Chartres and Orleans, back along the Loire Valley and then out again past Cherbourg. The Mk.VII Spitfires had an extra 28 gallons of petrol in tanks fitted in the leading edge of the wings, but to manage this long range mission they would also be carrying 90 gallon drop tanks.

## OUTBOUND

The 12 Spitfires took off from Culmhead at 2pm on August 7, with Sampson flying in a borrowed Mk.VII, coded 'NX-M', as wingman to Wing Commander Peter Brothers, the wing leader. They set off across the channel at 'zero feet' so as not to alert the German radar.

As they approached the enemy coast they climbed rapidly to cross it near Cherbourg at 10,000ft, then the gaggle of fighters dropped back down to 4000ft. With about 10 minutes to go to the turnaround point, some 400 miles from their base at Culmhead, the Spitfire pilots spotted two Bf 109s. Jettisoning their drop tanks they gave chase, but the 109s had too much of a head start and they had to call it off.

'Sammy' Sampson in the cockpit of his 131 Squadron Spitfire in early 1944.

Still image from a Spitfire gun camera film showing a Fw 190 under attack.

## COMBAT KILL

Shortly after this though, as the Spitfires passed to the west of Le Mans, the pilots spotted about a dozen Fw 190s, which they chased and were beginning to overhaul. The 190s then half rolled into a 'Split S', coming back on a reciprocal course towards the Spitfires and below them. The Spitfire pilots dived down on the enemy aircraft and, with his throttle wide open, Sampson could see that he was gaining nicely on two of the 190s as he chased them "on the deck".

He was now ahead of Wing Commander Brothers and at about 550 yards he opened fire in the hope of producing a reaction. It worked. The two Fw 190s split, both breaking away from each other. Sampson selected the right-hand 190 and Brothers followed the one turning to port. The Spitfire Mk.VII's turn rate was much superior to the Fw 190 and Sampson quickly closed the range. At 450 yards he fired a one-and-a-half-second burst of cannon and machine gun fire from 40° off the enemy aircraft's tail, with no result.

Closing to 300 yards, and now flying at 240mph, he fired another two second burst, again with no result. The 190 then began to jink hard left and right allowing Sampson to fire three more short bursts from almost line astern with his speed now at about 180mph. He saw his rounds striking the cockpit of the 190 and he probably killed or mortally wounded the German pilot because the enemy aircraft suddenly pulled up vertically to about 600ft, rolled over and went straight in, exploding on impact with the ground.

Sampson's kill was witnessed by two of 131 Squadron's pilots and so was confirmed. Meanwhile Peter Brothers had shot down the other of the two Fw 190s they had been chasing.

## FLAK

Forming up with another of the Spitfires on the way home at 4000ft, Sampson found himself subjected to some intense and accurate 88mm flak. As the flak exploded around them a near miss made a very large hole in the port wing of Sampson's aircraft. Fortunately it had not hit anything vital, but it certainly gave him a jolt.

Out over the sea, now back at "zero" feet he found that the Spitfire was flying perfectly, despite the hole in its wing. When he arrived at Culmhead he advised the control tower of his situation and they alerted the fire section and "blood wagons". In the event, the undercarriage and flaps worked as advertised and he landed 'NX-M' safely, three hours and 20 minutes after taking off.

When he climbed out of the Spitfire at 131 Squadron's dispersal he was greeted somewhat anxiously by the other pilots but got an entirely different reaction from the squadron engineering officer who could only say: "Oh, for Christ's sake, that's going to take some repairing!"

## IN THE NEWS

The next day Sampson was called to the AOC's office to report on the previous day's activities, at the end of which the AOC said: "That's it. You are a staff officer so no more operational sorties!" The AOC was probably even less enchanted when the press got hold of the story which appeared in *The Evening News* and started with: "Squadron Leader R W Sampson DFC took a day off yesterday and shot down a Fw 190..."

## SEQUEL

In November 1944, Sampson was allowed to return to operations, he became a Spitfire squadron commander and then wing leader, specialising in ground attack and dive-bombing until the end of the war in Europe. He retired from the RAF as a wing commander OBE DFC and Bar. ∎

Focke-Wulf Fw 190 similar to the one claimed by 'Sammy' Sampson on the afternoon of August 7, 1944, over France.

# Hawker Typhoon

The Hawker Typhoon Mk.IB ('Tiffy' in RAF slang) was the RAF's dedicated fighter-bomber aircraft on D-Day, with 20 operational squadrons available, 18 of them operating as part of 2 TAF.

Having overcome the difficulties that plagued the design in its early years, the Typhoon had now found its niche as a highly effective fighter-bomber, while retaining a useful air-to-air pure fighter capability at lower levels. The aircraft proved itself to be the most effective RAF tactical strike aircraft both on interdiction raids against communications and transport targets deep in North Western Europe prior to the invasion, and in direct support of the Allied ground forces after D-Day.

## TYPHOON VITAL STATISTICS

The Typhoon was a large and imposing aircraft for a single-seat fighter, measuring 32ft (9.75m) long with a wingspan of 41½ft (12.65m) and a massive three-bladed 14ft (4.3m) diameter propeller. Sitting high on its wide undercarriage, the cockpit was 8ft (2.4m) above the ground and pilots climbed in with the help of a pull-down 'stirrup' and steps hidden by sprung doors in the fuselage. While on the ground, there was no forward visibility at all for a pilot sitting in the cockpit.

Loaded for a fight, the Typhoon could have a gross weight of up to six tons (6000kg). It was fitted with a massive 'H'-layout, 24-cylinder Napier Sabre engine, one of the most complex piston engines ever built with a displacement volume of 36.7 litres and a power output in excess of 2000hp with the later versions having an astonishing 3000hp in reserve (with injection of a mixture of water and ethanol). The large chin intake underneath the nose contained the radiator and gave the aircraft its particular profile.

## TYPHOON PERFORMANCE

The 'Tiffy' was something of a 'beast' to fly. It cruised fast, typically 350mph, with a maximum level speed of around 400mph. In a dive it picked up speed very quickly, but was (officially) limited, for stability reasons, to 400mph loaded with bombs or rockets, although it was cleared to 525mph without them.

## TYPHOON ARMAMENT

Normally fitted with four 20mm cannons, the Typhoon was an excellent strafe platform with heavy hitting power, especially against unhardened buildings and unarmoured vehicles. From September 1943, Typhoons were also armed with eight 3in (75mm) unguided rocket projectiles

(RP-3), four under each wing, which could be fitted with different types of explosive warheads. The 6in (150mm), 60lb (27kg) high explosive warhead was the most commonly-used version, but the rockets could also be fitted with a 25lb (11kg), 3.44in armour-piercing warhead.

The rocket projectiles were unguided and inaccurate, with considerable gravity drop after firing and it took considerable skill and practice to aim them anything like accurately. However, the firepower of all eight RPs from a Typhoon was the equivalent of a navy destroyer's broadside.

The Typhoon could, alternatively, carry two 500lb (226kg) or two 1000lb (453kg) bombs, one under each wing. The first time that RAF single-seat fighter-bombers carried two 1000lb bombs each was on April 24, 1944, when the Typhoons of 438 Squadron were sent to attack bridges in northern France. This was to become standard practice and significantly increased the level of tactical firepower available to commanders. Although, in theory, the role equipment was easy to change, in actuality the Typhoon squadrons stuck to being either rocket-firing (RP) units (there were 13 of these squadrons available on D-Day) or bomb carriers – so-called 'Bomphoons'.

Hawker Typhoon Mk.IB, MN317, 'ZY-B', of 247 (China British) Squadron being re-armed at B2/Bazenville, Normandy, on June 15, 1944. The ground crews are loading 3in rocket projectiles, while the pilot waits in the cockpit for the next mission.

440 Squadron 'Bomphoon' RB389 'I8-P' named 'Pulverizer IV' taxies out for a sortie loaded with two 1000lb bombs.

## TYPHOONS VERSUS TANKS

The Typhoon's effectiveness against soft-skinned targets is widely accepted, but its ability to knock out German tanks has been the subject of considerable postwar debate, with some arguing that the relatively limited success rates were, perhaps, not worth the losses in aircraft and pilots.

Against the Wehrmacht's tanks, the Typhoon's rockets needed to hit the thin-walled engine compartment or the tracks to have any chance of destroying or disabling the tank. The 20mm shells from the Typhoon's cannons were only effective against armoured vehicles if they ricocheted off the ground into the lighter armour of the tanks' undersides, having been aimed short.

Inevitably, as in air-to-air combat, there was an element of confusion and over-claiming by the Typhoon pilots over the number of tanks destroyed. The results of their attacks were difficult to assess and they could not easily tell if a tank had already been attacked or previously abandoned. Operational analysis of destroyed tanks after the battles in Normandy indicated that actually only some 4% of German tanks had fallen victim to Typhoon rocket attacks.

However, these operational analyses also suggested that apart from the direct destructive effects of fighter-bomber attacks, the effects on the morale of the German troops caught up in Typhoon RP and cannon attacks were equally decisive, with many German tanks and vehicles being abandoned by their demoralised crews with only superficial damage.

One German tank commander said after the war: "We feared the Typhoons most of all. These aircraft continued to attack a target in spite of heavy ground fire, causing complete devastation, coming round again and again. It created a low morale from which we never recovered. I was lucky to survive; the only possible means of escape was to get out of our tanks and run."

## THE MORTAIN VICTORY

Evidence of German tanks being abandoned under rocket attack was seen in the only large-scale German armoured offensive in Normandy, which was mounted at Mortain, in the Falaise pocket on August 7, and which seriously threatened the American break-out from the beachhead. Despite determined defence, the credit for bringing the German attack to a halt on the afternoon of August 7, is generally regarded as belonging to Allied fighter-bombers, particularly RAF Typhoons, which were called in to intervene.

German accounts clearly attribute the failure of their attack to the fighter-bombers. The Typhoons first went into action against the armoured column just before 1pm, when early morning fog and mist had cleared. Finding a concentration of some 60 tanks and 200 vehicles grouped close together, many heavily camouflaged, the Typhoons commenced attacks against the front and rear of the column, which was immediately brought to a halt.

By the end of the day RAF Typhoons had flown 294 sorties in the Mortain area, firing 2088 rockets and dropping 80 tons of bombs. In addition, strafe attacks with the Typhoon's 20mm cannon had destroyed large numbers of unarmoured support vehicles laden with fuel and ammunition for the tanks. Three Typhoons and their pilots had been lost. Although the level of flak had initially been light, it had increased during the day with box-like patterns being put up over the tanks, and many of the Typhoons were found to have suffered damage from this and from small-arms fire. Interestingly, though, it was discovered in the aftermath that some 30% of the German tanks had simply been abandoned by their crews, who were, understandably, terrified by the Typhoon's rocket attacks. The tank crews knew that they were trapped and while the chances of a direct hit were low, their chances of survival were extremely small if they were hit.

The Supreme Allied Commander, General Eisenhower, said of the RAF Typhoon pilots' actions at Mortain: "The chief credit in smashing the enemy's spearhead, however, must go to the rocket-firing Typhoon aircraft of the Second Tactical Air Force... the result was that the enemy attack was effectively brought to a halt and a threat was turned into a great victory." ■

Hawker Typhoon Mk.IBs of 121 Wing assembled at B2/Bazenville, Normandy, for close-support operations. Second from the right is MN666 'C-G', the personal aircraft of Wing Commander C L Green, the wing leader. Note the mixture of three- and four-bladed propellers; the latter being a more recent modification.

'Clash of the Titans'. An RAF Hawker Typhoon Mk.IB fires 3in rockets at a German Tiger tank. Len Krenzler

# D-Day Typhoon Pilot

## Flight Lieutenant Ken Trott
### (197 Squadron Typhoon IB pilot)

**K**en Trott was born in Ilford, on the outskirts of London, in December 1922. He joined the RAF Volunteer Reserve in September 1941 and was posted overseas to Canada for flying training. In September 1942 he received his pilot's 'wings' and was commissioned as a pilot officer.

## TYPHOONS
After his return to England he completed his training on Miles Masters and was then sent to 59 OTU at Millfield, near Berwick-on-Tweed, to fly Hawker Hurricanes. Then in April 1943 he was posted to 195 Squadron, which was equipped with the mighty Hawker Typhoon, at Woodvale Airfield near Southport, Lancashire.

Soon after Trott's arrival, the squadron was moved to Norfolk and led a rather nomadic existence for several months, being based at Ludham, then Matlask, then Coltishall, before settling for a while at Fairlop in Essex from September 1943. During this time Trott carried out operations across the North Sea into Holland and over France. In early 1944, 195 Squadron was disbanded and Trott moved to 197 Squadron stationed at Tangmere Airfield, West Sussex. The Typhoons were then equipped with bomb racks under each wing to take 500 or 1000lb bombs. The squadron's main tasks were attacking radar and V-1 sites, as well as being on escort and standby duties.

## NEEDS OAR POINT AND 146 WING
In April 1944, 197 Squadron moved to the newly constructed temporary airfield at Needs Oar Point near the Beaulieu River, overlooking the Solent and the Isle of Wight. In preparation for D-Day, it became part of 146 Wing, 2 TAF, with 257, 266 and 193 Squadrons. In May 1944, the Typhoons were frequently called upon to make attacks against radar targets along the coast of France, as well as against V-1 sites.

On June 3, Trott was involved in a high-level dive-bombing attack on the radar site at Cap-d'Antifer, not far from Le Havre. This was part of the vital and carefully-planned campaign to blind the enemy prior to the invasion. The Typhoons crossed over the French Coast, high enough to avoid the light flak, and then turned through 180° into a steep dive-bombing attack on the German radar site with a final burst of cannon fire before levelling out over the sea at about 500mph. They then formed up into sections of four in battle formation for the return flight. Total flying time was one hour, 15 minutes. That night orders were received to paint the broad black and white invasion stripes on the wings and fuselage of the Typhoons.

## THE EVE OF D-DAY
On June 5, Trott air-tested a newly-delivered Typhoon, one of the first with a four-bladed propeller which were just starting to arrive at the squadrons. That evening he carried out another operation over the French coast, noting later in his logbook: "Large convoys of LCRs seen heading toward Cherbourg." In fact, the Channel was covered with boats of various kinds – a fantastic sight – and he thought that it was impossible that the Germans did not know what was happening.

After returning to Needs Oar Point, all the squadron pilots were ordered to the large

'Bomphoon' of 197 Squadron – as flown by Ken Trott – loaded with two 500lb bombs.

Typhoon IB loaded with two 1000lb bombs, taxiing through a large puddle at a forward airfield.

mess tent where a covered blackboard was set up. They were briefed by the wing leader, Wing Commander Reggie Baker DFC and Bar, that tomorrow, June 6, would be D-Day. The blackboard was unveiled to reveal the proposed landing beaches and other details of the invasion. The pilots were told to turn in early, as they would be on call from around 4am the next day, but the roar of aircraft overhead, heading towards France, made sleep almost impossible in their tents.

## D-DAY

After an early breakfast the pilots reported to their various dispersals, where the ground crew were already running up the Sabre engines of the Typhoons and then refuelling them. The pilots waited to be called to briefings while listening to the BBC radio broadcasts. 197 Squadron was the first to launch at 7.10am, eight aircraft being led by Wing Commander Baker (who lost his life over Normandy 10 days later, on June 16). The Typhoons attacked a German High Command headquarters in a chateau south of Bayeux. They encountered little opposition with only small amounts of light flak in the vicinity of their target. Bombing and strafing at will for 20 minutes, the Typhoons left the chateau a smouldering ruin. They all landed safely back at Needs Oar Point at 8.20am.

As soon as the aircraft from this first operation of the day had landed and taxied in, they were surrounded by both ground crew and the other pilots on standby, who were checking firstly to see if the muzzle covers had been blown off the cannons (which would indicate that each of the four 20mm cannons had been fired) and then if there was any flak damage to the aircraft. As soon as the pilots had climbed down, everyone wanted to know what it was like over the beachhead. "Any enemy aircraft seen? How much flak? The weather conditions? What targets had been attacked?"

Meanwhile, the squadron intelligence officer was hovering around, wanting to speak to each pilot who had taken part in

this first operation of D-Day. Having slung their parachutes over their shoulders, many pilots walked away to light a cigarette before giving way to the countless questions coming from all sides. The aircraft were now surrounded by the ground crews, busy refuelling and re-arming to get them ready as soon as possible for the next operation.

Trott was not involved in the early operations of the day, but he remained on call until 5.50pm when he and seven other pilots were briefed to carry out an armed reconnaissance south of Caen. Trott's logbook shows that this involved low-level bombing of an enemy supply dump, which was left with black smoke and flames coming from it. All the Typhoons on this mission returned safely at 7.20pm. The last operation for 197 Squadron on June 6 took off at 9.05pm, with eight aircraft on an armed reconnaissance in the Caen and Bayeux area. They landed back safely at 10.15pm, and so ended D-Day.

## NORMANDY

In early July, 197 Squadron moved from Needs Oar Point to Hurn in preparation for the move to their new airfield in Normandy. On July 8, the Typhoons landed at B3 St Croix-sur-Mer on the beachhead, due to stay for a few days. They were about to return to Hurn on the evening of July 13 when they were briefed to conduct an armed recce over the Caen area.

Four Typhoons, including one flown by Trott, took off led by Wing Commander Baldwin, who was due to become the wing leader. During the patrol Trott spotted an armoured carrier and requested permission to attack it with his wingman. With the necessary permission granted, the two Typhoons detached from the others, which held at higher altitude, while Trott and his wingman strafed and immobilised the vehicle. They were about to return for a second attack when they heard on the radio that the other Typhoons were being engaged by about 30 Bf 109s.

Destroyed German Würzburg radar on the cliff tops at Arromanches, similar to the site which was attacked by the Typhoons of 197 Squadron on June 3, 1944.

Climbing up into the fight above, Trott made a head-on attack against a Bf 109. As he broke away, the starboard wing of his Typhoon struck the Bf 109 with catastrophic consequences. Trott's head and shoulder struck the side of the cockpit as the canopy disappeared; his helmet, oxygen mask and goggles were torn off him and he was catapulted into the air from his disintegrating aircraft with only his parachute intact. He managed to pull the rip cord and then lost consciousness. When he came to, he was hanging in his parachute from a tree, surrounded by German soldiers. He was taken prisoner and subsequently spent the next 10 months as a prisoner of war, much of the time in medical care in the hospital at Stalag Luft III.

Ken Trott was finally demobilised from the RAF in November 1946 in the substantive rank of flight lieutenant. He passed away in September 2013, aged 90.

In total, during the 10 weeks of the battle of Normandy, 150 Typhoon pilots lost their lives, while many others became prisoners of war. ∎

'Storm Rising'. Two Hawker Typhoon Mk.IBs of 197 Squadron, coded 'OV-Z' and 'OV-C' taking off, roaring into the air, kicking up the dust. On D-Day, 2 TAF fielded 18 squadrons of Typhoon fighter-bombers. In the following weeks they played a vital role in the battle for Normandy, establishing a well-earned reputation for fast and accurate close support. By this time, most Typhoons were carrying rockets rather than bombs. In theory it was possible to re-role the Typhoons for the carriage of rockets or bombs quite easily, but in practice a number of squadrons, including 197 Squadron, retained bombs as their principle air-to-ground weapon. In this case the Typhoons are each carrying two 500lb bombs. These aircraft were referred to as 'Bomphoons'. Artwork: Adam Tooby adamtooby.artstation.com

# Flying the beast

## Flight Lieutenant 'Johnny' Colton (RCAF) (137 Squadron Typhoon pilot)

'Johnny' Colton with his 137 Squadron Typhoon in spring 1944.

Flight Lieutenant 'Johnny' Colton from Quebec, Canada, joined the RCAF in January 1942, aged 19. On completion of his training he joined 137 Squadron to fly Hawker Typhoons operationally.

At the time of D-Day, 137 Squadron was part of 11 Group ADGB and was based at Manston, Kent. Colton flew 104 operational sorties during the war and survived, an extraordinary accomplishment on both counts. 'Johnny' Colton passed away in Canada in May 2013. Here he describes what the Hawker Typhoon was like to operate:

"To start this monster, the Typhoon pilot had to set the throttle to five-eighth of an inch open and no more, otherwise there was a risk of drowning the carburettors in gasoline with a resulting engine fire. The ignition of the 24 cylinders, using what was called the Coffman System, was effected using a shotgun-style cartridge. As the cartridge exploded, the propeller rotated about 450°. At that point, with the cylinders full of gasoline, it was a must for the engine to start successfully, or it had an 80% chance of catching fire at the next attempt.

"The fuel had a very high octane rating at this stage of the war, the Typhoon used only 130 octane grade gas. Before starting the engine (and during the flight), the pilot was obliged to wear an oxygen mask because the cockpit immediately filled with carbon monoxide exhaust. The Napier Sabre engine had an awesome decibel output, sounding nearly five times louder than a Merlin. The vibration caused by this beast was quite disconcerting to an inexperienced pilot.

"While taxiing, it was recommended not to abuse the brakes, to avoid heating them and consequently decreasing their effectiveness. At the hold position, the pilot had to run up the engine 3000rpm to clear out the cylinders. At start-up and during taxi, the engine would spit plenty of hot oil, but the mechanic, who often guided the pilot by sitting on a wing, learned to have a cloth handy to wipe the windshield before the pilot took off. It was better not to wait too long before taking off, as the engine heated up quickly, easily reaching a temperature of 95°C.

Rocket armed Typhoons of 124 Wing taxiing on 'PSP' matting in the Netherlands in the autumn of 1944.

"With the massive propeller powered by the equally massive Sabre, the power on take-off was phenomenal, the torque being so strong as to frighten any unwary beginner pilot. On the take-off roll, the aircraft would veer violently to the right even with the rudder pedal fully depressed left. It was only with the proper rudder trim and the right mix of power that the pilots were able to keep the aircraft straight, the ailerons not being effective below 93mph.

"The flak that we experienced... you've heard the expression, 'it was so thick you could almost walk on it!' It was just black, and we suffered quite a few losses. We would start our dive at 6000ft and we'd be getting close to 500 miles per hour before we'd release our rockets and pull out. On the way down we had the 88mm anti-aircraft guns firing at us at five or six thousand feet, then 37mm, then 20mm, as we got lower and closer to the target. Then on the way out it was 20, 37 and 88mm in that order. They didn't have too hard a time picking off the boys.

"At the speed we were doing when we pulled out you could easily 'black out' for two or three seconds and when you came round you were going straight up. Frequently, when I got back to base the airframe mechanic would say to me, 'You know the rivets are pulled in the wings here. What happened?' This occurred quite often, the rivets would come loose from the stresses of the G-force."

# Group Captain Des 'Scottie' Scott (RNZAF) (Typhoon pilot with 198 and 486 (NZ) Squadrons)

Group Captain Des Scott, leader of 123 Wing, (wearing the mae west) having dismounted from his Typhoon behind him, converses with another RAF officer at B53/Merville, France, watched by an interested group of local boys.

Des 'Scottie' Scott was called up to join the Royal New Zealand Air Force (RNZAF) when war was declared in 1939. He joined 3 Squadron RAF in January 1941, as a sergeant pilot, flying Hawker Hurricanes.

He was commissioned in July 1942 and by August he was a flight commander, receiving a DFC and Bar before being promoted to squadron leader and rested from operations in a staff position.

In April 1943 he converted to the Hawker Typhoon and joined 198 Squadron. Despite some of his less than complimentary comments below, Scott loved this monster and mastered it thoroughly. Subsequently, he was posted to command 486 Squadron (NZ) Squadron. In August 1943 he received the DSO and became the Wing Leader at RAF Tangmere.

After commanding the airfield at Hawkinge in early 1944, during which time he was awarded the OBE for rescuing a pilot from a burning, crashed Spitfire, Scott enjoyed his greatest and most exhausting fighting days. Until February 1945, as the youngest group captain in the RNZAF, he commanded 123 Wing, a mobile wing of four Typhoon squadrons in 2 TAF, and led them from Normandy to Holland. His air-to-air combat claims for the war were five (plus three shared) confirmed destroyed, four (plus two shared) 'probables', and five (plus one shared) damaged.

Scott passed away in October 1997, aged 79. This is his description of flying the Typhoon:

"She roared, screamed, groaned and whined, but apart from being rather heavy on the controls at high speeds, as far as I was concerned she flew well.

"In stability terms, the aircraft was directionally and laterally stable but slightly unstable longitudinally, except at high speed, when it was just stable. Aileron control was light and effective up to

maximum speed, but at very low speed response was sluggish, particularly when carrying ordnance. The elevator control was rather light and could not be used harshly. There was a tendency to 'tighten up' in a looping aircraft. If 'black out' conditions were accidentally induced in steep turns or pulling out of a dive, the control column needed to be pushed forward firmly.

"Stalling speeds were quite low. The typical Typhoon trait, as with many aircraft at the time, was to drop a wing sharply at the stall either with flaps up or down. The stalling speeds varied depending on external load. At all-up weight plus two 500lb (230kg) bombs (12,155lb in total) with flaps up the Typhoon stalled at 90-100mph. With flaps down, the stall was initiated at 70-75mph. With all ammunition and nearly all fuel expended (9600lb) the stall occurred at 75-80 and 65-70mph.

"Should the Typhoon's temperamental engine stop in the air you were faced with two alternatives – over the side, or the gliding angle of a seven-ton brick; in a forced landing it was apt to somersault and either crush the pilot or explode."

# Squadron Leader Basil Gerald 'Stapme' Stapleton (Typhoon pilot with 247 and 257 Squadrons)

Squadron Leader Basil Gerald 'Stapme' Stapleton DFC was born in May 1920 in Durban, South Africa. He used the first name Gerald and was nicknamed 'Stapme' after a phrase used in his favourite cartoon strip Just Jane published in *The Daily Mirror*.

'Stapme' was a Spitfire pilot with 603 RAuxAF Squadron during the Battle of Britain. His personal score of six enemy aircraft destroyed, three shared destroyed, eight probably destroyed two damaged, all achieved on Spitfires during the battle, made him one of the outstanding fighter pilots of the period. He was awarded the Distinguished Flying Cross in November 1940.

Having subsequently served with various units, including flying 'Hurricats' with the Merchant Ship Fighter Unit, 'Stapme' converted to the Hawker Typhoon while serving as a flight commander with 257 Squadron when the unit re-equipped with the type in July 1942. Later, from August 1944 he commanded 247 Squadron, part of 124 Wing, 2 TAF, flying Typhoons in northern France.

On December 23, 1944, Stapleton was forced to land behind enemy lines and became a prisoner of war, after debris from

A salvo of Typhoon 3in rockets on their way to a target.

Typhoon Mk.IB MN234 'SF-T' of 137 Squadron, running up on an engine test at B78 Eindhoven, Holland. It is loaded with 3in rocket projectiles with 60lb warheads. 'Johnny' Colton flew this particular Typhoon while in Holland in 1944. The aircraft was eventually shot down during the Ardennes Campaign in December 1944.

an exploding train, which he had attacked, punctured the radiator of his Typhoon.

'Stapme' was one of the real 'characters' to survive the war, complete with his handlebar moustache and always with a mischievous twinkle in his eyes. The author had the privilege and pleasure of meeting him on many occasions in his later life and being regaled with his many wartime stories.

'Stapme' passed away in April 2010, a month before his 90th birthday. This is his 'take' on flying the Typhoon:

"The first thing that struck me when I climbed into a Typhoon was that you had to get used to the height you were sitting at. On take-off the Typhoon swung the opposite way to the Hurricane and Spitfire, so we had to unlearn that which had become second nature to us. Early Typhoon take-offs were nearly always in a climbing turn!

"The Typhoon was far more powerful than previous aircraft I'd flown. On an early flight I achieved 400mph on the clock at sea level; it really was a tremendous ground attack aircraft. The cannons were devastating for soft-skin targets, such as vehicles. If there was grass around the targets, it was like a wave when the shells

hit the ground and the turf seemed to ripple in retreat.

"There was no recoil when firing rockets. Having sighted the target, I lined up, dived, started to pull out and fired just as soon as it disappeared beneath the nose of the aircraft. Using this method, I reckoned that I couldn't miss.

"I found it best to stay low after an attack and utilise the speed to get away from the target, rather than attempting to climb away. This seemed to work and when I came down in December 1944, I wasn't shot down, I suppose I shot myself down when I flew through the debris of the locomotive I had attacked with my rockets!" ∎

The cockpit of the 'beast' – pilot's view as he climbs into the Typhoon cockpit.

# North American Mustang III

In addition to the Spitfire and Typhoon units, on D-Day the RAF also had at its disposal seven squadrons of Mustang IIIs, the British name for the North American P-51B/C with the Packard Merlin engine, which were acquired by the RAF under Lend-Lease arrangements.

The Mustang III entered service with 122 Wing (19, 65 and 122 Squadrons) in February 1944. The second Mustang wing was 133 Wing (306, 315, 316 (Polish) Squadrons) which re-equipped with the Mustang in April 1944, under the command of the Polish fighter ace Wing Commander Stanislaw Skalski, and which was subsequently joined by 129 Squadron RAF.

After these so-called 'razorback' Mustang III aircraft had been delivered to England, the RAF decided that the hinged cockpit canopy offered too poor a view for European operations. A fairly major modification was made in which the original framed hinged hood was replaced by a bulged Perspex frameless canopy that slid to the rear on rails. This canopy gave the pilot much more room and afforded a good view downwards and to the rear. This hood was manufactured and fitted by the British corporation R Malcolm & Co and became known as the 'Malcolm Hood'.

This hood was fitted to most RAF Mustang IIIs, and many USAAF Eighth and Ninth Air Force P-51B/C fighters received this modification as well.

The RAF found the Merlin-engine Mustangs to be robust and fast, capable of over 400mph level at 2000ft. Many pilots regarded the 'razorback' Malcolm-hooded Mustang III as the best of the entire series. It was lighter, faster, and had crisper handling than the later bubble-hooded P-51D/Mustang IV.

Prior to D-Day, being a scarce resource, the RAF Mustang IIIs were mainly employed on operations for which the aircraft's long range and high speed provided an edge over other RAF single-engine fighter types, such as long range fighter sweeps, and escort duties supporting USAAF heavy bombers or coastal command anti-shipping strikes by Bristol Beaufighters and DH Mosquitos.

On D-Day the Mustang III units provided fighter cover and subsequently some were deployed into France to provide ground support. In July half of them were pulled back to southern England to deal with the V-1 flying bombs, but they were soon back on the continent. The Mustangs continued to provide further long-range bomber escorts,

including some in support of RAF Bomber Command daylight raids.

During the Battle of Normandy, the RAF Mustang III really proved its worth as a true multi-role fighter. Very capable as a pure fighter in the air-to-air role at all altitudes, the Mustang was also an excellent ground attack strafe platform with its armament of four wing-mounted .50in (12.7mm) Browning heavy machine guns (with 350 rounds per gun (rpg) for the inboard guns and 280rpg for the outboard). It was also a very useful fighter-bomber able to carry two 500lb bombs or even two 1000lb bombs, one under each wing. ∎

'Malcolm' hooded Mustang IIIs of 19 Squadron, April 1944.

# Mustang – 'two up'
## Squadron Leader Eugeniusz Horbaczewski
## (315 Squadron Mustang III pilot)

Horbaczewski with his 315 Squadron Mustang III FB382 'PK-G' used in the rescue.

Squadron Leader Eugeniusz Horbaczewski climbing into his Mustang III.

One of the Polish fighter squadrons formed in Great Britain as part of an agreement between the Polish Government in Exile and the United Kingdom. One of several Polish fighter squadrons that flew and fought with the RAF during the Second World War, it was named after the city of Deblin, where the main Polish Air Force Academy was located.

The squadron was formed at RAF Acklington in January 1941. Initially equipped with Hawker Hurricanes, 315 was moved in March 1941 to RAF Speke (now Liverpool Airport) from where it made frequent patrols over naval convoys as part of 9 Group RAF. In July that year it moved to RAF Northolt and re-equipped with Spitfires. After only a month with Mk.IIa Spitfires, 315 Squadron received Mk.Vbs and, from then until March 1944, the squadron operated Spitfires on offensive fighter sweeps and fighter escorts over occupied Europe and defensive patrols

protecting the UK, later on with Mk.IXs. In March 1944, 315 Squadron re-equipped with Mustang IIIs, joining 133 Polish Mustang Wing of 2 TAF, operating from bases in southern England.

## SQUADRON LEADER EUGENIUSZ HORBACZEWSKI

Among the many Polish airmen who gave such valued service to the RAF, Squadron Leader Eugeniusz Horbaczewski, was one of the most distinguished.

Nicknamed 'Dziubek', Horbaczewski was a legendary Polish fighter pilot – the third highest scoring Polish fighter ace with a total of 16½ confirmed kills (plus one shared) – and an exceptional leader, highly respected by all those who knew him.

Horbaczewski had been a member of the special Polish unit consisting of 15 experienced Polish fighter pilot volunteers – the Polish Fighting Team (PFT) or 'Skalski's Circus' – that operated in North Africa with Spitfire Mk.IXs in the spring of 1943 and with which he destroyed eight enemy aircraft in combat.

Among the decorations Horbaczewski was awarded were the Virtuti Militari, four Polish Crosses of valour, the DSO and DFC and Bar. Horbaczewski took command of 315 Squadron in February 1944 just before the unit re-equipped with Mustang IIIs.

## 315 SQUADRON MUSTANG IIIS

During the invasion, the two RAF wings of Mustang IIIs were given responsibility for cutting off German forces behind the beachhead, with deep-penetration missions laid on at a rate of two to three missions per day, attacking both German ground targets and Luftwaffe aircraft in the air.

On the morning of June 12, 1944, Horbaczewski led four Mustangs of 315 Squadron on a dive-bombing mission north of Mortagne, during which they ran across seven Fw 190s at low level. The Poles shot down three of the 190s with Horbaczewski and Flying Officer Kirste claiming one each, while Flight Sergeant Bargielowski got two. On July 30 Horbaczewski destroyed a Bf 109 and shared a kill against another 109 with his wingman.

## HORBACZEWSKI TO THE RESCUE

On June 22, Horbaczewski led a formation of 12, 315 Squadron Mustang IIIs on a strafing attack against enemy ground positions in Normandy. Two of the Mustangs were hit by ground fire; Flight Lieutenant Henryk Stefankiewicz in FB398, 'PK-A' was killed and Warrant Officer Tadeusz Tamowicz's Mustang FZ157 'PK-J', was also hit by 20mm shells, slightly wounding the pilot in both legs.

Tamowicz managed to get his aircraft back into the beach-head area where he crash-landed in a marsh. Extricating himself from the cockpit of his Mustang which was sinking into the mud, Tamowicz crawled, with some difficulty due to his wounds, to a clump of bushes and used his shirt to dress his bleeding legs. Meanwhile, Horbaczewski found a short strip nearby, an ALG under construction by a group of American engineers. He circled it and decided to land to help his colleague.

Having landed safely on the strip, Horbaczewski was driven by the Americans in a jeep to the area where Tamowicz had crash-landed. On reaching the marsh about 30 minutes later, Horbaczewski and the American soldiers had to wade through mud and water for 400m, waist deep in places, to reach Tamowicz. With the Americans' assistance, Tamowicz was rescued, his wounds were tended and he was helped to the jeep and returned to the ALG.

## TWO-UP

Horbaczewski slid the seat of his Mustang as far back as possible and enlisted the further help of the American engineers to get Tamowicz into his Mustang (FB382 'PK-G'). Then Horbaczewski, who was

Flt Sgt Slon and Sqn Ldr Horbaczewski demonstrate for a press photograph (not very convincingly) how two can fit into a Mustang cockpit. (Tadeusz Tamowicz was recovering from his wounds when the picture was taken).

fortunately small in stature, climbed in and sat on Tamowicz's lap, started up, taxied to the end of the strip and took off.

The Mustang landed safely back at 315 Squadron's base at Coolham, Sussex, where the ground crews were understandably surprised to see two men emerge from the cockpit. Some of those who witnessed this return were deeply moved by Horbaczewski's actions and devotion to his men. The official RAF reaction was less benevolent in view of the many regulations that had been broken!

## TAMOWICZ'S LOGBOOK ENTRIES

Tamowicz was back flying on operations again five days later. His logbook contains two entries for June 22, 1944, the first stating: "Mustang III 'J' – Duty: Strafing south of 'Cher' – 1:40 – "shot down and crash landed south of Cherbourg. Ack. Ack". The second entry for June 22 states: "Mustang III 'G' – Pilot: Sqn Ldr Horbaczewski, Passenger: Self – Duty: Return with CO from France – 45 minutes passenger."

## HORBACZEWSKI'S FATE

In mid-July, 133 Wing was reassigned to Air Defence of Great Britain to participate in the anti-diver patrols against the newly introduced V-1 flying bombs. During this time, Horbaczewski shot down four V-1 flying bombs.

After a successful campaign against the V-1s, on August 18, 1944, Horbaczewski led 12 Mustangs of 315 Squadron on their first air-combat mission since their withdrawal from France – a 'Rodeo' fighter sweep against the Luftwaffe base at Beauvais. Despite being massively outnumbered, the Poles attacked a group of some 60 Fw 190s of Jagdgeschwaders 2 and 26 that they surprised over the airfield. A massive

dogfight ensued in which the Polish Mustang pilots were officially credited with 16 victories, one 'probable' and three damaged (German documents record the loss of 12 Fw 190s in the combat).

Sadly this victory haul cost the life of the 315 Squadron CO, Squadron Leader Horbaczewski, who had been seen to shoot down three of the German Fw 190s. As he opened fire on the last victim, a 190 rolled in on Horbaczewski's tail and delivered a fatal burst; the Mustang was seen to roll on its back and dive straight in, exploding on impact. In 1947 the wreck of Horbaczewski's Mustang, with his body still inside it, was found crashed near Valennes. ∎

Warrant Officer Tadeusz Tamowicz.

# 'Jammers' and 'Spoofers'

Boeing B-17G Fortress III 'BU-W' of 214 Squadron, in flight.

No account of Operation Overlord would be complete without mention of the deception operations conducted against the Germans. Since there was no disguising the imminence of the invasion, it was essential to its success that the enemy be misled about the actual location of the assault.

Imaginative, elaborate and realistic intelligence deceptions, for example utilising double agents, 'dummy' forces and 'spoof' radio traffic, played no small part in this campaign over the weeks and months preceding D-Day.

As the date for the invasion drew closer, the air campaign continued to sow confusion by attacking more targets north of the Seine and in the Pas-de-Calais area than in Normandy. However, on the eve of D-Day the lion's share of the credit for successfully blinding, confusing and misleading the Germans, must go to the air operations conducted by a relatively small number of

specialist aircraft and crews. So successful were these operations that the German High Command retained Wehrmacht divisions north of the Seine and in the Pas-de Calais, even after the invasion in Normandy had occurred, in the belief that this was where the main blow would fall. These enemy forces could, potentially, have made a major difference if they had been deployed to Normandy early enough. They might have turned the tide entirely and they would, at the very least, have inflicted greater casualties on the Allied troops during the initial break out from the invasion beaches.

## 100 GROUP RADAR COUNTER MEASURES

The Radar Counter Measures (RCM) units of RAF Bomber Command's 100 (Bomber Support) Group had become a standard part of offensive air operations by spring 1944, helping to reduce bomber losses on the Command's night-time raids. 214 (BS) Squadron, based at RAF Oulton in Norfolk,

flew Boeing B-17 Fortress IIs and IIIs, equipped with special RCM jamming equipment, as part of 100 Group. The RAF had adopted the B-17 Fortress for the RCM role because the aircraft's deep bomb bay was ideal for accommodating the special electronic countermeasures equipment; the B-17's ability to fly high above the bomber stream was also an asset.

The RCM Fortresses were painted with the standard Bomber Command brown/green camouflage pattern on the top surfaces, the black undersides extended up the sides of the fuselage and the fin was also painted black. The crew of these Fortresses was 10, with only a single pilot, assisted by a flight engineer who occupied the co-pilot's seat. They also carried a navigator, bomb aimer, wireless operator, top gunner, two waist gunners and a rear gunner. The 10th member of the crew was a German-speaking 'special operator'.

These special RCM Fortresses carried a radar jamming device codenamed Mandrel, which operated in the 85 to 135MHz band, to counter German ground radars, such as the Freya early warning radar. The Piperack equipment they carried was used for jamming the German night fighters' Airborne Intercept radars. The aircraft also carried and dropped 'Window' (now known as 'chaff') to confuse and swamp the enemy radar picture. On RAF Bomber Command main force bombing raids the RCM Fortresses flew just above the bomber stream or sometimes ahead of it as a 'Mandrel screen', throwing out a protective

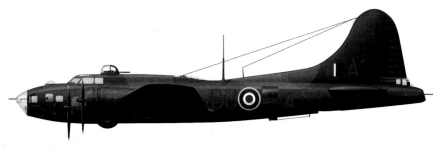

Boeing B-17 Fortress II 'BU-A' SR386 of 214 Squadron.

electronic 'cloak' to help conceal the attack. 214 Squadron Fortresses also carried 'Jostle' VHF radio jamming equipment, officially T3160, which had become known as ABC ('Airborne Cigar') and which had been used by 101 Squadron in its special Lancasters, with an eighth crewman, since 1943. It consisted of a panoramic receiver and three transmitters, which enabled the VHF ground-to-air R/T frequency being used by the German fighter controllers to be identified and then jammed.

The special operator used the equipment to listen in for a controller's transmissions. When he was sure that he was listening to the master controller, he jammed the frequency and if the Germans changed channels he had to find the new frequency and jam that as quickly as possible.

The Jostle equipment was large and heavy (it weighed over 600lb) and it replaced the underside ball turret fitted to the USAAF B-17s used on daylight operations (the use of the original 'ABC' Jostle equipment was terminated in July 1944, as it proved very easy for German night fighters to home onto it. It was replaced by Jostle IV).

The Short Stirling IIIs of 199 Squadron based at North Creake, Norfolk, and the Handley Page Halifax IIIs of 192 Squadron at Foulsham, Norfolk, were similarly equipped to the RCM B-17 Fortresses and they also played a part on the eve of D-Day.

## 'JAMMING' OPERATIONS FOR D-DAY

From the night of June 4-5, 1944, the specialist RCM aircraft of 100 (BS) Group, including USAAF B-17 Fortresses of 803 Squadron, which were attached to 100 Group, set up a radar jamming 'Mandrel screen' to cover the invasion fleet from the 'eyes' of those German radars which had survived the earlier attacks by Allied fighter bombers.

On the eve of D-Day, June 5-6, all the jamming squadrons of 100 Group were in the air performing their specialist duties. First up, around dusk, were 199 and 214 Squadrons. 199 Squadron Stirlings took up station at 15,000ft at intervals along the south coast of England, spread from Dorset to Dover.

Flying at precisely determined intervals, heights and bearings the aircraft jammed German radar across the entire central and eastern English Channel, masking the invasion fleet.

Meanwhile, B-17 Fortresses of 214 Squadron and a small force of 101 Squadron Lancasters were heading east to fly over Calais and along the Somme Valley, penetrating 80 miles into France then turning around to fly back and forth across the Channel.

On each inward run 'Window' bundles were tossed out as fast as possible. Just 10 aircraft created on German early warning radar a 'ghost' bomber stream of hundreds of non-existent raiders heading for precisely

those targets that would have been chosen if the invasion were taking place near Calais, distracting the German's attention from Normandy. The Fortresses also jammed the German fighter control radio frequencies with their special on-board equipment.

An electronic wall, blocking all German communications and radar, was established for several hours over northern France, masking the presence of the huge and vulnerable force of Allied transport aircraft and the gliders they towed, on their way to deliver airborne forces as the precursor to the invasion.

## D-DAY 'SPOOF' OPERATIONS

While the specialist 'jammers' of 100 Group did their work, three other special air operations added to the trickery that the Germans had to contend with on the eve of the invasion. Operations Taxable and Glimmer, flown by 617 Squadron Lancasters and 218 Squadron Stirlings, created 'spoof' invasion fleets, while Operation Titanic conducted by Special Duties Halifaxes and Stirlings generated decoy airborne landings. These operations are described in more detail in the following pages. ∎

The 10-man crew of a 214 Squadron RCM B-17 Fortress. Back row: Jimmy Pate (tail gunner), Jock Knox (flight engineer), Don Austin (pilot), Geoff Godfrey (navigator), Les Bostock (bomb aimer). Front row: Pip Piper (mid-upper gunner), Harry Richardson (wireless operator), Abe Levine (special operator), Chas Lewis (starboard waist gunner), Alf Butler (port waist gunner).

## 'WINDOW'

In early 1942, Joan Curran, a scientist and researcher, and the only woman 'boffin' at the British Telecommunications Research Establishment (TRE), suggested and then developed the idea of dropping aluminium strips from aircraft to generate a cloud of false echoes on enemy radars.

'Window' was the code name allocated to these small metallised strips, like tinfoil, designed to be dropped in bundles from RAF bombers. The strips of aluminised paper were cut to a half wavelength of the operating frequency to be jammed, although quarter-wavelength strips were later used as well.

When 'illuminated' by radar these strips re-radiated the signal. 'Window' appeared on enemy radar screens as a cluster of primary targets or,

alternatively, the screen would be swamped with multiple returns. Special treated paper was used to minimise the weight and maximise the time that the strips would remain in the air, to prolong the effect. The result was a gently drifting cloud of metallic strips that created confusing signals on German radar screens, either concealing the position of the actual bombers or generating a 'ghost' bomber stream.

One of the 617 Squadron Lancasters that took part in Operation Taxable on June 5-6, DV385, 'KC-A' 'Thumper Mk.III' was flown by Flt Lt Bob Knights and his crew.
Crown copyright

# 'Ghost' invasion fleets

## Operations Taxable and Glimmer

Operation Taxable and the similar Operation Glimmer were sophisticated deception operations simulating large invasion forces heading for Cap-d'Antifer and Pas-de-Calais. Both of these operations were conducted on the eve of D-Day, the night of June 5-6, 1944, while the actual invasion fleet was on the way to Normandy for the real landings.

To generate these decoy assaults two relatively small, specially trained forces of RAF bombers and Navy and RAF boats, set out to persuade German radar operators (and through them the high command) that major invasion fleets were sailing for and assembling off Fécamp and Boulogne.

### SELECTING THE SQUADRONS

Due to the complex nature of the task, Bomber Command's premier precision navigation and bombing unit, 617 Squadron (of Dambusters fame) was approached in early May 1944 to evaluate the feasibility of this deception plan. It was apparent that the operation would call for a high degree of flying ability, navigational accuracy and crew discipline. 617 Squadron was, of course, equipped with the Avro Lancaster four-engine heavy bomber and its success with target marking and precision bombing had proved that its aircrews possessed the necessary attributes in abundance.

Also during early May it was decided that 218 ('Gold Coast') Squadron would be used for the forthcoming operation to augment 617 Squadron. This decision was made due to the former's familiarity and expertise with the 'GEE' and 'G-H' radio navigation and 'blind-bombing' systems.

Based at Woolfox Lodge, Rutland, 218 Squadron was equipped with the Short Stirling Mk.III and was, at the time, the only front line heavy bomber squadron fully operational and trained within Bomber Command to use this equipment for 'blind bombing'. However, the poor performance of the Stirling compared with the later heavy bombers had meant that, prior to D-Day, 218 Squadron, which was now one of the last units using the Stirling as a bomber, had been relegated to mostly mining ('Gardening') operations and short penetration raids into the occupied territories.

During the spring of 1944 the squadron had executed a number of extremely accurate raids, utilising its expertise with the GEE and G-H equipment, including a precision attack on the Luftwaffe signals depot at Vilvoorde, north of Brussels on April 23-24, 1944, and an extremely accurate raid on the railway depot at Chambly on May 1-2, 1944; both raids causing extensive damage. The air staff's opinion was, therefore, that with their proven precision navigation skills, the crews of 218 Squadron could successfully complete the special and highly secret D-Day task without extensive additional training.

### PLANNING AND PREPARATION

On May 7, 1944, a meeting was held at 617 Squadron's base at Woodhall Spa, Lincolnshire, to discuss the 'spoof' raid. A number of high-ranking personnel from the Air Ministry and senior Bomber Command officers were present, along with the

Sqn Ldr Les Munro (back left), who led the Operation Taxable mission, with his regular 617 Squadron crew, posing alongside their Lancaster LM482 'KC-W'.

commanding officer of 617 Squadron, Wing Commander Leonard Cheshire.

A number of points were raised by Cheshire who was concerned about the complexity of the operation and the strain it would place on his crews. His concerns were acknowledged, and as a consequence it was decided that each of the crews for the operation would include a second navigator. New autopilots and new H2S radar navigation equipment would be fitted to the unit's Lancasters and an extra chute would be added to the squadron's aircraft to ensure the required amount of 'Window' (radar-reflective, aluminium foil strips) could be released quickly enough. In addition, extra relief pilots would be posted onto the squadron to augment the unit's already overworked crews.

As they had with the 'Dams Raid' exactly a year before, 617 Squadron now set about trying to achieve what seemed an impossible task; within a matter of days the aircraft modifications were completed and additional personnel had joined the squadron.

As an amusing aside, while the new equipment was being fitted to Lancaster ME561, the personal aircraft of American pilot Lieutenant Nick Knilans, it was discovered that the aircraft's ailerons had been fitted upside down at the factory. Correcting this mistake improved the aircraft's flying characteristics no end and sorted a problem which had led to Knilans being ribbed for his flying and especially for his landings.

A second planning meeting held 10 days later to finalise the preparations for the operation included representatives from the Royal Navy, including the Vice Admiral of Dover, Commodore Jessel, and the commanding officer of 218 Squadron, Wing Commander Royd Fenwick-Wilson. Among the decisions taken at this meeting, it was agreed that apart from the installation of an additional GEE set in the Stirlings, no other major aircraft modifications needed to be carried out to the 218 Squadron aircraft.

## TRAINING

When the crews of 617 Squadron were called together amid tight security for a special briefing by the air officer commanding 5 Group, Air Vice Marshal Sir Ralph Cochrane, to be told: "Gentlemen, the next time you are airborne operationally it will be D-Day", they all wondered what exciting task they would be given as Bomber Command's elite unit on such an historic occasion. It is easy to imagine that when the details of their diversionary task and the 'spoof' raid unfolded, there was a certain amount of disappointment. At the time they could not have realised the importance and enormity of what they were being asked to do.

From the middle of May, the two squadrons were kept off operations so that they could carry out weeks of extensive trials, training and equipment testing over the North Sea. For 617 Squadron these

training flights and the impending operation involved all of the crews, while 218 Squadron selected six experienced senior crews (and two reserve crews) under the leadership of the CO, Wing Commander Fenwick-Wilson, for their part in the operation.

Captured versions of the German radars were mounted on the headland at Flamborough Head to assess the effect of tactics as the training progressed. The weather for these training flights was often far from ideal with low cloud, heavy rain and poor visibility, but the bomber crews carried on regardless. The crews recorded these training flights in their logbooks with simple entries, such as 'special local flying' or other such mundane descriptions of the duty carried out.

## OPERATION TAXABLE

On D-Day, June 5-6, 1944, the first wave of eight 617 Squadron Lancasters took off from their base at Woodhall Spa shortly after midnight, each carrying a crew of between 12 and 14 men rather than the normal seven, with an additional pilot and navigator in each crew, as well as 'extra personnel' to assist with the task of dropping the bundles of 'Window'. The leader for the operation was one of the squadron's flight commanders, New Zealand Squadron Leader Les Munro, who had on board with him as his second pilot, the CO, Wing Commander Leonard Cheshire.

Les Munro takes up the story and describes the complexities of the operation in his own words (it should be remembered that this whole operation was, of course, carried out in total darkness):

"I have always believed that Operation Taxable was in one sense the most important that 617 carried out during my

time on the squadron. Not measured by any visual result, but because of the exacting flying and navigational requirements. There was absolutely no latitude for deviation from the correct ground speed, track, rate of turn and timing if it was to be successful.

"The object of the operation was to create the impression of a fleet of ships advancing at eight knots towards the French coast. To achieve this, two waves of eight aircraft were required, taking off two hours apart. Each Lancaster flew parallel oblong circuits (racetrack patterns) at 180mph at a height of 3000ft, maintaining a distance of two miles between them on both the outbound and return legs of each circuit, thereby creating a 16 mile front.

"From a predetermined start point each aircraft flew a straight course towards the French coast for two minutes 30 seconds, they then executed a rate one turn to port through 180°, lasting one minute, returning towards the English coast on an exact reciprocal track. After two minutes and 10 seconds the aircraft then carried out another 180° turn to port to arrive back over the original outbound track. The difference in the timing of the outbound and inbound legs resulted in the whole pattern advancing towards the French coast at the rate of eight knots, the average speed of a naval convoy.

"To create the impression of an armada of ships on the German radar screens, each aircraft dropped bundles of 'Window' of predetermined sizes every five seconds. The illusion of a convoy approaching the French coast was amplified by using progressively thicker window strips as the aircraft flew nearer to the coast on each outward leg, and lighter strips as they flew on the return legs. As well as the variation in the size of the 'Window' strips on each leg, the overall size was also increased every few circuits as the whole pattern

The 'ops log' on Flt Lt Bob Knights' 617 Squadron Lancaster DV385 'KC-A' Thumper Mk.III' included a 'D' on the bomb symbol for its 23rd 'op' indicating the D-Day Operation Taxable mission (the swastika on the 32nd bomb symbol indicates the shooting down of a German fighter by its crew). Crown copyright

advanced towards the French coast. No 'Window' was dropped during the turns.

The directions to crew members manning the 'Window' chutes as to when to commence dropping bundles of 'Window', when to cease and when to change the size, were relayed by a system of red and green lights operated by the second navigator.

"While we were doing our job in the air, a number of naval vessels on the sea directly below us were advancing at the same eight knots, using radar counter measures and broadcasting sound effects to simulate a large convoy at sea.

"Each aircraft flew those parallel circuits for two hours. The second wave of eight Lancasters took over from the first eight after two hours. Each aircraft of the second wave joined the circuits at precisely the same time as the first wave aircraft were starting their last circuit but 500ft above. When the first wave aircraft left, those of the second wave descended to 3000ft. A maximum of 90 seconds was allowed within which to complete the handover between the waves. Throughout the operation we flew without lights and in complete radio silence.

"Because of the tedious and repetitive nature of the operation, our crews were doubled up so that individual crew members could be rested periodically. I was once asked if I rested during my hour 'off', but with so many 'bods' on board, I stayed in my seat in the cockpit as there was nowhere else to go!"

The 'naval vessels' involved in Operation Taxable, which Les Munro refers to in his account above, were 18 small boats, a mix of Royal Navy Harbour Defence Motor Launches (HDMLs) and RAF Air Sea Rescue launches. The bad weather on June 5, 1944, and the heavy seas that resulted from it, caused the launches to struggle to converge at their meeting point on time. However, they all made it and between 2am and 4am, they advanced towards the French coast, operating specially fitted radar

counter measures (RCM) equipment, beneath the 617 Squadron 'Window' dropping aircraft.

The leading line of boats carried equipment that jammed the German radars, but not so effectively that they could not 'see' the 'fleet' behind them. The following boats each towed two radar-reflecting balloons which would reproduce big ship sized echoes on the enemy radar screens. They were also equipped with RCM devices known as 'Moonshine' (ARI TR1427).

'Moonshine' had originally been intended for airborne use; it was a pulse-repeater device which, when it received a signal from the German Freya radars, re-transmitted a portion of the signal as a greatly amplified, spread out pulse on the same frequency, giving the impression of a much larger radar return than was actually the case. Meanwhile, radio operators on the launches simulated the radio traffic that would be expected of a large fleet of ships.

Combined together, the jammers, 'Moonshines' and 'Window' dropped from above created a remarkably accurate simulation of a large invasion fleet, attempting to cover itself with RCM, on the German radar screens.

## OPERATION GLIMMER

The first three 218 Squadron Stirlings tasked for Operation Glimmer, plus the two reserve aircraft, took off from Woolfox Lodge during the 20 minutes leading up to midnight on June 5. The second wave of three more Stirlings took off 50 minutes later. Each Stirling carried a crew of 13 men: two pilots, three navigators, a wireless operator, a flight engineer, two air gunners and four 'Window' dispatchers.

As with Operation Taxable very precise flying and navigation was needed to achieve the desired effect. The timing called for an overall advance of 18 miles towards Boulogne at an apparent speed of seven knots. The front line of three aircraft needed to fly 23 orbits while the

second wave of three, which joined in after the first eight, would only fly 18 circuits. 'Window' was dropped in the same manner as Taxable and a naval task force of 12 HDMLs equipped with the same jamming devices, radar-reflecting balloons and radios sailed beneath the Stirlings. The boats began jamming operations at 1am followed by radio 'chatter' around an hour later.

## THE EFFECTIVENESS OF TAXABLE AND GLIMMER

The real D-Day assault into Normandy was supposed to have been completely masked by the radar jamming of the specialist 100 Group RCM aircraft.

That jamming, it transpired, was insufficient to overcome the powerful German radars that had survived earlier attacks, whose operators did in fact detect and report the real invasion fleet heading towards Normandy. By that point, however, the Germans were in a state of disarray and confusion, which had been added to by the 'spoof' invasion fleets simulated by Taxable and Glimmer.

While some German officers wanted to respond to the real invasion, others refused to accept it for what it was and would not believe the reports they were receiving. The fact is that potent German forces were kept in the Pas-de-Calais area, even after the invasion in Normandy had occurred, in the belief that this was where the main blow would still fall, proof indeed of the success of the numerous deception operations, including Taxable and Glimmer.

The commander in chief of RAF Bomber Command, Air Chief Marshal Sir Arthur Harris, sent a message to the air crews involved which said: "It is already established that the operations on which you engaged on the night of June 5-6 were very successful and it may well be when the full facts are known it will be found that you achieved results of even greater importance than can be known at present." ∎

Short Stirling Mk.III LF133, photographed here in the summer of 1944, was one of the 218 Squadron aircraft that took part in Operation Glimmer on June 5-6, 1944.

A wonderful colour shot of a Short Stirling bomber and some of the crew taken earlier in the war, showing the enormous size and ungainliness of the big aircraft on the ground.

# Operation Titanic
# Dropping the SAS and 'Ruperts'

Handley Page Halifax Mk.V (Special) JD319 NF-A of 138 Squadron at Tempsford.

The first Allied soldier to land in Normandy at the start of D-Day, June 6, 1944, was British Army Lieutenant Norman Harry 'Puddle' Poole of 1 Special Air Service (SAS). At 11 minutes after midnight, Poole jumped from a Handley Page Halifax Mk.V of No 138 (Special Duties) Squadron and parachuted into occupied France, landing two miles west of his intended drop zone, in a marshy area near Marigny, west of Saint-Lô in the Manche, 10 minutes ahead of schedule.

Poole was the first of a team of six courageous SAS soldiers out of the Halifax, the others being Lieutenant Frederick James 'Chick' Fowles and Troopers Dawson, Hurst, Merryweather and Saunders. These men had all volunteered for what they knew was quite likely to be a one-way mission.

Poole's arrival into enemy territory was not exactly what he had planned. He knocked himself out on leaving the aircraft and was unconscious on the ground for almost an hour after landing, eventually coming round with a cut lip and grazed chin.

## OPERATION TITANIC

The SAS team's mission was part of a 'spoof' deception operation, intended to decoy enemy forces away from the real Allied drop zones and invasion beaches by sending the Germans on a 'wild goose chase' responding to apparent but actually non-existent, mass paratrooper landings further inland.

The operation, codenamed Titanic, has subsequently captured people's imaginations and has featured widely in films and books about D-Day. As a result it has become immersed in myths, legend and inaccuracies, and sources vary wildly over the details, not least relating to the involvement of the SAS and their miniature 'friends'.

## SAS TEAM PARA DROP

The 138 Squadron Halifax from which Poole and his team parachuted was a Mk.V series 1 (special) from Tempsford. These aircraft were modified for 'special duties' with the

removal of the mid-upper, dorsal turret, the installation of additional fuel tanks and the fitting of a 'para' exit, along with other equipment to support clandestine parachute jumps and re-supply operations.

The Halifax was captained by Flight Lieutenant Johnson who, along with his crew, was well used to dropping agents and supplies into occupied Europe at night, to support the work of the Resistance movements.

For this drop the Halifax would have been at the usual speed and height of 140mph and 5-600ft. This was low, but gave sufficient time for the parachutes to open, while minimising both the time in the air under the parachute canopy and any drift away from the drop zone.

The crew's post-mission report for this sortie stated that: "The passengers jumped with alacrity", although it also admitted that the equipment containers holding the SAS men's heavier equipment, which were supposed to follow immediately after them, were delayed by a technical hitch and were not released until 10 seconds after the last man jumped. Unfortunately, this meant that, in the darkness, the SAS soldiers were unable to find the containers which held their Bren guns and additional ammunition, food and supplies, so they were left ill-equipped.

## SPECIAL DUTIES HALIFAXES AND STIRLINGS

Operation Titanic involved 34 RAF aircraft in all. 138 and 161 (SD) Squadrons, based at Tempsford, provided 12 Special Duties Halifaxes. 90 and 149 Squadrons, based respectively at Tuddenham, in Suffolk, and Methwold, in Norfolk, provided 22 Short Stirling Mk.IIIs. For the Special Duty Halifax crews this was the type of para-

Dispatchers inside a Special Duties Halifax using the 'para' hatch to drop supplies.

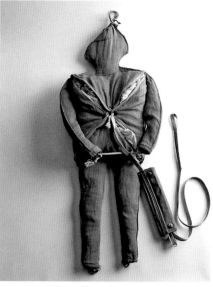

A surviving 'Rupert' – a dummy parachutist of the type used on Operation Titanic. Author

dropping mission that they carried out regularly and were expert in completing. The Stirling crews, however, were more normally employed on bombing operations as part of Bomber Command's 3 Group. The Stirlings' poor performance, especially their low operational ceiling, meant that the aircraft were now coming to the end of their useful lives as heavy bombers (some might argue that they were, in fact, already past it). 90 Squadron had begun the process of re-equipping with the Avro Lancaster, and 149 Squadron was similarly re-equipped in August 1944.

The Stirlings had been progressively withdrawn from main force bombing operations and since April 1944 both these squadrons had conducted a number of 'special operations' over France in support of the Resistance.

## 'RUPERTS'

The Operation Titanic aircraft were tasked with dropping large amounts of radar-reflective 'window' en route to the drop zones to mask from the German radar operators the relatively small number of aircraft actually involved in the operation and as a defensive tactic.

Apart from the Halifax flown by Flight Lieutenant Johnson, which dropped Poole's SAS team and their containers, the others carried between them some 450 dummy paratroopers, officially known as 'Paragons' but nicknamed, engagingly, 'Ruperts'. A surviving Second World War British Army infantryman told the author that it was common practice for the troops to refer to their officers in jest as 'Wuperts' in recognition of their likely background in British society. He believes that the nickname for the dummy parachutists came about because 'Wuperts' traditionally made a lot of noise but were actually completely useless!

The 'Ruperts' were 3ft tall. They were simply made from hessian sackcloth (burlap in the US and Canada) stuffed with sand, straw and wood shavings to form the crude

outline shape of a human figure. They were attached to scaled-down parachutes which were opened by static line just like real paratroopers. The static lines also activated a time-delay mechanism in the 'Ruperts' which caused them to ignite and self-destruct after reaching the ground, burning away completely. It was hoped that this might look, to any enemy troops finding the site, like paratroopers' attempts to burn their parachutes after landing. Some of the dummies were designed to produce sounds of gunfire or explosions after landing, before self-destructing.

The aircraft also dropped 'Pintail' bombs, which fell faster than the 'Ruperts' and landed first. These devices landed upright with a spike that stuck into the ground and they then fired off a Very light, giving the impression that there was a reception party on the ground to receive the 'paratroopers' and to illuminate the 'Ruperts' as they drifted down.

## THE SAS TEAM'S TASK

The SAS team, meanwhile, was to play amplified recordings of battle sound effects, such as bursts of small arms fire, mortar fire, explosions, screams and soldiers' shouted commands. The SAS men were also equipped with 20 Lewes bombs to create explosions and were to engage any German troops they saw.

Having created the noises of a large airborne landing for 30 minutes and created confusion among the defenders they were then to melt away into the countryside and allow silence to return. Subsequently, the SAS men were to conduct whatever sabotage or disruptive activity they could.

## TITANIC I-IV

Operation Titanic was originally conceived in four parts. Titanic II was cancelled before the event due to the high volume of air traffic in the planned area on a very busy night, but the other three parts of the

An unknown Halifax (SD) crew of 161 Squadron standing by their aircraft LL392 'MA-W' showing the special 'para' hatch.

Rare colour image of a 149 Squadron Short Stirling III coded 'OJ-B' taken in January 1942.

operation went ahead. Titanic I saw 11 Halifaxes and four Stirlings drop 200 'Ruperts' near Yvetot, Yerville, Doudeville and Fauville. Meanwhile on Titanic III, three Stirlings from 149 Squadron dropped 50 dummies in the Calvados region near Maltot and the woods to the north of Baron-sur-Odon to draw German reserves away from Caen. Titanic IV, which included the SAS team, was allocated 15 Stirlings which dropped 200 'Ruperts' near Marigny.

## STIRLING LOSSES

All of the Special Duties Halifaxes returned from the operation safely, but sadly two of the 149 Squadron Stirlings were shot down with the deaths of all but three of the 18 men on board the two aircraft.

Stirling III LK385, 'OJ-C', captained by Squadron Leader Hutchins, took off from Methwold at 10.28pm on June 5 to participate in Titanic IV. The aircraft is believed to have crashed near Baudre (Manche) 4km southeast of Saint-Lô. All those on board were killed. Four of the unusually large crew of nine are buried in Baudre churchyard; the others are commemorated on the Runnymede Memorial as having no known grave.

Stirling III LJ621, 'OJ-M', took off from Methwold at 10.09pm on June 5, also with a crew of nine and similarly tasked. It was shot down in the vicinity of Caen at 1am on June 6 and crashed at Marcelett (Calvados). The captain, Pilot Officer Mayo, and five other crew members were killed; they are all buried in the St Manvieu War Cemetery at Cheux. Three of the crew escaped the burning aircraft; Sergeants Heal and Wynne-Cole were captured and became prisoners of war. Sgt Heal was admitted to

hospital in Rennes with a broken leg; he was freed on August 4 when American forces entered the town.

Pilot Officer John Nind, one of the gunners, who had only been commissioned on June 4 and who had completed 20 'ops' on Stirlings (half of them special operations), hid in some woods for two days before being captured by the Germans on June 8. He was taken to a prison camp at Rennes, where he remained until July 6 when he was put on a prison train to be taken to Germany. For 10 days the train was stranded outside Tours, being unable to proceed because of Allied air raids. There were 40 POWs in the boxcar and they were given one loaf of bread and a small piece of meat each day between them. On July 23 he and the other POWs cut a hole in the end of the boxcar in which they were imprisoned and jumped out. Subsequently, Nind evaded recapture with the help of the French Resistance and was eventually handed over to Allied forces on September 5, 1944.

## THE AFTERMATH FOR THE SAS TEAM

The SAS team on the ground in Normandy also received assistance from a French Resistance worker, Monsieur Le Duc Edouard, as they laid low for a month and then tried to make their way back to the Allied lines in an area crawling with enemy troops. Unfortunately, they were surrounded and captured by German paratroopers on July 9 with three of the SAS team being wounded by a German grenade.

Le Duc Edouard, who was only 28 years old, was later executed by the Germans for assisting the SAS men. All six of the SAS soldiers became POWs; they were

eventually liberated, one by one, between August 1944 and August 1945 as the Allies overran their locations. Both of the officers were awarded the Military Cross for their exploits and the troopers received Military Medals. For them the operation had indeed been a one-way ticket, just like those on the ship it was named after.

## RESULTS

By 2am on June 6, the Germans had reported parachute landings east of Caen and as far west as Saint-Lô. Over half of the 12th SS Panzer Division was ordered to deal with an enemy parachute landing near Lisieux. The dummies and the SAS team of Titanic IV diverted a Kampfgruppe from the 915th Grenadier Regiment, which was the only reserve element of the 352nd Infantry Division, away from the Omaha and Gold beaches and the US 101st Airborne Division's drop zones.

The German regiment spent the morning of June 6 searching the woods for the parachutists, believing an airborne division had landed in the area, instead of supporting their colleagues at the coast. 'Enigma' intercepts from the area of Titanic I, revealed that one German commander was reporting a major landing up the coast from Le Havre (well to the north of the landing beaches) and that he had been cut off by them!

Overall, Operation Titanic achieved its objective of adding to the confusion the Germans were experiencing as a result of all the various deception operations surrounding the invasion. In addition, German forces were decoyed away from the actual Allied airborne landing zones and invasion beaches. ■

# Airborne operations
## Transport aircraft, glider tugs and para-droppers

While the RAF's offensive aircraft types were fully engaged in operations during the build-up to D-Day, aside from those aircraft involved in 'Special Duties' operations in support of the Resistance movements, the remainder of the RAF's transport aircraft and glider-towing fleet of 38 and 46 Groups did not have an operational role to play prior to June 5-6.

The pilots and crew of these transport aircraft had been training hard in formation flying and partaking in large-scale airborne exercises to ensure that they were ready for what was required of them. On D-Day their turn came to do it 'for real' in the airborne assault phase of the great invasion.

Halifax tugs with Horsa and Hamilcar gliders waiting to go, at Tarrant Rushton airfield, June 6, 1944.

## RAF TRANSPORT SQUADRONS

On the eve of D-Day 38 and 46 Groups had some 337 aircraft available, compared with the 876 transport aircraft which made up the US 9th Air Force's IXth Tactical Carrier Command.

The RAF order of battle included 15 squadrons of transport and glider-towing aircraft. 46 Group consisted of five squadrons of Douglas C-47 Dakotas, while four squadrons of Armstrong Whitworth Albemarles, four of Short Stirlings and two of Handley Page Halifaxes made up 38 Group's assets.

Attached to these groups were a total of over 700 gliders with another 400 in reserve, mostly Airspeed Horsas with some of the larger, light-tank- and heavy-load-carrying General Aircraft Hamilcars. The crews for these gliders were provided by the Glider Pilot Regiment of the Army Air Corps.

## OPERATION TONGA

Before the Allied heavy bombers and then the naval artillery started to pound the enemy beach defences and the seaborne assault went in, the massive airborne operation in support of the invasion was already under way.

The lifting capability of the relatively limited number of aircraft available to 38 and 46 Groups made it impossible to transport all of the British 6th Airborne Division to Normandy in a single wave. The plan, therefore, was for two lifts, the first of which, codenamed Operation Tonga, was executed overnight during the early hours of D-Day, six hours before the seaborne assault commenced. On this lift the RAF aircraft transported the 3rd and 5th Parachute Brigades into Normandy, together with over 80 gliders, some targeted against specific high-priority objectives and others carrying the Divisional HQ and as

many anti-tank guns as possible.

These paratroopers and glider-borne troops were dropped on the eastern flank of the invasion area, tasked with capturing two strategically important bridges over the Caen Canal and Orne River, destroying other bridges and securing several important villages. The Merville gun battery which could, it was believed, have inflicted heavy casualties on the troops landing on Sword beach was also to be assaulted and destroyed. The division was then to create and secure a bridgehead around the captured bridges until they linked up with the advancing Allied ground forces.

## OPERATION TONGA – TIMELINE

Operation Tonga commenced at 10.30pm on June 5, when six Halifaxes, three each from 298 and 644 Squadrons, began to take off from Tarrant Rushton airfield each towing a Horsa glider carrying the 'coup de main' force tasked with capturing the vital bridges, codenamed 'Pegasus' and 'Horsa'.

Wing Commander Duder DSO DFC, the commanding officer of 298 Squadron, led the formation, towing the glider on board which was Major Howard who led the assault on the bridges. The brilliant success of this mission is now a well-known part of D-Day history. It is rather beyond the scope of this publication, which focuses on the RAF involvement, but the outstanding flying

Halifax tug towing one of the large Hamilcar gliders.

Paratroopers landing on a drop zone in Normandy.

skill and courage shown by the Army glider pilots, who put their five gliders down safely, on the spot, in the dark, coming to a halt within yards of their objective, must be considered one of the finest pieces of operational flying of the entire war.

At 11pm 28 Albemarles of 295, 296, 297 and 570 Squadrons took to the air from Harwell and Brize Norton. They were transporting the pathfinders of the 22nd Independent Parachute Company, who were to mark the three drop-zones to be used by the airborne troops of the division, and also the advanced parties of the 3rd and 5th Parachute Brigades.

About 30 minutes later the main body of the 5th Parachute Brigade left the airfields of Fairford and Keevil. 38 Group contributed a total of 109 aircraft for this lift, with 190, 196, 299 and 620 Squadrons each providing 23 Stirlings, and 296 and 297 Squadrons providing eight and nine Albemarles respectively. These forces were due to land in their respective drop zones at 12.50am.

At the same time, the Dakotas from the five squadrons of 46 Group, 48, 233, 271, 512 and 575 Squadrons, took off and headed for their drop zones, with 108 aircraft carrying the 3rd Parachute Brigade and a further 17 towing Horsa gliders. The Albemarles of 38 Group's 295 and 570 Squadrons contributed additional support to this lift, carrying between them 20 loads of paratroopers and towing four Horsas.

Several hours later, at about 1.40am on June 6, having allowed enough time for the Army Engineers to clear the landing strips, the remaining aircraft of 38 Group took off with the main glider lift. The Halifaxes of 298 and 644 Squadrons each towed 17 gliders, included among which were four of the large Hamilcar gliders. Albemarles of 295, 296, 297, and 570 Squadrons towed 41 Horsas. The troops on this second part of the lift were planned to land at 3.20am. The final part of this wave towed the three Horsa gliders carrying the sappers and men from the 9th Parachute Battalion, who were to land atop Merville battery at 4.30am.

## OPERATION TONGA – EXECUTION

The towing of gliders was always a precarious business and it was common for a small number to cast-off prematurely, due to broken tow-ropes or similar malfunctions. Several gliders came down over England only minutes after take-off, while others ditched in the English Channel and some, having made it to the French coast, fell several miles short of the landing zone.

The flight across the Channel was uneventful, but as soon as the aircraft crossed into France, sporadic bursts of light flak came up at them. Flying slowly and at a very low altitude, they were easy targets for the anti-aircraft gunners to hit and a number were damaged, to a greater or lesser degree, while others were shot down.

In addition to the losses among the gliders, eight towing aircraft also failed to

Operation Mallard: Halifax tugs, towing Hamilcar gliders approaching Normandy on the evening of June 6, 1944.

return: five Stirlings, one Albemarle, one Halifax and two Dakotas. 620 Squadron suffered the worst, with three of its Stirlings brought down, aboard one of which all six aircrew and 19 men of the 7th Battalion and 591st Parachute Squadron were killed following a direct hit as the aircraft struggled to locate its drop zone. In comparison to what might have been expected, however, resistance was relatively light.

In fact, the main source of problems was the weather. Conditions for the airborne drop were, as they were for the troops at sea, not ideal. Patches of low cloud had gathered over Normandy and obscured some of the terrain, making navigation more difficult. From the air, the River Dives and the River Orne appeared very similar and, in poor visibility, a number of aircrew mistook one for the other, causing some errors in the landing areas for paratroopers and gliders.

## OPERATION MALLARD

On the evening of D-Day, after only a short respite for the air crews, Operation Mallard, the second lift of the day, delivered the balance of the 6th Airborne Division's equipment, including the light tanks, artillery and the glider-borne infantry. The first of 256 aircraft/glider combinations to take off from seven airfields in southern England were the Dakotas of 271 Squadron towing Horsa gliders, the first of which lifted off from Down Ampney at 6.40pm.

Over the next one hour and 20 minutes the remainder of the force took to the air and slowly made their way across the Channel to France. This time the gliders that the large aircraft towed included 30 Hamilcars as well as 226 Horsas. From this vast air armada, one Horsa crashed on take-off, three broke their tows en route and three were forced to ditch in the Channel. The remaining gliders, including all the Hamilcars with their precious heavy weapons and armoured vehicles, made it safely down to their landing zones. A further 50 RAF Dakotas undertook supply-dropping missions.

This lift occurred in daylight and so required a fighter escort. For the British and American airlifts combined the overall air escort comprised 110 Spitfires, 72 RAF and 98 USAAF P-51 Mustangs, and 96 P-47 Thunderbolts. As it happened, the air armada was not threatened by the Luftwaffe and the escort fighters' presence was almost, with the benefit of hindsight, unnecessary.

Losses in this second phase were 13 transport aircraft: nine Dakotas, two

Albemarles, one Stirling and one Halifax. The Halifax that did not make it home from this mission was from 298 Squadron. Flying Officer Carpenter's LL407 '8T-H' was hit by flak after releasing its glider over the drop zone. It staggered away, but was forced to ditch in the sea eight miles from the French coast. Another Halifax crew from the same squadron saw Carpenter's aircraft go down and circled the area until a naval vessel arrived to pick up the crew, who were all returned safely to England.

Considering the scale of the assault and the intensity of the flak these losses were surprisingly light. That said, these bald numbers do not in any way convey the fear that must have been experienced by the transport aircraft crews as they plodded through the flak over enemy territory, low and slow, to get into their drop zones and out again, nor the courage it must have taken to do so and then go back for more.

## BATTLE OF NORMANDY

After D-Day the air dropping of supplies continued. When there were sufficient advanced landing grounds constructed to allow it, RAF transport aircraft began landing in France to deliver supplies. On June 13, three of 233 Squadron's Dakotas had the honour of being the first Allied transport aircraft to land in France since the invasion, arriving on the B2/Bazenville airstrip with four tons of freight on board.

During the following months the battle for Normandy was supported by a several-times-a-day shuttle service of transport aircraft, flying military supplies, equipment and ammunition into France, and evacuating wounded on the return flights. Meanwhile, resupply drops to the troops on the front line continued when needed. ∎

British Army Glider pilots pose in front of a Horsa glider. Pictured from left are Lt J F Hubble; S/Sgt B L Morgan; S/Sgt J L Crone; Sgt R Biagott.

# Armstrong Whitworth
# Albemarle

Albemarle Mk.V of 297 Squadron complete with invasion stripes. Note the glider towing hook.

The Armstrong Whitworth Albemarle is a lesser known aircraft type of the Second World War, which in fact played a major role in the D-Day airborne operations.

## CONCEPTION

Originally conceived by the Bristol Aircraft Company as a medium bomber, intended to be constructed by subcontractors from readily-available materials, such as steel and wood, the design was taken over by Armstrong Whitworth, who reworked it as a reconnaissance bomber.

Although the type was occasionally used on offensive operational duties, it was apparent that its performance was no improvement over other aircraft already in service and it had obvious shortcomings in the bomber role compared with the RAF's new four-engine heavy bombers, the Halifax and Lancaster. Only 32 Mk.I Series 1 bomber Albemarles were made before it was decided to produce all subsequent Albemarles as Special Transports (ST.1) or General Transports (GT.1). The first ST.1 and GT.1 Albemarles entered RAF service in mid-1942 and early 1943 respectively.

The entire production run of just over 600 Albemarles was assembled by A W Hawksley Ltd of Gloucester, a subsidiary of the Gloster Aircraft Company formed specifically for the purpose of constructing the Albemarle. The individual parts and subassemblies for the Albemarle were produced by about 1000 subcontractors.

## DESIGN

The Albemarle was a mid-wing, cantilever monoplane with twin fins and rudders. The fuselage was built in three sections; the structure being of unstressed plywood over a tubular steel frame. The forward section used stainless steel tubing to reduce interference with the magnetic compasses. It had a hydraulically operated, retractable tricycle landing gear (one of the first UK production aircraft to do so). The main wheels retracted backwards into the engine nacelles, and the nose wheel also retracted backwards into the front fuselage (there was also a semi-concealed 'bumper' tail wheel).

Most of the transport versions of the Albemarle retained the Boulton-Paul designed dorsal turret with four .303 machine guns. The original bomber design had a crew of six including two gunners; one in a four-gun dorsal turret and one in a twin-gun ventral turret, but in the transport role the normal crew was five, with a single pilot (who was the captain), navigator, bomb-aimer, wireless operator and air gunner. When used as a paratroop transport, up to 10 fully armed troops could be carried. The paratroopers were provided with a dropping hatch in the rear fuselage, and there was a large loading door in the fuselage side. The ST Mk.I Series 2 aircraft were equipped with the necessary gear for towing gliders. The Mk.V was essentially the same but also had a fuel jettison capability. All production Albemarles were

powered by a pair of 1590hp (1186 kW) Bristol Hercules XI radial engines, giving the aircraft a cruising speed of 170mph and a maximum speed of 265mph. A former pilot said of the Albemarle that it had "no virtues but no vices either".

## OPERATIONS

During the build-up to D-Day the Albemarles were involved in dropping supplies to SOE agents and the French Resistance in enemy territory, as well as training with Airborne forces.

The pinnacle of the aircraft's career though was its involvement in the airborne operations in support of the D-Day invasion, Operations Tonga and Mallard, and then on Operation Market Garden, the Arnhem para drop.

On June 6, 1944, the four Albemarle squadrons of 38 Group and the Operational Training Unit (OTU) were fully committed to Operation Tonga. 295 Squadron towed 21 Horsa gliders, although it lost six in transit; 296 Squadron used 19 aircraft, some towing Horsas; 570 Squadron sent 22 aircraft with 10 towing gliders and 42 OTU provided four aircraft and crews. On Operation Mallard, later in the day, the Albemarle squadrons towed 220 Horsas to Normandy.

During these D-Day operations the Albemarle proved to be a real success. Of the 602 Albemarles delivered to the RAF, only 17 were lost on operations, while another 81 were lost in accidents.

# Albemarle pilot

## Flight Sergeant 'Bernie' Johnson of 296 Squadron

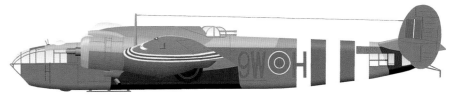

When the Second World War broke out, John Bernard Johnson, of Wigan, Lancashire, was 15. In 1942, at 18, he was accepted for pilot training. In early 1944, Johnson joined 296 Squadron, which operated Armstrong Whitworth Albemarles in the transport, para-dropping and glider-towing roles.

In mid-March 1944, 296 Squadron was based at Brize Norton, in Oxfordshire, which was to be its base for the forthcoming D-Day operations. The squadron consisted of three flights, each with 10 aircraft and there were an additional three spare aircraft in the 'reserve pool'. 'Bernie' Johnson, as he was known in the RAF, served on 'B' Flight.

### SOE OPERATIONS

Most of the flying being conducted by the squadron at this time was training with the Airborne Forces, both for para-dropping and glider towing, in preparation for the impending D-Day invasion. Johnson and his crew were heavily occupied with these training exercises during the run-up to D-Day.

Occasionally, the squadron was tasked to send individual aircraft out at night, over enemy occupied territory, to conduct clandestine supply drops to the Resistance movements in Europe on behalf of the Special Operations Executive (SOE). By May 1944, Johnson was considered ready to take his crew on one of these operations. Taking off from Tarrant Rushton, in Albemarle Mk.V, V1775, on the night of May 6-7, 1944, the crew flew their first operational sortie to drop supply canisters to the French Resistance. They landed safely back at Brize Norton six hours and 15 minutes after take-off.

On May 21, 1944, the 296 Squadron Operational Record Book (ORB) recorded that a News of the World article had been published stating that the RAF glider tug pilots were usually older men, unfit for combat duties! Bernie Johnson was 20 and ready and fit for all combat duties. It seems that the report caused some amusement!

### TRAINING AND TONGA

From June 2, all personnel at Brize Norton were confined to camp as a security precaution and preliminary aircrew briefings for the forthcoming operation were conducted. On June 4, some air tests were flown and briefings continued with crews being shown film of the run-in to their drop zones. Also on this day, Air Chief Marshal Sir Trafford Leigh Mallory visited the station and addressed the crews.

For Operation Tonga, the first Airborne Forces air lift, which was executed overnight during the early hours of D-Day, 196 Squadron initially provided three Albemarles to drop the Parachute Brigade Pathfinders. Then 30 minutes later, having given enough time for the Pathfinders to set up lights at the landing zones, another 17, 296 Squadron Albemarles carried troops of the 5th Parachute Brigade, to Normandy.

Nine of the Albemarles, including Johnson's, carried nine paratroopers each, while the other eight towed Horsa gliders. Johnson and his crew took off at 11.48pm on June 5, in Albemarle II, V1744. They dropped their nine paratroopers and six kitbags on to a drop zone near Caen, and also released six containers of supplies.

The Albemarles experienced considerable light flak and some aircraft received minor damage; one rear gunner from the squadron, Flight Sergeant Jones, was unfortunately killed when his aircraft was hit by ground fire. Johnson and his crew returned safely, landing at 3.07am.

### OPERATION MALLARD

Having returned from Operation Tonga at dawn, most of the squadron's aircrew went to bed. They were awakened at midday to be briefed for Operation Mallard which was to take place that evening.

The 296 Squadron Albemarles were tasked to tow 20 Horsas, but in fact only 19 made it as one had a structural failure on take-off and crashed. Johnson and his crew took off at 7.36pm on June 6, in Albemarle II, V1696, towing a Horsa glider loaded with troops and equipment of the 6th Air Landing Brigade, which they released near Caen.

Near the release point the German flak gave the 296 Squadron Albemarles some trouble and several were hit. However, Johnson and his crew landed safely at 10.34pm. Their D-Day was over.

### A TRAGIC END

After D-Day, Johnson and his crew were not required to fly operationally again until the night of July 11-12, 1944. This time they were not so lucky. It was their turn to fly another SOE clandestine supply operation.

Johnson took off at 12.15am with his usual crew plus a passenger, Sergeant Dace of the Parachute Regiment, who was assistant to the station army liaison officer. The planned drop zone was near Marolles-les-Braults, Sarthe, about 25km southeast of Alençon. Exactly what happened is not known, but the aircraft, Albemarle Mk.V, V1744, failed to return; all on board were posted missing and have never been found. Flight Sergeant 'Bernie' Johnson was still only 20 years old when he was killed. ∎

Albemarle towing a Horsa glider off the runway during training for the D-Day invasion.

Albemarles towing gliders over some of the Allied invasion fleet on the evening of June 6, 1944, during Operation Mallard.

Short Stirling Mk.IVs towing Airspeed Horsa Gliders. In the early evening of D-Day, June 6, 1944, as part of Operation Mallard, 36 Short Stirling Mk.IVs of 620 and 190 Squadrons, based at Fairford, towed the Horsa gliders of the British 6th Airborne Division to their landing zones in Normandy. The Airspeed Horsa gliders cast off and landed troops and equipment near Ranville. The gliders carried 254 men, 33 jeeps, 29 trailers, 11 motorcycles and eight 75mm Pack Howitzers. One of the Stirlings involved in this operation was LJ849 of 620 Squadron, coded 'QS-E', captained by Flight Lieutenant Gordon Thring DFC (RCAF). Moments after releasing its glider, LJ849 was hit by German anti-aircraft fire. A petrol tank in the port wing blew up and the aircraft rolled upside down. Fortunately, Thring managed to make a successful crash landing. All the crew survived and their remarkable story 'The Tables Turned' is told on pages 71-72. Artwork: Adam Tooby adamtooby.artstation.com

# Short Stirling

The prototype Short Stirling, which was designed to meet Air Ministry Specification B12/36 for a four-engine heavy bomber, first flew on May 14, 1939, before the Second World War had started. The original design had been compromised by the Air Ministry's insistence that the aircraft's wing span should not exceed 100ft (30m). In order to generate the necessary lift from a shorter span, the wing was thickened and reshaped, which subsequently had an adverse effect on the aircraft's performance, particularly at altitude.

## OPERATIONAL DEBUT

After various early problems had been cured, initial deliveries of the big new bomber began in August 1940 to 7 Squadron based at Leeming. The Stirling's operational debut was on the night of February 10-11, 1941 when aircraft from 7 Squadron took part in a raid on Rotterdam.

## STIRLING PERFORMANCE

A consequence of the Stirling's thick wing was a low ceiling and many missions were flown as low as 12,000ft. On combined operations with other RAF bombers which could fly higher, the low-flying Stirlings took the brunt of the enemy's firepower. Within five months of being introduced, 67 out of the 84 aircraft delivered had been lost to enemy action or written off after crashes.

Despite the disappointing performance, Stirling pilots discovered that the thick wing endowed the big aircraft with an excellent turn rate and radius, allowing it to be flung around the sky in evasive manoeuvres. Its handling was much better than that of the Halifax and some pilots actually preferred it to the Lancaster.

However, the Stirling's maximum bomb load could only be carried for a short distance of around 590 miles. On typical missions deep into Germany or Italy only some 3500lb (1590kg) of bombs could be carried. This was the sort of load being

Stirling Mk.IV glider tugs of 196 and 299 Squadrons lined up at Keevil on June 5, 1944, in preparation for Operation Tonga – the airborne operation that launched D-Day.

carried by the RAF's twin-engine medium bombers such as the Vickers Wellington.

Another problem was that, although the Stirling's bomb bay was large at 40ft long (12m), it was divided into separate compartments, so it could not carry bombs larger than 2000lb (907kg). As the RAF started using the 4000lb (1815kg) 'cookie' and even larger special bombs, the Stirling became less useful.

The Handley-Page Halifax and especially the Avro Lancaster offered better performance (the Lancaster could carry twice the Stirling's bomb load over long distances, it was at least 40mph faster and could operate significantly higher) so when they became available in greater numbers from 1943, it was decided to withdraw the Stirlings to secondary tasks. Their final Bomber Command operation was flown by Stirlings of 149 Squadron against Le Havre on September 8, 1944.

## A NEW ROLE – GLIDER TUG

As the Stirling became surplus to requirements as a bomber, it was realised

that it could fulfil the need for a powerful glider tug to tow heavy transport gliders such as the Hamilcar and the Horsa.

By mid-1944 the Stirlings had found a new lease of life, being modified to Mk.IV standard for the glider-towing and para-dropping role, with the removal of the front and dorsal gun turrets (to save weight), and the addition of a para-exit hatch in the rear fuselage and glider towing equipment.

In August 1943, the first of at least 130 Mk.III bombers were modified to Mk.IV specifications and production was switched to building new Mk.IVs, with a total of 577 eventually being built.

The Stirling fulfilled its new role admirably, its low operational ceiling was not an issue as 2000ft was now the normal operating altitude, and its manoeuvrability was a positive asset. It could carry 20 paratroopers and as a tug it could tow the large Hamilcar glider, two Horsas or up to five Hotspurs. On D-Day the RAF's 38 Group transport forces included four squadrons, 190 and 622 at Fairford and 196 and 299 at Keevil, equipped with the Stirling Mk.IV. ∎

Short Stirling Mk.IV LK203, '8E-B', of 295 Squadron, taxiing from its dispersal at Mount Farm, Oxfordshire, during a glider towing exercise in August 1944.

# 'The tables turned'

## The remarkable story of the crew of a 620 Squadron Stirling glider-tug, shot down on D-Day

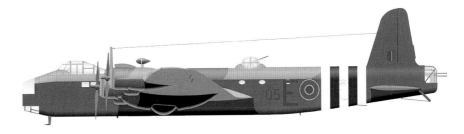

During the early evening of June 6, 1944, still in daylight, Short Stirling Mk.IV, LJ849, 'QS-E' ('E' for 'Easy'), rumbled into Normandy, towing a Horsa glider behind it, as part of Operation Mallard. This second massive airlift of D-Day, involved over 250 aircraft and glider combinations with a huge escort of over 370 Allied fighter aircraft.

'E-Easy's crew of six – Flight Lieutenant Gordon Thring RCAF (pilot), Flying Officer M E Price (navigator), Flying Officer H Braathen (bomb aimer), Flight Sergeant R W A Burgess (wireless operator), Sergeant W Buchan (flight engineer) and Flying Officer Gerry McMahon DFM (rear gunner) – had played their part in the first airlift, Operation Tonga, about 19 hours earlier, when they dropped paratroopers of the British 5th Parachute Brigade into a drop zone near Ranville. Now, on this, their second mission in the 24-hour period, they were towing a Horsa glider containing soldiers of the 6th Airborne Division, reinforcements for the paratroopers delivered overnight.

### FLAK

On the way to the drop zone, 'E-Easy's rear gunner, Gerry McMahon, noticed some very accurate anti-aircraft gunfire coming from the corner of a wood; a number of tugs and gliders were hit by the flak from this position. McMahon reported the location of the battery to his pilot, hoping that on the

way out, after releasing their glider, he might get the opportunity to engage the enemy position with the intention of putting it out of action.

### SHOT DOWN

Stirling LJ849 released its glider in the briefed location and then proceeded to drop containers of supplies for the troops, from its bomb bay. Turning for home, they headed back towards the wood they had passed on the way in, as the gunner, McMahon, had hoped they would. However, the enemy anti-aircraft gunners must have spotted the Stirling returning and before McMahon got the chance to open up against the flak position, 'E-Easy' was targeted by the battery and hit several times, sustaining heavy damage.

At such low altitude and short range the effect of the flak salvo was devastating. One of the petrol tanks in the port wing took a direct hit and exploded, the port outer engine caught fire and the Stirling was blown violently upside down. In the rear turret McMahon's ammunition fell out of

the magazines, hitting him in the face.

Struggling with the controls, the pilot, Gordon Thring, managed to right the aircraft at the last moment and made a controlled 'belly landing' in a ploughed field near Plumetot, the Stirling skidding to a halt in a cloud of dust and soil. Fortunately none of the crew were injured in the crash landing and all escaped the burning aircraft, moments before it blew up. 'E-Easy' was not going home and the crew was down in enemy territory; their chances did not look good either.

### 620 SQUADRON

620 Squadron was one of the four glider-tug units equipped with Short Stirling Mk.IVs, as part of the RAF's 38 Group, which provided airborne support on D-Day and afterwards. The Squadron had been formed from a nucleus of 'C' Flight of 214 Squadron in June 1943.

Initially based at Chedburgh and equipped with Stirling Mk.Is, it was used on night bombing raids, carrying out its first operational sorties two days after its

British paratroopers preparing to board Stirling Mk.IVs of 620 Squadron at Fairford.

formation. The Squadron re-equipped with Mk III Stirlings in August 1943 and flew its last mission for Bomber Command on November 19, 1943. Three days later its 20 aircraft moved to Leicester East for conversion to the Airborne Forces role. In five months of bomber operations, the squadron had lost a total of 26 aircraft; at least 19 more were to be destroyed in their new role.

Over the following months, the aircrews practised the techniques for towing gliders and for dropping parachutists and supply containers. The chief features of the training were day and night cross country navigation exercises and glider-towing. By February 1944, 620 Squadron was ready to undertake the first of numerous sorties over France on behalf of the Special Operations Executive (SOE), dropping arms and supplies to the Resistance forces, frequently using Tarrant Rushton as a forward base.

On March 18, 1944, the Squadron was moved to Fairford, which it shared with 190 Squadron, and training continued apace for the impending invasion. During the remainder of that month alone, its aircraft carried out six exercises with airborne troops, each involving between eight and 16 aircraft.

## D-DAY – OPERATION TONGA

On the first night of the Normandy landings, 620 and 190 Squadrons were both heavily involved in Operation Tonga. Commencing their take-off at 11.30pm on June 5, the Stirling Squadrons carried between them 887 men of the 5th Parachute Brigade, to a drop zone near Ranville.

Twenty-three of 620 Squadron's Stirlings were used on this first lift, not without loss; three were shot down by anti-aircraft fire, and a further four received damage.

Upon their return to Fairford, it was discovered that no fewer than 27 aircraft from the two squadrons were in an unserviceable condition. The ground crews worked feverishly throughout the morning, and by the afternoon all but two had been repaired.

In the foreground of this formation of Short Stirling Mk.IVs of 620 Sqn is 'QS-E' ('E for Easy') flown by Flt Lt Gordon Thring RCAF. This is actually LJ566, the replacement aircraft for Thring's LJ849, 'QS-E', in which he and his crew were shot down on D-Day.

## D-DAY – OPERATION MALLARD

On the evening of June 6, as part of Operation Mallard, 18 Stirlings from each squadron helped to transport the main glider element of the 6th Airborne Division to their landing zones. The Horsa gliders that they towed carried 254 men, 33 Jeeps, 29 trailers, 11 motorcycles, and eight 75mm Pack Howitzers. All but one of 620 Squadron's Horsas managed to reach their intended landing zone. The only Stirling lost on this operation was Gordon Thring's LJ849, although six more were damaged by light anti-aircraft fire.

## ON THE GROUND IN NORMANDY

As German troops appeared on the scene of Stirling LJ849's crash site in Normandy, hunting for the crew, the airmen hid together in a wheat field. After dark, when things had quietened down somewhat, the crew began to make their way back towards the Normandy coast. Unfortunately, in the early hours of the morning they mistook two passing German soldiers for Americans and, having hailed them, they were taken prisoner and were held in the barn of a French chateau.

## TABLES TURNED

The next morning the chateau was attacked by RAF Hawker Typhoons. The Germans and the RAF crew all took shelter in a slit trench together during the Typhoons' attacks, which soon reduced the chateau to rubble. At this point the Germans' morale began to crumble and the officer in charge, believing that he and his men were surrounded, decided that they were now on the losing side, and offered to surrender with his 40 men to the RAF crew of six. Exploiting the situation, Thring, McMahon and the rest of the crew agreed to accept the German troops' surrender on condition that they marched up formally to the Allied lines with them and gave themselves up.

## RECEIVED – 62 PRISONERS

Over the next four days, as the RAF crew and their charges made their way to the Allied invasion beaches, the number of German prisoners swelled to 90 as more and more gave themselves up in the hope of saving their lives. Unfortunately, some of the Germans were killed during the march, mainly by Allied snipers. When they finally reached the safety of Allied lines the number of prisoners stood at 62. Handing the Germans over to the Canadian Army on June 11, four days after they themselves had been captured, the RAF crew demanded and received a receipt for their prisoners (in finest military tradition)!

## SEQUEL

The Stirling crew were returned to England courtesy of the Royal Navy, to discover that they had been posted as missing in action and that most of the squadron who had witnessed their crash believed that they had been killed. They were given 'survivors leave' and when rear gunner, Gerry McMahon went home, he met his parents on their way to attend his own requiem mass; his poor mother promptly fainted!

Gordon Thring and his crew all returned to 620 Squadron and flew with the unit for the rest of the war, including the other major airborne operations, such as Market Garden (Arnhem) – they all survived the war, with a remarkable story to tell. ■

Stirling Mk.IV towing a Horsa glider.

# Douglas C-47 Dakota

Douglas C-47 Dakota of 233 Squadron with invasion stripes. Crown copyright

The most numerous and probably the most famous transport aircraft of the Second World War was the Douglas C-47 Dakota, the military freighter version of the DC-3 airliner. The type saw widespread use by the Allies during the war and went on to become one of the most successful aircraft designs in history, used by air forces and civilian operators worldwide.

## DC-3 ORIGINS

The DC-3 airliner first flew in 1935 and was used extensively thereafter by America's airlines. Recognising the aircraft's great potential as a military transport, the United States Army Air Command specified a number of changes needed to make the aircraft suitable for military use, including more powerful engines, the replacement of airline seating with utility seats along the walls, a stronger rear fuselage and floor, and the addition of large loading doors. The double, port side loading door was close enough to the ground, thanks to the aircraft's tail wheel configuration, for heavy or unwieldy military freight to be loaded relatively easily. Deliveries of the military version of the DC-3, which was designated C-47 'Skytrain' in the United States, commenced in October 1941. When production finally ended, a remarkable total of 10,692 DC-3/C-47 aircraft had been built.

## RAF DAKOTAS

Under the Lend-Lease programme large scale deliveries of C-47s were made to the UK; over 1900 Dakotas, as the aircraft became known in RAF service, had been delivered by the end of the war. The first

Dakotas to enter service with the RAF arrived in 1942. The delivery of large numbers of Dakota IIIs revitalised the RAF's transport capacity, which until then had been based around a number of obsolete bombers and general purpose aircraft, which were poorly adapted for the role. The Dakota III eventually equipped 22 RAF squadrons and three RCAF squadrons under RAF operational control.

## D-DAY DAKOTAS

In June 1944, RAF Transport Command's No 46 Group comprised five squadrons, each equipped with 30 Dakotas, based at Broadswell, Down Ampney and Blakehill Farm. These Dakotas dropped the main elements of the 3rd Parachute Brigade into Normandy on D-Day, as well as towing

Horsa gliders across the Channel. After D-Day Dakotas were also used as freighters, air ambulances and personnel transports.

## DAKOTA SPECIFICATIONS

The Dakota was fitted with two Pratt and Whitney Twin Wasp radial engines producing 1200hp each and giving the aircraft a typical cruising speed of 160mph. The Dakota III could carry a payload of 8000lb (more than double the original specification), 28 fully-equipped soldiers or paratroopers, or 18 stretcher cases. In practice, the aircraft's specified load limits were often exceeded and its ruggedness became legendary. The C-47 was actually overbuilt, making it almost indestructible. As one pilot put it: "You can wreck a Dak, but you can't wear it out!" ■

Paratroopers jumping from a C-47 Dakota of 271 Squadron. Crown copyright

'Operation Tonga'. Shortly after midnight on June 6, 1944, the great D-Day invasion got under way with Operation Tonga when 108 RAF Douglas C-47 Dakotas dropped paratroopers of the British 3rd Parachute Brigade into Normandy. Illuminated by searchlights and 'flak', Dakotas of 233 Squadron from Blakehill Farm are seen over Drop Zone 'K', near Caen. In the foreground is C-47 Dakota FZ692, named 'Kwicherbichen' by its crews. All 30 of 233 Squadron's Dakotas flew to Normandy on Operation Tonga; two of them failed to return, victims of German 'flak'. Artwork: Adam Tooby adamtooby.artstation.com

# RAF Dakota
## D-Day experiences

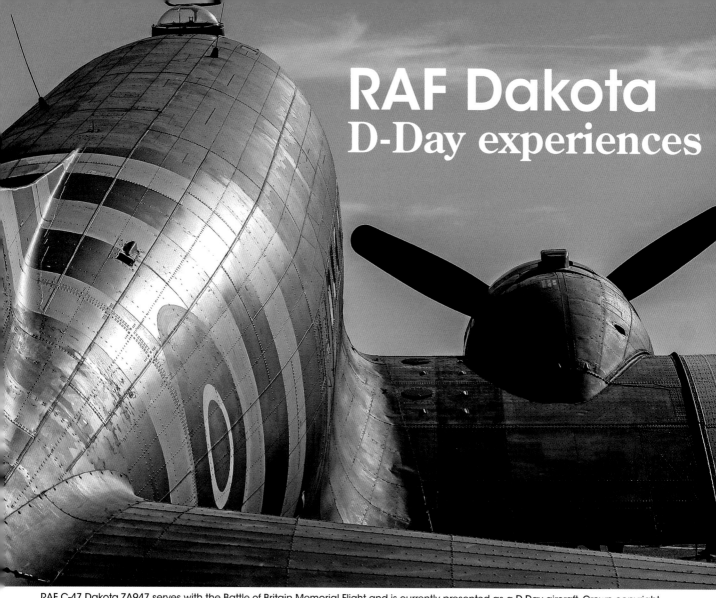

RAF C-47 Dakota ZA947 serves with the Battle of Britain Memorial Flight and is currently presented as a D-Day aircraft. Crown copyright

**FLIGHT LIEUTENANT ALEC BLYTHE – A PILOT WITH 48 SQUADRON BASED AT DOWN AMPNEY – FLEW A C-47 DAKOTA ON OPERATION TONGA ON THE EVE OF D-DAY. THIS IS HIS STORY:**

"My DZ was one-and-a-half minutes' flying time from crossing the French coast to dropping. The briefing for the mission had been tremendously detailed. Accurate models of the Normandy coast and hinterland had been constructed. From these models, cine films were made of the tracks to each of the dropping zones. So we were prepared with a mental picture of what we would expect to see as we flew in.

"As we crossed the coast, my navigator reported two large houses which we expected to see before a line of trees came out of the murk. I was getting ready to drop my troops south of the road to Caen. There was a fair amount of moonlight and I could see that the Germans had flooded the area south of the road where we were supposed to drop. I didn't have much time to think, but I decided that I had better drop to the north of the road rather than in the water.

"The red light was on and the Royal Engineer paras were standing ready to jump. There was some flak. But I hadn't had to take any evasive action. I was intent on making as steady a run as possible when suddenly the aircraft banked almost 45°. In a flash of light from the ground I saw a Stirling passing very close in front of us. Clearly, we had been caught in his slipstream which threw us off course. I brought the wings level and regained heading as quickly as possible. The paratroopers in the back were no doubt hurled about and were probably cursing me.

"I would like to think that my engineers were dropped accurately, especially as the two bridges assigned to them were subsequently blown up."

British paratroopers inside a RAF C-47 Dakota, ready to go.

## PILOT OFFICER GEORGE 'PETER' BRETT BAILEY – A DAKOTA PILOT WITH 233 SQUADRON BASED AT BLAKEHILL FARM. HE TOWED A GLIDER FOR THE 'COUP DE MAIN' ATTACK AGAINST 'PEGASUS' BRIDGE, AND ALSO DROPPED SUPPLIES ON OPERATION MALLARD:

C-47 Dakota towing a Horsa glider.

"I was a pilot on 233 Squadron and towed gliders on the D-Day operations. All the RAF glider-tug and glider pilots carried out extensive training early in 1944 prior to D-Day. I was flying Dakotas from Blakehill Farm in Wiltshire and was fortunate enough to team up with a particular Horsa glider crew. The glider captain was Staff Sergeant Richard Banks, known, for some reason, as 'Admiral' Dickie Banks, and his co-pilot was Sergeant Brian Hebblethwaite.

"On the night of June 5-6, I took off from Blakehill Farm at 10.50pm towing the Horsa flown by Dickie and Brian, to Drop Zone 'K', near Caen. The glider was loaded with Royal Engineers of the 6th Air Landing Brigade and their stores. The engineers were tasked with blowing up certain bridges at Troarn, east of Caen. Ours was the second of five gliders to be released.

"On crossing the French coast we flew into cloud, necessitating instrument flying by me and the glider crew to keep in the proper tow position. When the gliders were released, their pilots found that their

planned landing zone had not been prepared and was not lit. Only two of the five gliders made it to the correct landing site, one of them ours.

"Banks and Hebblethwaite landed their glider successfully in the correct place in the dark, despite the poles which had been set up by the Germans to prevent landings. The paratroops were successfully unloaded, with a firefight occurring only about 200 yards away. The bridges were blown and the operation was a complete success. Banks and Hebblethwaite returned to our unit unscathed about two weeks later amid much celebration!

"Dickie Banks was awarded the Distinguished Flying Medal for his part in the operation. Both Banks, who was 25, and

Hebblethwaite, who was only 21, were later killed in action on September 19, 1944, during Operation Market Garden (Arnhem), after having successfully landed a glider in enemy territory for a second time.

"On the evening of June 6, I was flying a resupply mission to the troops who had landed earlier in the day, when I saw a Dakota of 575 Squadron shot down in flames. I watched helplessly as the Dakota crashed somewhere near Giberville and later discovered that it was being flown by my friend Pilot Officer Errol Wood. I was sure that he and his crew must all have been killed. It was not until the 1960s that I learned that they had all survived the crash, but were captured and became POWs for the rest of the war before finally being liberated."

## FLYING OFFICER RONALD WARREN – A NAVIGATOR WITH 575 SQUADRON BASED AT BROADWELL. ON OPERATION TONGA HIS DAKOTA WAS THE FIRST TO CROSS THE ENEMY COAST:

"We were detailed to take paratroops from Broadwell in Oxfordshire to a field beside the river Orne at Ranville near Caen. The first 'vic' of three Dakotas, led by Wing Commander Jefferson, was due to drop at 12.57am. The second 'vic', led by Squadron Leader Cragg, was due to drop 20 seconds later. I was the navigator of the lead aircraft of the third 'vic' piloted by Flight Lieutenant Dixon. Our dropping time was 20 seconds after that.

"We took off in loose formation and I was busy for some time making sure that we were on the right course at the right speed to arrive at Ranville at the right time. Twenty seconds between aircraft is not a big margin so, as soon as things were running smoothly, I looked through the astrodome to see how close we were to the six aircraft in front. To my horror there was nothing there but empty black sky! What had I done wrong? Where had I boobed?

"I looked back and saw the lights of aircraft stretching back as far as the eye could see and probably beyond. For some reason the first two 'vics' had not formed up

in front. Finding myself in the lead, I shot back to my position and for the next hour worked like never before making sure that we were on course and time to arrive at Ranville at the correct time.

"We crept very slightly ahead of our time so that our ETA became 12.57am. I should perhaps have instructed the pilot to knock two or three knots off our speed but I figured that with nobody in front and the whole invasion behind us, early was better than late, and in any case 12.57am was the leader's dropping time. We arrived and Jock Young our fourth crew member took over the map reading for the last few hundred yards. Then the fun started.

"Gerry Brown, the wireless operator went to the rear to see the boys out. The first four left in orderly fashion, they were Military Police, but the fifth man with a mortar barrel stuffed up his jumper fell in the doorway and blocked the way for the others. By the time they got him back on his feet we were past the drop zone. Gerry passed the information on but, because he forgot to release his microphone button he didn't hear Dixon say that we would go round again so I had to nip back and tell him. They all went out in good order the second time round.

"With all the excitement only Jock noticed that we were being fired at, but nothing hit us, and we made our uneventful way back to base. Because of the delay we

A 'vic' of Dakotas dropping paratroopers.

were on the end of a very long queue for landing. It was a bit of an anti-climax and I didn't mind the mild telling off I got for being 40 seconds early over the drop zone."

## FLIGHT SERGEANT J A DALDORPH – A DAKOTA CO-PILOT WITH 233 SQUADRON BASED AT BLAKEHILL FARM. THIS STATEMENT IS FROM AN OFFICIAL REPORT WRITTEN ON JUNE 17, 1944:

"At 11.17pm on the night of June 5-6, Dakota KG356 took off from Blakehill Farm as part of Operation Tonga. The captain was Flying Officer Harvey Edgar Jones (RCAF), the remainder of the crew being Flying Officer LN Williams, navigator, Warrant Officer 'Cobby' Engleberg (RCAF), wireless operator, and myself as second pilot.

"The aircraft was carrying paratroops and containers. In the circuit, while climbing, we lost sight of the 'vic' leader and did not regain contact again, so the captain decided to proceed independently. Just after crossing the French coast we were hit by light flak which must have caught one of our starboard petrol tanks alight. It could have been an underslung container holding petrol, although we did not realise that possibility at the time.

"At the correct point the order was given to drop the containers and the wireless operator reported this had been done. With the aircraft now on fire the paratroops were also dropped. Just afterwards Flying Officer Jones gave the order to abandon aircraft, although the rest of the crew could not hear this command as the intercom was dead. The fact that the intercom was unserviceable made things rather confused. As far as I could make out Flying Officer Jones refused his own parachute when it was offered and wanted us to get out.

"The navigator and myself went back to the door at the rear of the aircraft and found the wireless operator pulling in the static lines. He then went to get his parachute. We waited at the door for a short while and as neither the captain nor the wireless operator came back, we abandoned the aircraft. A few seconds later

C-47 Dakota of 233 Squadron.
Inset: Fg Off Harvey Jones RCAF.

the aircraft dived into the ground. During Tuesday morning we returned to the aircraft crash site and found that Flying Officer Jones was dead and that the wireless operator was unconscious but being attended by the villagers (Engleberg received severe internal injuries and was taken to the beach by stretcher bearers. He was still unconscious three days later, but was eventually evacuated to Britain and recovered from his injuries).

"We also found that the containers had not been dropped as previously thought, as apparently the electrical circuit must have been rendered unserviceable by the fire.

"The crash occurred on the outskirts of Bassenville, a village east of Caen. In my opinion Flying Officer Williams and I were able to bale out safely due to the fact that Flying Officer Jones remained at the controls in spite of the fact that the aircraft was alight." ∎

Crashed and burning C-47 Dakota.

## RECOMMENDATION FOR THE VC

Further to this personal report, a recommendation, dated June 30, 1944, for the award of the Victoria Cross to Flying Officer Harvey Jones was made:

"Flying Officer H Jones was the captain of a Dakota aircraft detailed to drop parachute troops in the Caen area on the night of 5-6 June, 1944. The approach was made at a height of 600ft above ground, in the face of heavy anti-aircraft fire. "About four miles from the Dropping Zone the aircraft was badly hit and set on fire. Flying Officer Jones continued heading towards the dropping zone and gave the signal for the parachute troops in the aircraft to jump, which they did successfully. He then ordered his crew to abandon the aircraft. Flying Officer Jones could himself have abandoned the aircraft through the pilot's escape hatch at the same time as the crew were ordered to jump. Although well aware of the danger of remaining in the aircraft, he refused his parachute pack when it was brought to him and stayed at the controls to keep the aircraft on an even keel and maintain sufficient height for his crew to jump safely. Two of the crew jumped successfully after which the aircraft crashed and Flying Officer Jones was killed.

"By his premeditated action in remaining at the controls until the mission was completed and the crew had left the aircraft, Flying Officer Jones deliberately sacrificed his life to carry out his orders and to ensure the safety of his crew. The dauntless courage and self-sacrifice displayed by this very gallant officer are a glorious example to all pilots in his Majesty's Service."

This VC recommendation was approved by the Blakehill Farm Station Commander, by 46 Group and by the AOC Transport Command. However, it was denied by the Air Ministry and Harvey Jones was simply awarded a Mention in Dispatches for his actions.

# 'The Flying Nightingales'

## Dakota casualty evacuation from Normandy and the WAAF air ambulance nurses

On the morning of June 13, 1944, (D-Day +7) three Douglas C-47 Dakota transport aircraft of 233 Squadron, took off from Blakehill Farm, Wiltshire, and flew across the Channel to France, escorted by a squadron of Spitfires. They landed at the newly-completed B2 airstrip at Bazenville near Bayeux, thereby gaining the honour of being the first Allied transport aircraft to land in France since the invasion.

The three Dakotas were carrying four tons of military freight, mostly ammunition. After the supplies had been unloaded, 14 casualties on stretchers and some sitting wounded were loaded on to each of the aircraft ready for an immediate return to England.

The three Women's Auxiliary Air Force (WAAF) air ambulance nurses, one on board each Dakota, who cared for the wounded soldiers on the return flights became the first females to fly into the combat zone in Normandy and the first British women to be sent into a war zone on active service by the British Government.

### 'CASEVAC' OPERATIONS

These first air ambulance casualty evacuation flights were something of an experiment, but the military was keen that they should succeed. They did, and they paved the way for the large-scale evacuation of casualties from the battle areas.

Full scale 'Casevac' air operations began on June 18, 1944, when 11 Dakotas landed on the airstrip at B4/Bény-sur-Mer in Normandy. They were loaded with 183 casualties who were flown back to Down Ampney, to be followed by 90 more, three days later.

By the end of June, 1092 stretcher cases and 467 sitting wounded had been evacuated from Normandy by 233, 271 and 48 Squadrons. This was the beginning of a regular casualty evacuation service by air that continued up until the end of hostilities in May 1945.

### WAAF NURSES

Carrying up to 24 wounded soldiers on each return trip, with one WAAF nurse on board each Dakota to care for them, these operations played a vital part in speedily evacuating casualties to hospitals in the UK which could provide the necessary life-saving operations and treatment.

The nurses had to deal with horrifying injuries. Many of the young soldiers were

The first 'Flying Nightingales', from left, LACW Myra Roberts, Cpl Lydia Alford and LACW Edna Birkbeck, photographed with a 233 Squadron Dakota on June 13, 1944.

missing limbs or had their faces burnt or blown away; treatment such as amputations, transfusions and colostomies had often been improvised in the field.

During the course of the remainder of the war, two WAAF air ambulance nurses were killed on active service; many others suffered subsequent mental breakdowns because of the horrors they witnessed, but the women received little official recognition and no medals for their bravery.

### 'FLYING NIGHTINGALES'

The first casualty evacuation flights on June 13, 1944, with the female nurses on board, were met by members of the press on their arrival at B2/Bazenville and, later, on their return to Blakehill Farm, by dozens more press correspondents, representing many British, Canadian and American newspapers.

The WAAF nurses were immediately dubbed the 'Flying Nightingales' by the press, a name that was to remain with them

for the rest of the campaign. A photograph of the three 'Flying Nightingales' from that first operation, standing together in front of one of the 233 Squadron Dakotas, was published in the newspapers the next day. The three nurses were LACW Myra Roberts, Corporal Lydia Alford and LACW Edna Birbeck. These are their individual accounts of what it was like for them.

Casualties being loaded onto RAF Dakotas at an ALG in Normandy in June 1944.

## LACW MYRA ROBERTS – 233 SQUADRON DAKOTA AIR AMBULANCE NURSE:

Myra Roberts was part of a large family of eight children and came from the Midlands area of the UK, near Birmingham. She started to train as a nurse at the Angel Hospital in Birmingham before the war broke out, but had to give it up and return home when her father was taken ill with duodenal ulcers. Her mother needed Myra's help with him and the six youngest children who were still at home. Myra was naturally disappointed at the time, but the war gave her a further opportunity to take up her vocation as a nurse.

"I joined the air force, the WAAF, to get away. I was sent first to Bridgnorth in Shropshire, and did all the 'square bashing'. I wasn't all that enamoured with that marching and saluting stuff so I was very glad when I was directed into the medical section for we never had to do a lot of saluting again – even for our pay!

"From here I was sent to further my nursing experience at a school in Sidmouth in Devon. After that I was in Sawbridgeworth in Hertfordshire for a couple of years. Just when this hospital patch was becoming a bit humdrum, and I was wishing for a change, the medical officer had a talk with me: 'We've been asked to find people for flying duties, air ambulance duties. But you've got to volunteer before we can recommend you.' He warned me I'd have to do some extra, hard training. I volunteered immediately. He was right, they did put us through the mill in our training.

"Not long after, I had orders to go to a place called Blakehill Farm. I was to pack all my stuff and get on a train to this place near Cricklade in Wiltshire. When I got there, good gracious. It looked like a place that had been torn out of fields. There were buildings going

up, and roads being made. An aerodrome was being built, but it was grim. You had to wear boots or wellingtons everywhere because you were knee-deep in mud.

"I was told that I was going to become part of the air crew of a Dakota. Ten of us, from different parts of the country, were billeted in Hut 5. Among them was Minnie from Trinidad, she was a great big tall girl. We shared a double bunk. Eventually there were about 20 of us at the station. This training of ours was for D-Day, but nobody knew that. We just did as we were told, but we realised that there was something big happening. We had to have flying experience. So we went up in the Dakota whenever the crew of our plane went up. Sometimes they'd do glider towing; and they'd practise circuits and bumps, they called it; sometimes they'd be taking six of the airborne, paratroopers, up and letting them jump out. Day or night, whenever you were allotted you had to go with it, you were part of the crew.

"The pilot of the Dakota in which I did my training flights was Scottish, Warrant Officer Jock McCannell. After the first few trips I had the feeling he didn't want me aboard and eventually I asked why. He said it was nothing personal. He'd come from a fishing family and fishermen would never put out to sea with a woman in the boat. It was considered bad luck. During that first week of June we girls were grounded, while all the planes took part in the landings. Jock's was one of the few that didn't return on June 6, 1944. I thought about the woman in the boat.

"On June 12, the air ambulance pool were summoned to the headquarters and given a pep talk by Sir Harold Whittingham, the Director-General of RAF Medical Services. He chose three of us: Lydia Alford, Edna Birkbeck (Morris now) and me. We were taken to collect our gear and

LACW Myra Roberts after returning to Blakehill Farm on June 13, 1944, holding the bunch of flowers given to her by a French girl in Normandy earlier in the day.

be fitted with parachutes, told that we were operational the next day, and spent the night in sick bay headquarters.

"We were awakened before dawn on the 13th, given our 'flying meal' and then taken to an aircraft each with our medical panniers of equipment and large flasks of hot tea. My panniers went aboard the plane, which was already loaded with supplies – mostly ammunition, so there was no Red Cross insignia on it. But we were given fighter air cover for this first flight into Normandy.

"My first flight to France began with a handshake and 'bon voyage' from the air marshal, and he gave me a newspaper to read on the outward journey. I remember thinking, silly chap, does he really think that I shall be reading a paper? I'd be too busy wondering what the next few hours had in store for me.

"We flew in over the coast, which was an indescribable scene with boats and ships of every size and shape, barrage balloons, and all the debris of the landings. Our three planes landed in Normandy on an airstrip which was a cornfield with a metal strip laid down the middle as a runway, about two kilometres from the shore where the boys had just gone in and the Germans had just vacated their trenches.

"Our planes were quickly unloaded of supplies and then loaded with the wounded. Lydia's plane took off almost immediately but the weather closed in and Edna and I were told there would be a delay until the weather improved. We were taken by a newspaper correspondent on a short tour of the area towards Caen where the action was fierce. We could hear the bombing and see the shelling and sense the snipers in the trees! As we made our way back to a farm where there were some refreshments, we passed convoys of soldiers who, when they

RAF Blakehill Farm airfield with C-47 Dakotas lined up in preparation for a training exercise in April 1944.

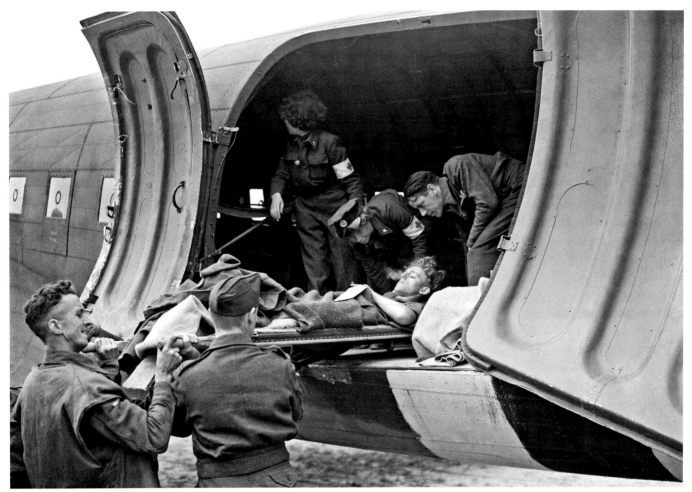

Loading a wounded soldier on a stretcher into a 233 Squadron Dakota at an ALG in Normandy in June 1944.

saw us in the jeep, yelled 'Blimey! Women!' I was given a bouquet of flowers by a very pretty French girl called Giselle. Then it was back to the aircraft and Edna's plane took off.

"Just as we were closing our doors, an ambulance came tearing up. 'Sorry to do this to you,' said this young MO. 'I have a badly wounded soldier and no place to keep him. He probably won't make it, but for God's sake don't let him die on the plane – do your best.' My first thought was 'Why me?' while I was fixing this dying soldier up with oxygen, slowly to begin with, gradually increasing it. And as I did, he started to use the most frightful words in Welsh. He was badly injured internally – he was minus a leg, and an arm had gone. I thought, he'll not last 10 minutes, let alone make it back to the base.

"I got hold of his hand, and told him I was sorry that I couldn't speak Welsh but I could understand it! I read his label and he was from Tywyn. I told him I knew his home-place very well and not to worry, he'd be back there. And then I got the wireless operator to ask for a medical officer on the base as soon as we landed. The soldier had to be seen immediately. I was glad to hand him over still alive, and I wondered if he'd make it.

"Do you know what? Six years later, I was married by then and living near Tywyn, my husband Jack came home one day and said: 'Guess what? I met this chap on a kind of trolley wheelchair who asked me who was the girl he saw me with the other day. I

told him it was you, my wife. And he told me you were the girl who'd fetched him back from France.' In the hospital they'd shown him a picture of me, which had been in the papers. And he'd remembered the face. So next day we went down to the pub and had a drink with him. And he lived for a good 20 years, you know.

"Anyway, to go back to that first successful ambulance lift that he'd been on. After all the casualties had been removed and all the equipment had been put into the ambulances, just as I was coming out of the Dakota I was asked to pose for a picture with my bunch of flowers from Giselle in my arms. There was a sea of cameras and all the army big wigs and the air force hierarchy were there. This trip was a feather in their caps. It was a boost for everyone to know that if any of our troops were wounded they could be brought back swiftly and safely.

"After that, we followed the fighting. They'd make an airstrip near the latest fighting, we'd take in supplies and bring the wounded out. We went right into where the action was going on.

"One trip I'll never forget. I prayed more earnestly than I have ever prayed in my life. The weather was grim, one of the casualties started being sick and more followed. I was trying to wedge sick-bags under them. One soldier had a tracheotomy tube in. I had to undo this and clear the inner tube so he could breathe and fix it back. And I began to feel so sick myself. Please, please God, don't

let me start vomiting now, I begged, because once you start you can't stop. So I kept my head back and prayed.

"Another time for prayer was when we had to crash-land. We'd taken some casualties to Oxford and were returning to Wiltshire, empty. And I couldn't understand why the pilot was circling, and circling, until they explained that we were going to have to crash land. I put myself with my hands behind my head and curled up into a ball. This way you could roll and take the impact. I ended up at the foot of the plane, but it wasn't too bad a crash-landing; we just skidded along.

"We were overworked, really. You could be on duty that afternoon, come back at night and find you had to stay put for the next flight back. We had very little leave at all and it was dangerous work, though none of us seemed to suffer from nerves. We were carrying ammunition. We had bombs at our feet, and once I had to sit on the edge of one, because there was nowhere else, and you couldn't stand.

"At the time you didn't think anything of it. You became acclimatised to it. I don't know why, your brain realised you were helping, you were doing your duty, kind of thing, and if it was your duty, you did it. There was an urgency. You didn't have time to think, really. Once or twice it was a bit harrowing. The war taught me to stand on my own two feet, I suppose, and keep an eye on other people at the same time. It made me feel capable of taking things in my stride."

Cpl Lydia Alford on June 13, 1944.

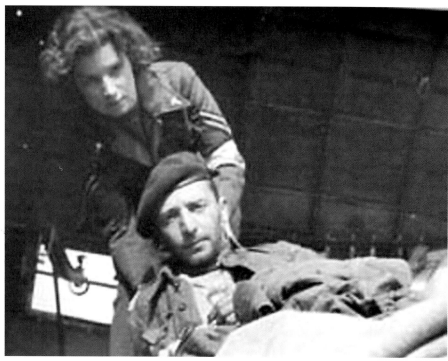

Cpl Lydia Alford loading a casualty into a Dakota.

## CORPORAL LYDIA ALFORD – 233 SQUADRON DAKOTA AIR AMBULANCE NURSE:

Lydia Alford was born in July 1916 and grew up in the village of Horton Heath, near Eastleigh, Hampshire. She was the fourth child in a family of six. After leaving school she spent a period in domestic service and then trained to become a nurse at the South Hants Hospital, Southampton, before joining-up as a WAAF nursing orderly.

"I responded to a call in routine orders asking for volunteers from suitably qualified medical personnel to train for air ambulance duties. Within weeks of applying, I was sent on an intensive air ambulance training course at Hendon for special training. This included instruction in the use of oxygen, injections, learning how to deal with certain types of injuries such as broken bones, burns and colostomies, and to learn the effects of air travel and altitude.

"When I had completed the course, I was posted to Blakehill Farm, near Cricklade. The training continued with a 'brush-up' course at the nearby RAF hospital at Wroughton, dinghy drill in the swimming pool at Bath and several hours of flying experience often in night glider exercises. These were pretty terrifying, as they were carried out with the aircraft cargo door removed, and when the glider was released the whole plane juddered. During the tense days of waiting we were put through a tough routine of physical training and helped with building roads on the newly-built airfield.

"It was raining slightly when we boarded the planes at 5am on June 13, wearing our mae west life jackets and parachutes and carrying the first-aid panniers. Flying over the Normandy coast, we could see the aftermath of the D-Day landings strewn across the beaches; abandoned landing craft, broken tanks, craters and scattered

discarded equipment. The thing I remember chiefly about that first time on the ground in Normandy is the dust which was everywhere, coming up in great clouds. While the freight was being unloaded I tried to make the wounded men as comfortable as possible in all that dust. I had water to give them and panniers of tea. There was a little stray dog that came up from somewhere or other and started to play with the wounded – it cheered them up no end.

"After the supplies were unloaded, we immediately loaded the wounded on board

and took off again. Unfortunately, the weather closed in and the other two girls had to wait for it to clear. Most of my wounded men were stretcher cases. One man required oxygen; a few hours earlier he had been shot in the chest and back by a German sniper.

"As the first back, I was overwhelmed by dozens of press men. The story that appeared in the newspapers the next day was the first that my family knew of exactly what I was doing."

(Lydia Alford died in 1993)

Checking on a wounded soldier at an ALG in Normandy in June 1944.

## LACW EDNA BIRKBECK – 233 SQUADRON DAKOTA AIR AMBULANCE NURSE:

Edna Birkbeck was born in Northamptonshire in August 1924. After leaving school she became a trainee nurse and in February 1943, still aged only 18, she joined the WAAF as a nursing orderly "for excitement". She was trained at Morecambe and Sidmouth before moving to RAF Medmenham in Buckinghamshire. Shortly afterwards she responded to a call for volunteers for air ambulance duties, although she was not entirely sure what was involved.

"I had, like Myra, volunteered to become an air ambulance nurse. We met with the other 'Nightingales' at Blakehill Farm, before we went into action.

"About a week before the first operation, we had to go to the RAF hospital at Wroughton for a refresher course. When we got back we found that the camp was all under curfew – no one could get in or out without passes – so we knew something was going to happen. Then D-Day came, when the planes all took off, and a few days afterwards we were called up to a marquee, a field hospital ready to take the wounded.

"A senior medical official gave us a pep talk, and said that we would soon have to be doing the work we'd trained for, and then pointed to Myra, myself and Lydia. He said: 'You three stay here. All the rest can go.' Then he told us he wanted us to go and pick up a mae west – a life-jacket – and a parachute, and take it up to the crew room.

"In the crew room, of course, there were one or two of the air crew, and one of them, sounding a bit miffed, remarked that it looked like the girls were going over before them. They'd flown over, but they hadn't landed, you see. From now until we left, we were not allowed to go back to our own WAAF quarters at all. They sent someone to get our night clothes, and our instructions were not to go out, not to speak to anyone.

"The WAAF sergeant came along: she gave us best hospital blankets to sleep on, not the old grey ones, and a tray with cocoa on it. Lambs to the slaughter! Someone came in and said my boyfriend was outside and wanted to speak to me. I'd only been going out with Glyn a short time then (Glyn Morris and Edna later married). Well, of course, I wasn't supposed to, but I popped out and had a few words with him. I could see he was worried about me, and wanted to make sure I was all right before I went.

"The airstrip we landed on was only a cornfield that had been flattened down, and it still had poppies round the edge, but all the rest was barren. There was a concrete dugout, a German dugout, so I went investigating there. It was strange to think that only a few days before, Germans had been walking round in the dugout. I picked up a German helmet, a gas mask and a bayonet. I've still got the bayonet, and also a hand grenade – I was very naive about hand grenades in those days. I'd never seen one

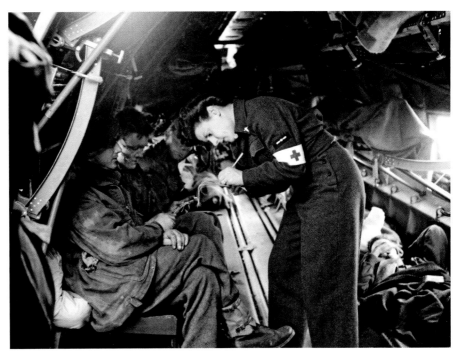

Checking the casualties' details inside a Dakota.

An RAF Servicing Commando introduces himself to the girls in Normandy.

before. Anyway, back in barracks it went up on the shelf above my bed, and there it stayed for 12 months, until I got married. When Glyn my husband saw it. 'Good God,' he said, 'it's live', and he promptly took it off to the armoury. It could have gone off at any minute if it had fallen and the pin had come out. I had no idea.

"By the end of the war I had done about 70 flights with 233 Squadron. Some of the wounded were very badly injured but you couldn't let it get to you. None of my patients ever died on any of my flights. They always wanted tea, those that could drink. We'd carry an industrial-sized urn. And they'd always want to know when we were over the coast. I'd tell them that and say: 'It won't be long before you're home.' And they'd cheer. All this changed me certainly, because I was a really shy person when I joined up and before I started flying, but that gave me a lot of confidence."

(Edna Morris died in 2004) ■

LACW Edna Birbeck on the steps of her Dakota after returning to Blakehill Farm on June 13, 1944.

C-47 Dakota ZA947 of the RAF Battle of Britain Memorial Flight is currently painted to represent Dakota FZ692 of No 233 Sqn, which was named 'Kwicherbichen' by its crew. 'Kwicherbichen' was involved in the D-Day operations and in subsequent casualty evacuation missions, as shown by the mission symbols on the side of the cockpit. Photo: John Dibbs, The Plane Picture Company

# The 'Heavies'

## The RAF heavy bombers' contribution to Operation Overlord

Three Avro Lancaster B Mk.Is of 44 Squadron, based at Waddington, Lincolnshire, on a daylight operation.

U p until the end of March 1944 the heavy bombers of RAF Bomber Command had been totally committed to the campaign against German cities and Berlin in particular, with the so-called 'Battle of Berlin' officially lasting from November 1943 to March 1944.

The commander-in-chief of Bomber Command, Air Chief Marshal Sir Arthur Harris, had believed for some time that an all-out bombing campaign against Germany, with the combined might of the British and Americans, might bring about the downfall of the Nazis and bring the war to an end without the need for a prolonged land offensive. By the end of March 1944, however, it had become apparent that the war would only be ended by the defeat of Germany in the field.

The costly Nuremberg raid of March 30-31, 1944, when 95 of the 795 bombers on the operation failed to return and another five were written off in crashes, was temporarily the last of Bomber Command's major offensives against the German homeland. In preparation for Operation Overlord the emphasis was switched to targets in occupied Europe and the transportation system in western Germany, although there were still some occasional raids against cities further east in an effort to keep the German night fighters and flak defences as far east as possible.

### LANCASTER AND HALIFAX

By this stage, the two principal types of heavy bomber in use by Bomber Command were the Avro Lancaster and the Handley-Page

Halifax, the few remaining Short Stirlings having been more or less withdrawn to second line duties. The Halifax had entered service with the RAF in November 1940 with 35 Squadron and flew its first operational raid on March 11-12, 1941.

The Lancaster, on the other hand, had evolved from the less-than successful Avro Manchester and did not carry out its first operational sorties until almost a year later, on March 3-4, 1942. By June 1944 though, there were twice as many Lancaster squadrons in Bomber Command as there were Halifax-equipped units.

ACM Harris had been very critical of Handley Page and the performance of the Halifax in comparison with the Lancaster, which had proved to be the better of the two designs in terms of bomb-carrying capability and survival rates. The later variants of the Halifax, powered by Bristol Hercules radial engines and fitted with the Perspex nose and modified tail, were almost on a par with the Lancaster in terms of speed and altitude performance and bettered it on loss rates and crew survival statistics. However, Harris did not alter his opinion and the Lancaster remained his heavy bomber of choice.

If he had his way, he would have had all production switched to the Lancaster. As it was, while new manufacturing facilities were devoted to the Lancaster, Halifax production continued at Handley Page's existing manufacturing facilities because it was considered more efficient to allow this, rather than to stop production for an unknown period while the factories converted to building Lancasters. However,

Halifaxes were progressively relegated to secondary theatres such as North Africa and Italy, while many were converted to or built new as glider tugs, transports and maritime reconnaissance variants. Meanwhile, the Lancaster became Bomber Command's pre-eminent heavy bomber and, of course, it was also the 'darling' of its crews.

### TARGETS IN FRANCE

In the two months before D-Day the RAF Bomber Command Lancasters and Halifaxes were increasingly tasked against targets in France. In April 1944 less than half of the bomb tonnage dropped was directed against targets in Germany. In May three-quarters of the heavy bomber sorties were against targets in France and other occupied territories outside Germany.

In the final weeks before D-Day much of the heavy bombers' work was directly in support of the impending invasion, with their efforts directed at destroying the German lines of communication in France and attempting to destroy the German coastal batteries covering the French channel ports.

### 'EASY' TARGETS?

For the crews of the bombers, the attacks on the French targets brought a welcome relief from the assault on Germany. The 'Battle of Berlin' and the winter were behind them, and the spring brought lengthening odds on each man's survival.

Their morale plunged, however, when word came that Bomber Command intended to recognise the relative ease of attacking targets in France by making each

Halifax B Mk.III, LV857, of 51 Squadron, was one of the 95 aircraft lost on the costly raid on Nuremberg on the night of March 30-31, 1944. It was shot down by a Me 110 night fighter flown by Oberleutnant Martin Becker of I/NJG6. The crew of seven, who were only on their third operation, were all killed.

of these sorties count as only one third of an operation towards a man's tour. Crews with only three or four trips left to complete their tour of 30 'ops', which most did not live to see, were appalled by the prospect that these remaining hurdles to survival might stretch to nine or 12 trips.

In May 1944 two bombing raids on French 'tactical' targets demonstrated why this invidious idea was so ill-conceived. On May 3-4 a force of 348 Lancasters, led by 14 Mosquitos, was sent to bomb a large German Wehrmacht depot at Mailly-le-Camp southeast of Paris. The enemy troops and tanks in this depot could have been used to resist the Allied advance after the invasion.

Problems with marking the target accurately and then with radio communications between the master bomber and his force, resulted in the bombers being delayed on their attack runs and being forced to orbit in bright moonlight. The German night fighters got in among the bombers and caused carnage, proof indeed that the Allies did not have the same air superiority at night as they enjoyed by day.

From the point of view of the bombing results, the operation was a success; 1200 tons of explosives were dropped on the German camp, 220 Wehrmacht soldiers were killed and another 150 wounded, and 37 tanks were destroyed. However, of the 362 aircraft on the operation 42, or 11.3%, were shot down, overwhelmingly by the night fighters. It was a high cost and one that could not be justified.

On May 10, 89 Lancasters were sent to bomb a target at Lille. There was a prolonged delay in the middle of the attack, when the target indicators were blown out and the target had to be remarked. Twelve aircraft, 13.5 per cent, were destroyed.

These were two exceptionally bad nights, but they were a brutal reminder of

what the Luftwaffe night fighters could still do, given the chance. Lingering around a target for accurate visual marking could be fatal. There was no more talk of French targets counting as a third of an 'op'.

## DESTROYING THE RAILWAYS

By June 3, the RAF heavy bombers had attacked every one of their allotted pre-invasion targets. A total of 54,869 tons of bombs had been dropped, of which the Lancasters contributed just over 33,000 tons. The devastation inflicted on the railway system in France and Belgium was extensive.

Every important railway junction through which German reinforcements and supplies could reach Normandy had been severely damaged or destroyed. By D-Day the capacity of the lines had been reduced to six trains a day when German plans had counted on 48 trains a day to reinforce the possible invasion areas.

German defences all along the French coast had been pulverised by the heavy bombers, which had flown some 1700 sorties on 30 separate raids on gun emplacements and batteries. Throughout these operations, the continuing deception of the Germans demanded that three times as many bombs fell east of the Seine as did to the west.

## D-DAY

On the night preceding the invasion itself, June 5-6, 1944, the 'Heavies' targeted the coastal batteries overlooking the actual planned invasion beaches. Bomber Command set a new record that night with 1211 aircraft despatched on missions of all types, most of them in direct support of the invasion. Of the heavy bombers targeting the coastal batteries, four Halifaxes and four Lancasters failed to return, most shot down by German night fighters. Cloud cover

meant that most of the bombing was carried out 'blind', but these raids helped to create a 'shock and awe' effect as well as putting some of the batteries out of action.

## BATTLE OF NORMANDY

After D-Day the heavy bombers continued to be used against tactical targets and in support of the Allied ground forces, targeting communications, railways, ammunition dumps, enemy troop positions and other specific targets.

More than 4200 Lancaster sorties were flown during June against these types of targets and in direct support of Operation Overlord and the Battle of Normandy. On June 14, as a result of the overwhelming daylight air supremacy achieved by the Allies, Bomber Command was able to resume daylight operations for the first time in years. Fighter cover was provided for these relatively short penetration operations.

From mid-June much of Bomber Command's efforts were directed against the German 'V'-weapon sites, which could have directed their missiles against the Allied forces in Normandy as well as against the UK mainland.

## THE 'HEAVIES' CONTRIBUTION

The heavy bomber operations of the RAF have been covered in myriad books, documentaries and accounts, but they are often taken in isolation. Most people would, perhaps, not consider that the heavy bombers played much of a direct part in the success of the Allied invasion of Europe. In fact, though, the 'heavies' part in Operation Overlord, the D-Day invasion, and the subsequent 'Battle of Normandy' was extremely important and actually contributed significantly to the ultimate success of these operations as well as to the final victory. ∎

'Spitfires Escorting Lancasters on a Daylight Raid'. Operations like this were part of the massive Allied air effort against German forces after D-Day in 1944, when the hard-won Allied air supremacy permitted daylight bombing operations by RAF heavy bombers. As the number of daylight raids increased, the Lancasters received fighter cover from the RAF for the first time in the war. 617 Squadron Lancaster pilot Bob Knights later said: "The Spitfires were a very welcome sight and would accompany you to the target; they would hang around and see you were all right." Artwork: Gary Eason

# 'Lost and found'

## Lancaster shot down on D-Day found 68 years later

Lancaster Mk.III PB410 'OF-J' of 97 Squadron. Note the H2S radar blister under the rear fuselage.

On June 5, 1944, 83 and 97 Lancaster Pathfinder Squadrons, based at RAF Coningsby in Lincolnshire, received the details of the target for the night at about 1pm. It seemed like a normal operation to start with, the target being a battery of coastal heavy guns on the French coast at a point called St Pierre-du-Mont, situated on the southeast corner of the Cherbourg Peninsula.

Then various other pieces of information relating to the night's operations trickled in, details such as convoys to be avoided, keeping strictly on track and at the briefed altitude, news of impending naval actions to the east, and so on.

It became obvious to those piecing together the plan for the night that the great day they had all been waiting for had arrived, the invasion of Europe was about to commence and they would have a part to play in it. The commanding officer of 97 Squadron, 24-year-old Wing Commander Edward James 'Jimmy' Carter DFC, was heard to exclaim: "Thank God I'm still on ops and not at an OTU (Operational Training Unit)." He would not have time to regret that statement and he was not to know it, but his desire to be involved in the great enterprise was going to cost him his life.

### 'JIMMY' CARTER

'Jimmy' Carter had been in the RAF throughout the war; he was now a very experienced bomber pilot, as his DFC from a previous tour of operations showed. He had assumed command of 97 Squadron, which was then based at Bourn, in January 1944, after completing a tour as an instructor on a Vickers Wellington training unit. 97 Squadron moved to Coningsby in April 1944. Since taking over the squadron, Carter had led the unit's crews on pathfinder target marking operations to Berlin, Leipzig, Essen, Lille, Brunswick, Schweinfurt, Kjeller (Oslo), the Philips Works at Eindhoven and the German artillery battery at Maisy on the French coast. For the operation on June 6, Carter was nominated as the deputy master bomber.

### CARTER'S CREW

Carter's crew were at least as experienced and decorated as their pilot and captain; in all they boasted no fewer than nine Distinguished Flying Crosses or Medals between them. The crew consisted of: Pilot Officer Guy Dunning DFM (flight engineer), Flight Lieutenant Ron Conley DFC RAAF (navigator), Flight Lieutenant Herbert Rieger RCAF (bomb aimer), Flight Lieutenant Albert Chambers DFC and Bar (wireless operator), Warrant Officer Frank Watson DFM (mid-upper gunner) and Squadron Leader Martin Bryan-Smith DFC and Bar (rear gunner). Two of the most experienced of these crew members were the leaders for their aircrew trades on the squadron; Squadron Leader Bryan-Smith was the gunnery leader, and 23-year-old Flight Lieutenant Chambers, who had flown 58 'ops', was the signals leader.

It was not uncommon for pathfinder Lancasters to carry an eighth crew member on some 'ops', who sat alongside the navigator and operated the H2S ground mapping radar for blind bombing and accurate target marking. This was the case in Carter's aircraft on the night of June 6 and Flying Officer 'Hank' Jeffery DFM flew with the crew as the second navigator/bomb-aimer in this role, as he had done on a previous occasion. Jeffery had already completed a tour of 30 operations on Lancasters with 9 Squadron at Bardney, being awarded the DFM in December 1943. Having been 'screened' as an instructor at the heavy conversion unit at Winthorpe he was now flying regularly on

Wg Cdr 'Jimmy' Carter, OC 97 Squadron.

Some of Carter's crew, from left, wireless operator Flt Lt Chambers, second nav/bomb aimer Fg Off Jeffery, bomb aimer Flt Lt Rieger RCAF and rear gunner Sqn Ldr Bryan-Smith.

'ops' again with 97 Squadron, although he had told his mother that he had volunteered for just one last flight.

This crew which was, at the time, probably one of the RAF's most decorated, was also a very valuable team of experts.

## D-DAY 'OP'

Excitement among the Lancaster crews was at a fever pitch as they went through the routine build-up to a night on 'ops', including the necessary planning and briefing. The popular station commander at RAF Coningsby, Group Captain Anthony Evans-Evans, kicked off the briefing and set the scene for the crews. Evans-Evans was one of the great characters at Coningsby, a big cheerful man he flew on 'ops' occasionally, but his age (he was 42), his rank and his sheer size were against him in this. Most of the aircrew believed that he would never fit through the escape hatch if he needed to bale out! Sadly, he was eventually killed in an 83 Squadron Lancaster on an operation over the Mitteland Canal in February 1945, only a few days after being awarded the DFC.

The crews of the 18 Lancasters flying on the operation from Coningsby on June 6, were driven to their aircraft which were dispersed around the airfield. Carter and his crew were flying Lancaster Mk.III ND739, 'OF-Z', which was loaded with 11 1000lb bombs and four 500lb bombs. They must have been feeling good about their chances as they lifted off from Coningsby's runway at 2.56am, not only because they were going to be part of a momentous event but also because the target was barely inside enemy territory and their exposure to enemy defences, flak and night fighters was surely only going to be brief. As they climbed to their briefed operating height and cruised southwards over England and the English Channel the cloud cover below them did not allow them to see the armada beneath them.

## ON THE GERMAN SIDE

Across the Channel, at Évreux airfield in Normandy, Hauptmann (Captain) Helmut Eberspacher of 3/SKG (Schnellkampfgeschwader) 10 was on alert. SKG10 was a Luftwaffe fast-bomber, ground-attack unit equipped with Focke-Wulf Fw 190G-3s and G-8s. Twenty-eight-year-old

Eberspacher, a holder of the Iron Cross first and second class, had been promoted to Staffelkapitän to lead the 3rd Staffel of the 1st Gruppe in May. SKG10 flew 'hit and run' fighter-bomber missions with their Fw 190s over southern England both by day and by night. Due to the lack of regular night fighters in France and in view of the increasing number of night bombing missions being flown by the RAF over France, from April 1944 onwards the Fw 190s of SKG10 were also employed on Wilde Sau ('Wild Boar') free-ranging, night-fighter missions against the British bombers on the brighter moonlit nights. It was for this purpose that Eberspacher and some of his pilots were sitting on alert at Évreux.

Earlier that night, warnings of enemy glider and paratroopers landing in Normandy had reached Évreux, but the Fw 190 pilots that were scrambled had found no enemy air activity. They were rather downcast by this lack of success and failure to see anything of the enemy. Then at about 4.30am information came into the Gruppe HQ that Allied bombers were pounding the coast between Carentan and Caen.

Eberspacher was ordered to scramble with three other Fw 190s into that sector. There was very limited assistance from the German fighter controllers whose radars had mostly been destroyed, while the surviving parts of the air defence system were being heavily jammed. However, there were so many RAF bombers in such a small area that it was almost inevitable that the Fw 190 pilots would stumble across some. Fate was about to bring Eberspacher's Fw 190 and 'Jimmy' Carter's Lancaster together.

## THE BOMBING ATTACK

The heavy bombers' attack against the coastal battery at St Pierre-du-Mont started at 4.50am, about 30 minutes before dawn, with a red target indicator (TI) which was dropped accurately on the target by an 'Oboe'-equipped Mosquito Pathfinder. It was instantly backed up by green TIs dropped visually by Mosquito aircraft of 627 Squadron. These latter TIs were not as accurate as those dropped with 'Oboe'. However, by the time the main force came in to bomb, the target was well marked. The bombing was extremely accurate and the whole point was flattened.

## THE COMBAT

Carter and his crew had dropped their bombs on the target and had turned for home when they were found by Eberspacher in his Fw 190 shortly after 5am. It would not be true to say that they came 'face to face', because the bomber crew probably never saw the Fw 190 and never knew what hit them. Eberspacher spotted several Lancasters silhouetted against the moonlit clouds below him. He dived down on Carter's 'Z-Zebra' and attacked from the Lancaster's blind spot underneath, avoiding engaging the bomber from any other angle out of a healthy respect for the RAF gunners. He later said: "Similar to a shadow theatre, the bombers stood out against the clouds. However, they could not see me against the dark ground. We were at war, the enemy had to be combated and I was in a favourable position."

At 5.04am a transmission from Carter on the Force radio frequency, acknowledging a message from the master bomber, was suddenly cut short. Cannon shells and machine gun fire from the Fw 190 ripped into the underside of the Lancaster, causing immediate catastrophic damage, probably wounding and killing some on board and setting the bomber on fire. It is almost impossible to imagine the adrenalin-pumping terror that would be felt by a bomber crew on the receiving end of a

Hauptmann Helmut Eberspacher, Fw 190 pilot.

sustained burst of cannon fire from a completely unseen foe.

Eberspacher reported no return fire from the Lancaster and knew it was fatally damaged. He immediately attacked a second Lancaster and then a third, shooting down all three within three minutes, with the loss of all on board except one of the gunners. One of the other pilots in his flight, Feldwebel Eisele, claimed another of the RAF heavy bombers, so when they landed back at Évreux they were able to claim a total of four bombers shot down, the first air combat action and the first kills for the Luftwaffe on D-Day.

## LOST WITHOUT TRACE

None of Carter's crew escaped from the burning Lancaster; the bombing height was lower than usual and there was little time for any survivors of the Fw 190 attack to bale out before the bomber ploughed into the Normandy fields and exploded. All eight of the crew were still on board and all were killed. They were proof that experience, expertise, skill and alertness were not enough to survive in the bomber crews' war and, in the end, it was just a lottery that came down to sheer luck. They were lost without trace.

Many, indeed most, of the heavy bomber crew members who were killed over enemy territory during the Second World War received a decent burial from the Germans. However, in this instance the location of the crash site, near Carentan in Normandy, quickly became a battlefield and was, therefore, not dealt with in the usual way. The war rolled over the site and the men's bodies were never recovered. Their names were listed on the Runnymede memorial which commemorates 20,389 airmen of the Second World War with no known graves.

Fw 190s of SKG10 in their camouflaged 'hides' on an airfield in Normandy.

## FOUND 68 YEARS LATER

Sixty-eight years later in 2012, British aviation historian and archaeologist Tony Graves was taken to an aircraft crash site in Normandy by French locals. Some farmers had found part of a wheel protruding from the soil and a local metal detector had found a gold ring, which bore the initials 'AC' on its face, and the inscription 'Love Vera' engraved on the back. Some detective work by Mr Graves led him to realise that the 'AC' referred to Albert Chambers (Carter's wireless operator) who had married Vera Grubb, aged 21, at St Giles' Church, Normanton near Derby, in October 1943, just eight months before he died on D-Day.

Permission was obtained from the land owner and from the French Government to excavate the site, where some 300 rounds of British .303 ammunition was still lying on the surface. The excavation uncovered two of the inner Merlin engines, one outer engine and several propeller blades, one of the Lancaster's wheel hubs, the back of an armour-plated seat, one of the bomb bay doors and all the bomb racks clamps.

The fragmentary wreckage that emerged convinced the aviation archeologists that these were the remains of ND739, Wing Commander 'Jimmy' Carter's Lancaster, which had been missing from Coningsby since June 6, 1944. A number of personal items found during the dig were the most poignant: a silver-plated cigarette case twisted by the impact, a watch torn from the wrist of an airman, a mangled Bomber Command whistle, a forage cap, a silk flying glove, and remains of wool serge battledress jackets, one with a DFM ribbon, one with the remains of a Waterman pen in the pocket and one with a German 7.92 bullet lodged inside a sleeve. Lancaster ND739 and some personal reminders of its crew had finally been found 68 years after they went missing on D-Day.

The motto of 97 Squadron was 'Achieve your aim'. These eight airmen gave their lives on D-Day doing just that.

(Helmut Eberspacher was later awarded the coveted Knight's Cross in January 1945 after he had flown 170 fighter-bomber and night-fighter missions and shot down seven enemy aircraft. He survived the war and died in June 2011). ∎

A Lancaster bombing blind through cloud.

# 'Sledgehammer to crack hard nuts'

The major Bomber Command effort on the night of June 8-9, 1944 (D-Day +2) involved 483 bombers attacking rail centres at Alençon, Fougères, Mayenne, Pontaubault and Rennes. Four aircraft were lost on these raids. One of the most significant attacks that night was made by 617 Squadron against the Saumur railway tunnel and involved the first operational use of a new 'special weapon', the Tallboy earthquake-effect bomb.

## SAUMUR RAILWAY TUNNEL

As the invasion unfolded, the French Resistance and British intelligence reported to Allied headquarters that the German Wehrmacht was planning to move a Panzer armoured division by rail from the Bordeaux region to Normandy. If they had succeeded, this division could have been used to initiate a powerful counterattack against the break out from the beaches. The railway line that would be used to transport the division crossed the Loire River over a bridge and then immediately passed through a tunnel near the town of Saumur in the Loire valley, some 125 miles south of the battle area. A raid against this important target was planned in great haste and was a classic example of the heavy bombers being used tactically, with the specific aim in this case being to block the route of the German reinforcements to the ground battle.

Just after 2am on June 9, the Saumur target area was illuminated by flares dropped by four Lancasters of 83 Squadron, although it was reported that most of them were dropped inaccurately, too far away, and only the last two or three were of any use.

Nonetheless, at 2.06am Wing Commander Leonard Cheshire, the Officer Commanding 617 Squadron, who was flying Mosquito VI MS993, with navigator Flying Officer Kelly, dived on the southern entrance of the tunnel from 3000ft down to 500ft and released four red spot fire

Tallboy bomb being manoeuvred for loading by RAF armourers.

markers, one of which fell on the railway cutting just at the mouth of the tunnel.

A second Mosquito, flown by 617 Squadron's 'Tom and Gerry' duo of Flight Lieutenant Gerry Fawke and Flying Officer Tom Bennet, dropped flares to illuminate the target area, followed by three red spots which landed 50 yards from the north end of the tunnel.

Twenty-five Lancasters of 617 Squadron (a new squadron record for an operation), 19 of them carrying the new Tallboy bomb and the others with eight 1000lb general purpose bombs each, then bombed the tunnel and the bridge. The 1000lb bombs were dropped against the bridge, but the bombing was inaccurate and the bridge was left undamaged. The 19 Tallboys which

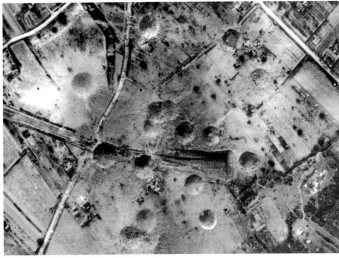

Post-raid reconnaissance photograph of the Saumur railway tunnel, showing the Tallboy craters, two of which are on the line and one penetrating the tunnel itself.

The hole in the roof of the Saumur railway tunnel cause by a Tallboy on June 9, 1944, after the debris had been cleared.

were dropped against the tunnel from between 8000 and 10,500ft were much more effective. Although the clouds of dust caused by the bombs temporarily blotted out the marker flares and caused some delays, many of them were dropped with great accuracy; 50% of the bombs fell within 100 yards.

Reconnaissance photographs taken the next day showed the full extent of the damage caused by 617 Squadron's attack and the Tallboys in particular. The railway track at the southern end of the tunnel was broken by two huge Tallboy craters and a third Tallboy actually pierced the roof of the tunnel and brought down a huge quantity of rock and soil, some 15,000 cubic metres of it. The tunnel was blocked for a considerable time and the Panzer unit was badly delayed in its movement to the battle area. The Saumur railway tunnel had still not been completely cleared by the time that part of France was liberated and this stretch of line remained unusable to the Germans. No aircraft were lost on this, the first Tallboy raid.

## TALLBOY

Designed by Barnes Wallis, the Tallboy bomb was a remarkable weapon, combining the explosive force of a large, high-capacity bomb and the penetrating power of armour-piercing munitions. When it was introduced it was the only weapon in the Royal Air Force's inventory capable of breaking through the thick concrete structures of the German U-boat shelters, E-boat pens and V-weapon sites.

Tallboy measured 21ft (6m) long and contained 5200lb of Torpex explosive. With a streamlined (ogival) shape, it was fitted with a long, light-alloy, conical tail with four small square fins. These fins were offset by 5°, causing the bomb to spin during its fall, aiding stability and improving its accuracy. To increase its penetrative power, the nose of the bomb contained a specially-hardened and precisely-machined, steel plug. Tallboy was ballistically perfect and in consequence had a very high terminal velocity. Released from an altitude of 18,000ft, a Tallboy took only 37 seconds to fall to the ground; when it hit, it was supersonic and still accelerating. It could penetrate 16ft (5m) of concrete or 90ft of earth and made a crater 80ft (24m) deep and 100ft (30m) across, which would have taken 5000 tons of earth to fill.

The bomb was designed to detonate below ground, transferring all of its energy into the target structure. This earthquake effect caused more damage than a direct hit, as it shook the whole target structure, causing major damage to all parts of it and making repair impossible or uneconomic.

The fuses in the rear of the bomb could be set to give it sufficient time to penetrate before exploding. The time delay could be set to between 11 seconds and 30 minutes after impact.

A 12,000lb Tallboy bomb being loaded on to 617 Sqn Lancaster ED763, 'KC-Z' 'Honor'. This aircraft led a charmed life and served with the squadron to the end of the war.

## STABILISING AUTOMATIC BOMB SIGHT (SABS)

To achieve accuracy with these large single bombs, 617 Squadron used a special bombsight – the Stabilising Automatic Bomb Sight (SABS) Mk.IIA – which, for the first time in the RAF's history, permitted true precision bombing from medium altitude.

These special bomb sights were hand-made, precision instruments, produced in small numbers and used only in specialist roles. With a well-trained and practiced bomb-aimer, able to keep the SABS aiming graticule exactly over the aiming point during the approach to the target, the sight automatically calculated the aircraft's ground speed and wind drift. These were the principal factors which led to inaccuracies with earlier bomb sights, like the Mk.XIV in use with the rest of Bomber Command.

The SABS fed information to a Bombing Direction Indicator mounted in front of the pilot, which showed him whether any course correction, left or right, was required. It also calculated the bomb release point and released the bomb automatically at the correct moment.

Given optimum conditions, a well-trained crew could reliably place a bomb within 80 yards of the target from 18,000ft. Achieving this level of precision required extremely accurate flying. Unfortunately, it also required a long straight run-up to the target of between five and 10 minutes, during which no evasive action was possible, making the

Lancaster a sitting target for the defences, especially radar-directed predicted, flak.

The combination of SABS and Tallboy was effective only if the aiming point could be clearly identified and tracked visually by the bomb aimer. Some missions were aborted or unsuccessful because this was not possible and, due to the cost and complexity of their manufacture, Tallboy bombs which were not dropped were brought back to base.

## DUSK RAID AGAINST E-BOAT PENS AT LE HAVRE, JUNE 14, 1944

After the initial success at Saumur, Tallboys were used against a wide range of targets in France over the summer of 1944, especially against the German's heavily hardened concrete structures, such as U-boat and E-boat pens and 'V'-weapon sites.

One such raid, on the evening of June 14, was Bomber Command's first daylight raid over enemy occupied territory since 1941 (actually it was a last-light, dusk raid). A total of 221 Lancasters bombed the German E-boat pens at Le Havre, including 22 from 617 Squadron carrying Tallboys. Being relatively close to the invasion beaches, these fast German motor torpedo boats were a significant threat to the hundreds of Allied ships crossing the Channel daily with men and supplies for the Second Front. The destruction of this naval target would safeguard the Allied shipping. The heavy bombers were escorted

Two of the 617 Sqn Lancasters that took part in the dusk raid against the E-boat pens at Le Havre, en route to the target on June 14, 1944. In the foreground is Lancaster DV385, 'KC-A', 'Thumper Mk.III', flown by Flt Lt Bob Knights. Leading him is Sqn Ldr Les Munro in his trusty LM482 'KC-W'. On this raid Thumper Mk.III was hit by flak but only lightly damaged. It was flying again the next day, dropping a Tallboy against the E-boat pens at Boulogne.

by Spitfires which prevented any Luftwaffe fighters from interfering with the raid, but the enemy flak was still a problem and some bombers were hit.

Tallboy was on the secret list, so the other Bomber Command crews had not been briefed about it. Flight engineer Ken Down, of 550 Squadron, who was on the raid said: "...when I saw 617 Squadron's bombs explode it was as if the whole surface had erupted. We hadn't been told anything at the briefing about the Tallboy bombs, but when I saw them go in, it was obvious that this was something special."

The long straight run in to the target, required for the SABS bomb sight to function correctly, nearly cost Flying Officer Michael Hamilton and his 617 Squadron crew dear in their Lancaster DV403 'KC-G', as he later recalled:

"We went into the target and immediately the flak started. The first shot burst under the Tallboy, which deflected the shrapnel into the aircraft and we lost our hydraulics. More shots went through the Lancaster; one bent the bomb bay doors, another broke the lock on the starboard undercarriage, causing the wheel to come down. The drag from that was pulling us to the right. We were still on our 12 mile bomb run.

"The next flak burst went straight through the starboard middle tank and we lost 140 gallons of petrol, which sprayed on to the rear gunner through his clear vision panel. It felt like a fortnight, but it was only 14 seconds.

"We dropped the Tallboy and the bomb aimer (Flying Officer Duck) shouted: 'We've hit it.' Just as he said that the nose of the aircraft was shattered; the escape hatch had gone and all of the Perspex too. A terrific draught came in and blew window all over the place as well as all of the navigator's papers. The bomb aimer was writhing around in agony. The crew tried to help. The engineer said: 'I don't know what he's making

all the fuss about, he's only got a small hole in his leg'. They tried to put a tourniquet around it, but he wouldn't let them.

"I was now totally engaged in flying the aircraft. Even though we had climbing power on, we were sinking. It was chaos with the drag, the undercarriage half down, the draught, and the bomb aimer, who in his writhing had kicked the throttles and pitch levers. I shouted at them to get him back to the rest bed. By this time we were down to about 3000ft over the Channel."

Hamilton fully expected that he would have to ditch in the Channel and he put out a distress call so that an Air-Sea Rescue boat would be launched. Somehow, though, the battered Lancaster managed to get its crew back to England and to RAF West Malling with its grass runway. The crew blew the undercarriage down using the emergency

air system and managed to get it locked down, but it was not possible to get all of the flap down for the landing. Hamilton was very concerned about the damaged undercarriage collapsing and also knew that they would be coming in to land faster than normal, so he had all of the crew in their crash positions. His landing was, "one of the smoothest I have ever done", the undercarriage held and the aircraft rolled to a halt.

After the Lancaster had stopped and fallen silent, one of the West Malling crash crews appeared at the front of the aircraft, looked up through the wrecked nose and said: "God, how the bloody hell did you get this thing back?" The bomb aimer was taken to hospital, where doctors found he had 27 pieces of shrapnel in his body between his chest and his legs. He survived. ∎

Oblique recce photograph showing one of the destroyed E-boat pens at Le Havre after the Tallboy raid on June 14, 1944.

Between 2013 and 2016 the RAF Battle of Britain Memorial Flight Avro Lancaster PA474 was painted to represent 617 Sqn Lancaster DV385, 'KC-A', 'Thumper Mk III'. The real 'Thumper' was the regular aircraft of Flt Lt Bob Knights and his crew. It flew on the 'spoof' chaff raid, Operation Taxable, on the even of D-Day, and on many of the squadron's 'Tallboy' bombing raids, including the first against the Saumur railway tunnel on June 8-9, 1944, and the dusk raid against the E-boat pens at Le Havre on June 14. The real 'Thumper' survived the war but was later scrapped. Photo John Dibbs. The Plane Picture Company

# Victoria Cross

## Lancaster gunner, Pilot Officer Andy Mynarski, was awarded the VC for his actions on the night of June 12-13, 1944.

In addition to the special operations conducted in concert with 617 Squadron and their 'Tallboys', the Bomber Command 'Main Force' heavy bombers flew a huge number of other sorties in support of the initial phases of the Battle of Normandy. They attacked road and rail targets, enemy troop concentrations, military barracks, radar installations and fuel depots.

In the week immediately after D-Day, the Bomber Command Lancasters alone flew 2689 operational sorties, of which 1856 were flown against road and rail targets. These operations were not without risk and there were significant losses to enemy flak and night fighters; a total of 77 Lancasters were lost on these raids.

## VICTORIA CROSS

One of the Lancasters lost during this period was that of Flying Officer Art De Breyne and his crew from 419 'Moose' Squadron of the RCAF. This Lancaster was one of three from 419 Squadron shot down during an attack against a rail yard at Cambrai, in northern Picardy on the night of June 12-13, 1944.

The actions that night of one of the gunners in De Breyne's crew, Pilot Officer Andy Mynarski, resulted in his later award of the Victoria Cross (VC), the highest award for gallantry in the face of the enemy that can be made to members of the British and Commonwealth forces.

The VC is awarded only for "most conspicuous bravery, a daring or pre-eminent act of valour, self-sacrifice or

extreme devotion to duty in the presence of the enemy". During the whole of the Second World War, only 30 awards of the Victoria Cross were made to airmen serving in the Royal Air Force, its Volunteer Reserve and those serving with the air forces of the Commonwealth countries. The VC awarded to Andy Mynarski was the only one that was made to an airman during the immediate D-Day period.

## 419 SQUADRON

419 'Moose' Squadron was a heavy bomber unit of the RCAF, part of the all-Canadian 6 Group, embedded within the RAF and Bomber Command, based at Middleton St George (now Teesside Airport). When Canadian pilot Flying Officer Art de Breyne and his crew joined 419 Squadron the unit was still flying Handley-Page Halifaxes, but soon afterwards the squadron re-equipped with Canadian-built Lancaster Mk.Xs. The de Breyne crew actually flew only one operation in a Halifax with 419 Squadron before converting to the Lancaster.

## THE CREW

Art de Breyne's crew consisted of flight engineer Sergeant Roy Vigars (the only Englishman in the otherwise all-Canadian crew); navigator, Flying Officer Robert Body; bomb aimer, Sergeant Jack Friday; wireless operator, Warrant Officer Jimmy Kelly; mid-upper gunner, Andy Mynarski who was commissioned as a Pilot Officer on June 11, 1944 and rear gunner, Flying Officer Pat Brophy.

Individually skilled in their own areas of expertise, the seven members of the Lancaster crew welded together into a close-knit, disciplined and professional team in the aircraft, each reliant totally on the others not only for success but also for survival. On the ground they were friends, especially the two gunners who, despite their age difference (Mynarski was 27 and Brophy was 22) enjoyed socialising together in the English pubs. In early June the crew was allocated its 'own' Lancaster Mk.X, KB726, VR-A', making the team complete.

## JUNE 12-13, 1944

On June 12-13, 1944, 16 Lancasters from 419 Squadron were detailed to participate in a night bombing raid on the rail marshalling yards at Cambrai, as part of a force of 40 Lancasters from 6 Group. It was to be a relatively low-level attack, bombing from a height of only 2000ft. For Art de Breyne and his crew, this was their 13th 'op' and they were planned to be over the target on Friday the 13th. For the superstitious among the crew, there were some bad

omens here. Lancaster KB726, VR-A', with de Breyne at the controls, lifted off from Middleton St George at 9.44pm on June 12.

In the Lancaster's bomb bay were 16, 500lb GP bombs and two 500lb GP long-delay bombs; a total of 9000lb of high explosive. The weather conditions were favourable, promising good visibility over the target.

## NIGHT FIGHTER ATTACK

After encountering flak over the coast and having briefly been illuminated by searchlights, the Lancaster began its bombing run. Suddenly, a Junkers Ju 88 night fighter bored in from the Lancaster's port beam in a lightning attack, sweeping up from below and astern, raking the bomber with its angled-up Schrage Musik cannon fire. In the rear turret, gunner Pat Brophy saw the Ju 88 at the last moment, yelling a command to 'corkscrew' to the pilot, he swung his turret 45° to the port side of the bomber, depressed his four .303 machine guns down and fired at the night fighter. It was too late.

The cannon fire from the Ju 88 tore into the Lancaster's port wing, knocking out both port engines and setting the wing ablaze. The hydraulic pipes to the rear turret were hit and a fine spray of hydraulic fluid ignited, starting a raging fire in the rear fuselage. All the bomber's electrics failed, the cockpit was thrown into darkness and the intercom, used by the crew to communicate with each other, also failed.

The captain – de Breyne – realised that the situation was hopeless and, with no intercom system available, flashed the pre-arranged signal of the letter 'P' in Morse code on the crew-station lights, to order the crew to bale out.

## TRAPPED IN THE REAR TURRET

In the rear turret, Brophy was not surprised to get the bale-out signal, as he could see the mass of flames spreading back from the port wing. In the Lancaster

Flying Officer Art de Breyne RCAF.

Lancaster Mk.X KB745 'VR-V' of 419 'Moose' Squadron, flying over a bomb-cratered Normandy during the summer of 1944. This aircraft was lost on October 4, 1944, during an attack against the U-boat pens at Bergen; all of the crew were killed.

the gunners could not wear their chest parachutes in their turrets; there simply wasn't room. The rear gunner's parachute hung on the wall of the Lancaster behind his turret doors. In order to bale out, the gunner first needed to get his turret straight, open the doors, get his parachute and clip it on to the chest harness, and then bale out from the aircraft, either through the main entry/exit door just ahead of the tail, or by rotating the rear turret through 90°, so that the back of it pointed sideways, and then doing a back flip out into the night sky.

With this desperate need in mind, Brophy tried to rotate his turret straight, but with the hydraulic pipes ruptured it would not move. No problem, there was a manual back-up handle, but as Brophy started to wind that, it snapped off in his hand. He was now stuck with his turret pointing 45° to the Lancaster's port side, with the guns pointing down where he had last fired at the German night fighter. He opened the turret doors, but could only just get his left arm through the small gap. He reached his parachute, pulled it into the turret and clipped it on to his chest

harness, but he could not get out of the turret either into the aircraft or into the airflow. He was trapped.

## MYNARSKI

Through the open doors of his turret and the side Perspex, Brophy saw his friend Andy Mynarski, the mid-upper gunner, climb out of his turret, get his parachute off the wall of the Lancaster, clip it on to his chest harness and move to the side door. As he was about to jump, Mynarski looked to his right and saw the rear turret askew with no movement in it and realised that his

The crew (l to r): Brophy, Kelly, Vigars, de Breyne, Mynarski, Friday and Body.

Pilot Officer Andy Mynarski VC.

friend Pat Brophy was trapped. With complete disregard for his own safety and survival, Mynarski made his way to the rear of the Lancaster, crawled through the flames, and started trying to hack a way out for his friend with the fire axe. When that failed, he tried to force the turret straight with brute strength.

As Brophy watched, he was horrified to see Mynarski's clothes catch fire up to the waist, as he became soaked with burning hydraulic oil. He realised the hopelessness of the situation and yelled and gesticulated at Mynarski to leave him and to save himself. The anguished look on Mynarski's face showed how he felt about leaving his friend, but he knew he had no choice and backed off through the flames. By the time he reached the Lancaster's door, Mynarski was on fire from head to foot; the parachute on his chest was also burning. Even so, before he jumped, he straightened up and saluted his friend in the rear turret who he thought was going to die. He then baled out.

When his parachute opened it was on fire and he descended far too rapidly. Although Mynarski was alive when he hit the ground in France, he died shortly afterwards from a combination of the impact and the severe burns he had received. Andy Mynarski is buried in Méharicourt Cemetery, France.

## THE PILOT

In the Lancaster, the pilot, de Breyne, with no intercom to communicate with the crew, thought he had given enough time for everyone to bale out, certainly the crew members at the front had gone. To give himself a chance of getting out too, he throttled back the two starboard engines, to balance the dead engines on the port side, and he trimmed the aircraft for wings level and a gliding attitude. He then left his seat and baled out through the hatch in the bomb aimer's compartment.

## A MIRACLE

The Lancaster was now gliding down in the dark, pilotless, with Brophy trapped in the rear turret, no doubt expecting to die. The pilot must have done a good job because the aircraft remained wings level in a gentle descent and that was how it hit the ground. At over 100mph it slid along on its belly and into some trees. The first thing to hit the trees was the port wing; this swung the aircraft so violently that the whiplash effect freed the rear turret and whipped it round so that the open doors at its rear faced the starboard side. Brophy was flung out of his turret backwards and found himself sitting against a tree, with his unopened parachute on his chest and the Lancaster, with the bombs still on board, exploding some 200

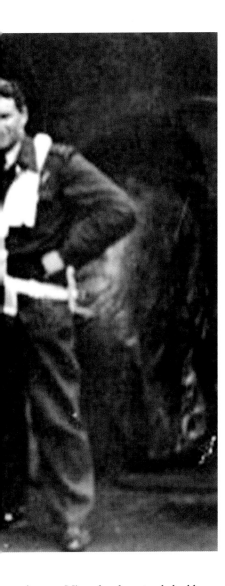

yards away. Miraculously, not only had he survived, but he was completely unscathed!

## THE AFTERMATH

Brophy was picked up by the French Resistance and hidden for six weeks, by which time the Allies had advanced further into France and he was handed over to them. Three other members of the crew, de Breyne (pilot), Body (navigator) and Kelly (wireless operator), also evaded capture and were eventually repatriated. The other two became PoWs for the duration of the war.

## THE VC

In 1945, Pat Brophy was reunited with Art de Breyne and the rest of the crew and the details of the final moments in the aircraft that night were revealed, including the valiant efforts made by Mynarski in trying to free Brophy. In late 1945, de Breyne started the process of getting Mynarski's extraordinary deed recognised with an award. The recommendation worked its way slowly up the command structure of the RCAF and the RAF and, on October 11, 1946, the award of a posthumous VC to Andy Mynarski was finally announced, for his supreme sacrifice in giving his own life to try to save that of his friend and colleague on June 12-13, 1944. ■

Rear gunner, Flying Officer Pat Brophy.

B-25 Mitchells of 320 (Dutch) Sqn under attack from Luftwaffe Fw 190s and being defended by their escort of Spitfire Mk IXs of 602 Sqn (Aux AF) during a daylight raid around D-Day. Artwork by Wiek Luijken

# Medium bombers & intruders

**T**he twin-engine medium bombers and intruders were a relatively small, but nonetheless effective, component of the RAF's order of battle during the D-Day period. In June 1944, the RAF's 2 TAF fielded six squadrons of De Havilland Mosquito fighter-bomber FB Mk.VIs, four of North American B-25 Mitchells, and two of Douglas A-20 Bostons. The Boston was gradually being phased out and replaced by the other two types; by the war's end there was only one Boston unit still operating (342 Free French Squadron).

These squadrons of Mosquitos, Mitchells and Bostons conducted tactical precision-strike, interdiction and intruder operations by day and by night, during the build-up to D-Day and the subsequent Battle of Normandy, frequently operating at low level. Targets were numerous and varied and included fuel and supply dumps, barracks and headquarters, airfields, communications targets – such as railway infrastructure, bridges, road transport and convoys – and 'V'-weapon 'Noball' sites. Some attacks against pinpoint targets from very low-level, such as against certain Gestapo headquarters, were spectacularly successful. Fighter escorts and the hard-earned Allied air supremacy allowed

daylight operations without too much interference from the Luftwaffe, but the enemy 'flak' was still very dangerous and caused some losses.

During the build up to D-Day, the pace of operations for these units intensified and it continued to do so after the invasion. To take just one of the Mosquito FB VI units as an example, 464 Squadron (RAAF) alone, flew 350 sorties in July 1944 and another 400 during August.

Concentrating mainly on night-time intruder attacks on German transport and

infrastructure in France, they lost three aircraft during this time. Taken together, these day and night operations by the medium-bomber/intruders added to the havoc being wreaked in enemy-occupied Europe by the RAF and Allied air forces.

## DE HAVILLAND MOSQUITO

The 'Wooden Wonder', affectionately known to its crews as the 'Mossie' will need no introduction to most readers. This twin-Merlin-engine, two-crew aircraft, of almost entirely wooden construction had originally

Mosquito FB VI of 418 Sqn (RCAF).

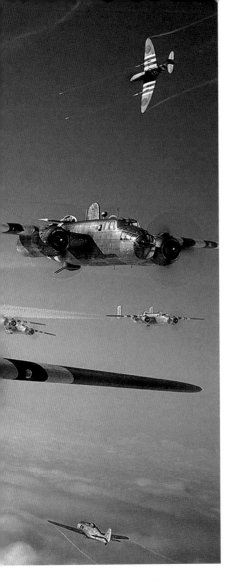

Loading 500lb bombs into the internal bomb bay of a Mosquito FB VI.

been conceived as an unarmed fast bomber. It first entered service with the RAF as a photographic reconnaissance aircraft in September 1941, at which time it was one of the fastest operational aircraft in the world. By 1942 it was in widespread service with the RAF and was being adapted to fill many roles. Its performance remained impressive, later marks being capable of over 400mph, and it had a good range and altitude capability.

From late 1943, Mosquito bomber units were formed into the Light Night Strike Force often dropping 4000lb (1812kg) HC blast bombs, 'cookies', in high-altitude, high-speed raids that German night fighters were almost powerless to intercept. They were also used as pathfinders for RAF Bomber Command's heavy-bomber raids.

As a night fighter, from mid-1942, the Mosquito not only defended the United Kingdom against German night bombing raids, but was also employed offensively as a night intruder, conducting raids over Luftwaffe airfields and as a night fighter supporting RAF Bomber Command's heavy bomber raids. In these roles it played an important part in reducing bomber losses during 1944 and 1945.

The Mosquito's survivability was enhanced not only by the capability of its wooden structure to soak up battle damage, but also by its legendary ability to fly on one engine, quite happily, if required.

The Mosquito FB VI, operated by 2 TAF at the time of D-Day and the Battle of

A Mosquito FB VI flying effortlessly in close formation alongside the camera ship, with the port engine feathered.

Normandy, had first entered service in May 1943. Powered by two 1460hp Rolls-Royce Merlin 21s or two 1653hp Merlin 25s, the Mosquito FB VI introduced a restressed and reinforced wing, capable of carrying a single 250lb (113kg) bomb on racks in streamlined fairings under each wing (increased to 500lb (227kg) bombs on Series 2 FB VIs ), or up to eight 3in rocket projectiles. Alternatively, a 50 gallon or 100 gallon fuel drop tank could be fitted under each wing. The usual armament was four .303 Browning machine guns in the solid nose and four 20mm Hispano Mk II cannons under the cockpit section of the

fuselage. The ventral bay doors were divided into two sections; the forward pair giving access to the 20mm cannon breeches and ammunition feed, while the rear pair covered a bomb bay which could hold two 250lb bombs. The top speed of this mark of the Mosquito, with the more powerful engines, was over 370mph. As well as being extremely effective against ground targets with its bomb and gun armament, the FB VI was quite capable of holding its own against single-engine fighter aircraft and 'Mossie' crews did indeed claim numerous Luftwaffe Fw 190s and Bf 109s on their intruder missions.

RAF B-25 Mitchell II with D-Day invasion stripes applied.

# NORTH AMERICAN B-25 MITCHELL

The North American B-25 Mitchell was an American twin-engine medium bomber, which was widely used by the USAAF and other air forces during the Second World War. The RAF received nearly 900 B-25 Mitchells under the Lend-Lease programme and it was the only air force to operate the aircraft from the UK on raids against targets in Europe. The majority of the aircraft delivered to the RAF were B-25Cs and Ds, which the British designated Mitchell II. The first RAF operation with the Mitchell took place on January 22, 1943, when six aircraft from 180 Squadron attacked oil installations at Ghent. It was not a good start to the aircraft's operational career as one aircraft was shot down by 'flak' over the target and two others were lost when attacked by Fw 190 fighters. This was an aircraft that needed air superiority to operate without high loss rates.

The Mitchell II was powered by two Wright R-2600-13 radial engines, producing around 1700hp each, giving the aircraft a cruising speed of 230mph and a maximum speed of about 270mph at 13,000ft. The defensive armament consisted of a dorsal turret with a pair of 0.5in (12.7mm) heavy machine guns, a retractable, remotely-operated ventral turret also fitted with two 0.5s, and a further two 0.5s in the Plexiglass nose, one fixed forward firing and one flexible. The Mitchell could carry up to 3600lb (1600kg) of bombs in its bomb bay.

The Mitchell was an amazingly sturdy aircraft that could withstand tremendous punishment. It was also a safe and forgiving aircraft to fly. With one engine out, it was possible to fly 60° banking turns into the dead engine and control could be easily maintained down to 145mph. However, the pilot had to remember to maintain engine-out directional control at low speeds after takeoff with rudder; if this manoeuvre was attempted with ailerons, the aircraft would snap out of control. The tricycle landing gear made for excellent visibility while taxiing and on landing. The only significant complaint from its crews about the Mitchell was the extremely high noise level produced by its engines.

The Mitchells were sometimes used on daylight short-penetration raids with a fighter escort, and they also flew night operations, including illuminating targets with flares for Mosquitos to make night attacks against ground transport targets. As the invasion approached, they flew night attacks against 'V'-weapon, 'Noball' sites and against communications targets.

After D-Day the Mitchells operated in support of the ground action, bombing enemy positions and attacking concentrations of armour and fuel depots, as well as making more attacks against 'Noball' sites. With air supremacy achieved, the Mitchell crews found, as did the other medium bomber crews, that enemy fighters were not a particular threat, but the 'flak' certainly was.

RAF B-25 Mitchell of 226 Sqn over the invasion fleet.

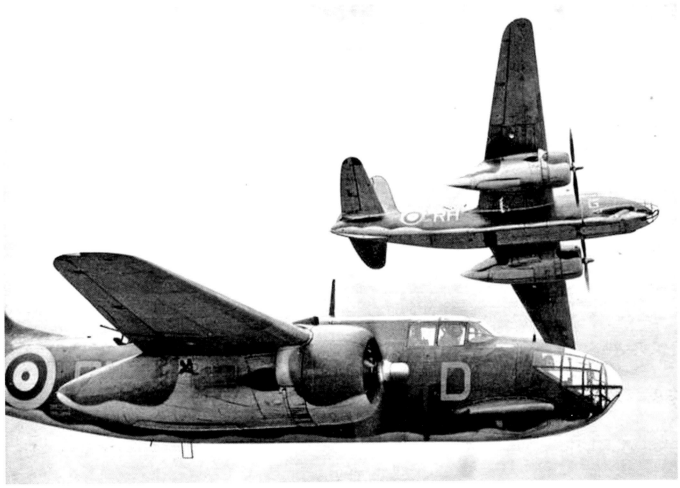

RAF Douglas A-20 Boston IIIs of 88 Sqn.

# DOUGLAS A-20 BOSTON

Largely replaced by the other two medium bomber types by the time of D-Day, the two units still operating the Douglas A-20 Boston were Nos 88 and 342 (Free French) Squadrons based at Hartford Bridge, in Hampshire. Along with No 226 Squadron, equipped with the Mitchell II, these units made up No 137 Wing, part of 2 Group of 2 TAF.

Variously known as the DB-7, A-20, Havoc and named Boston by the RAF, this was the most-produced American attack bomber of the Second World War, with over 7000 built. The DB-7B was the first batch of the aircraft to be ordered directly by the RAF, in February 1940. Three hundred were delivered and the British designated this version 'Boston III'. Although not the fastest, nor endowed with the longest range or great load-carrying capability, the Boston was a tough, dependable and manoeuvrable medium bomber with a decent turn of speed and a good reputation among its crews. Powered by two Wright R-2600-A5B Twin Cyclone radial engines producing around 1700hp each, the Boston III had a maximum speed of just over 330mph and a service ceiling of over 23,000ft, although it was more often employed at low level.

The Boston had a crew of three and was armed with four fixed forward-firing 0.303 Browning machine guns, plus a dorsal turret with two .303s and a ventrally mounted Vickers K .303 machine gun. It could carry 2000lb (910kg) of bombs in its bomb bay.

The RAF Bostons took part in a number of spectacular low-level raids against targets in occupied Europe. In the first half of 1944, from their base at Hartford Bridge, they concentrated on attacking invasion targets in northern France, including coastal defences, Luftwaffe airfields and communication targets. On D-Day, the two Boston squadrons were charged with the important and dangerous task of laying the smoke screen to hide the first wave of landing craft from the enemy gunners on the shore. After D-Day, 137 Wing moved to France as part of the tactical air forces supporting the Allied armies as they advanced. ■

RAF Douglas DB-7 (A-20) Boston III.

'RAF Bostons on a Low-Level Strike'. Eight RAF Douglas Boston medium bombers from 342 (Free French) Squadron streak across northern France in loose formation at low level in one of the many attacks on communications and transport targets in the build-up to the Allied invasion in 1944. Artwork: Gary Eason

# 'Smokers'

Boston IIIs of 88 Sqn flying low over the sea to avoid detection by enemy radar as they head towards a target in Europe prior to D-Day.

As the invasion forces on the surface headed towards the Normandy beaches at 5am on D-Day, June 6, 1944, their first visible evidence of 2 TAF's support for them was the arrival of the Bostons of 137 Wing's 88 and 342 (Free French) Squadrons, laying a smokescreen off the beaches to cover the dash to the shore by the first wave of landing craft. 88 Squadron covered the eastern half of the invasion area, while 342 Squadron took the west. It was a precision operation, with 12 Bostons from each unit arriving singly from each flank at 10 minute intervals in order to maintain a continuous smokescreen.

The Bostons hurtled along the Normandy shoreline at 250mph and at only 50ft laying a thick trail of smoke to shield their comrades from the view of the enemy gunners. As they did so, they ran the gauntlet between the devastating barrage of naval heavy gunfire and that of the German artillery defences. The operation was deemed completely successful in its aims, although each of the two squadrons suffered the loss of an aircraft (both Bostons crashed into the sea with the loss of all on board).

A second 88 Squadron aircraft was hit by 'flak' and shortage of fuel forced the pilot to land downwind at Hartford Bridge. The Boston ran off the end of the runway and into sand pits, killing the navigator.

## BOSTON PILOT – LESLIE VALENTINE

One of the Boston pilots on the D-Day smoke-laying operation was 24-year-old Flying Officer Leslie Valentine. Valentine had originally joined the army and saw action in France in 1940 with the Highland Light Infantry. Gaining selection for pilot training in the RAF he was sent to Canada for training, returning to 13 Operational Training Unit at Bicester in January 1943.

He joined 88 Squadron in May 1944 and he had already completed operational sorties over France, attacking vital supply lines to disrupt the transportation of enemy reinforcements. Describing these operations, he said: "We flew in very close formation, an arrowhead of six aircraft. We had a lead navigator who got you over the target. He was in charge.

"You needed a very good navigator. You were always a bit apprehensive, but once you'd started the job you had to concentrate on what you were doing."

On D-Day, Valentine was flying Boston IIIA 'RH-E', 'E-Easy'. As he roared along the invasion beaches at 50ft, the trajectories of shells from the big guns of the naval gunships offshore arced overhead, and enemy gunfire came from the other direction. He later said: "I'd anticipated that it was going to be a little hairy. I had just 44 seconds to let off four canisters of smoke. The Germans were only half a mile back from the beach.

"The noise of the shells was deafening. Not only was there the chance of being hit in the crossfire but also, as the Allied ground forces were unsure who the aircraft flying so low above them were, they also let fly with small arms fire. I was flying at 250mph at only 50ft and I had to hold it very steady, as at that speed and height if I'd even sneezed that would have been it."

Valentine returned safely to RAF Hartford Bridge from the D-Day operation and subsequently went on to fly many more sorties against tactical targets by both night and day. He survived two tours of operations, 60 'ops' in all and said: "After a while you felt you had become lucky." Leslie Valentine celebrated his 95th birthday in 2013 and is the only surviving British serviceman to have been awarded the French Croix de Guerre with Silver Star, one of the country's highest accolades, for heroic deeds performed in the liberation of France.

Fg Off Leslie Valentine (Boston pilot).

## BOSTON NAVIGATOR – 'JOCK' LOUDEN

Flying Officer George 'Jock' Louden was the navigator in Boston IIIA, BZ292 'RF-L' of 88 Squadron for the D-Day operation. He later recalled: "At 0436 hours we were airborne and heading for the 'big one'.

"Our task was to lay smoke at sea level (our aircraft had been specially adapted with canisters in the bomb bays and funnels projecting out through holes in the bomb doors), to protect the Royal Navy ships and also the invasion troops as they forged ashore.

"We flew from Hartford Bridge to Selsey Bill at about 500ft and descended to wave top height as soon as we reached the Bill, then on course for the beachhead. I was to call up the battleship HMS *Ramillies* on the radio transmitter while en route and inform them that we were ready and about to lay smoke. I am still awaiting their reply!

"However, as we flew below her decks at sea level the *Ramillies'* acknowledgement

Boston IIIAs of 88 Sqn with smoke laying equipment fitted, at Hartford Bridge.

was to give us everything she'd got by way of tracer gunfire and what have you, this despite the fact that we were painted like a humbug!

"Our next pin-points on the lead into the beach area were the battleships HMS *Warspite*, *Rodney*, and *Renown*, they handled us more gently, but inevitably we were in the middle of it and were catching it from both 'Jerry' and our own forces.

"We found out afterwards that commanders were anticipating 75% losses from this smoke laying operation. Our final pin-point before hitting the beaches was a Naval Monitor, this was merely a barge with one bloody great gun on it. My memory is that as we flew below the deck height of the battleships I could hear their big guns going, "wuff, wuff, wuff" at the enemy, while the Naval Monitor was covered in black smoke and it was delivering a massive, "crump, crump, crump" towards the 'Jerries'.

"We were going in to the beachhead at intervals to lay smoke and, approaching the Naval Monitor, I could already see the smoke screen laid by our leading aircraft, Wing Commander Paddy Maher. We hit the beach slightly to the North West of Bayeux turned to port and laid our smoke slightly inshore of the Wing Commander's. I'm glad we were on the deck although I suppose it didn't make much difference as we were getting attention from our own and the German forces.

"Having pressed the tit and laid the smoke we turned to port to come home, and immediately we were over the port entrance of Le Havre, where we got a rough

reception from German E-Boats and their harbour defences.

"Then we were home: a cigarette, a pint and a good meal. A wonderful, hairy, scary and sad day; a proud success. I shall never forget the sight of the English Channel that day, nor of those mates that 'bought it'."

## BOSTON GUNNER – BILL MORRIS

Sergeant William 'Bill' Morris was a 23-year-old British wireless operator/Air Gunner (WOp/AG) serving with 342 (Free French) Squadron on the D-Day smoke-laying operation. These are his recollections:

"My crew and I went to breakfast then gathered in the briefing room. After we were all settled in and all crews were present and accounted for the doors to the room were locked.

"A high-ranking officer said: 'Good morning gentleman, today is D-Day. What you have been trained to do, you will do today.' Of course those words provoked a murmur of excitement from all of us gathered there.

"At around 5am we took off from Hartford Bridge aerodrome in our trusty Boston aircraft, in relays of two, to lay smoke for the invasion fleet.

"We flew 50ft above the waves and as we were coming up to our target my pilot Hank said: 'Bill, helmet off, gas mask on', as sitting in an outside turret I could otherwise be choked by the smoke. Each aircraft carried four canisters that were timed 11 seconds per canister to discharge the smoke. This took 44 seconds and we had to fly straight and level during this time.

I wasn't in contact with the rest of the crew inside the aircraft during this part of the operation, so 44 seconds to me felt like forever. As Hank pulled away I was glad to get my mask off and helmet on and to be back in contact with my mates again.

"It was pretty scary flying so low and when we started to climb it was a relief. The pilot Hank said excitedly: 'Bill, did you see them?' (meaning the invasion fleet). I said: 'Yes! Who the hell's going to stop that lot?'

"We were all so elated and proud to have done our little bit on that very special day." ∎

Sgt Bill Morris (Boston gunner) on the left, with some of his mates.

# 'On a wing and a prayer'

Mosquito FB VI MM417 'EG-T' of 487 Sqn (RNZAF) carrying a 250lb bomb under each wing.

Flight Lieutenant Charles Derek Bovet-White (RAFVR) was a de Havilland Mosquito FB Mk.VI pilot with 487 Squadron (RNZAF) during 1944. His route to the Mosquito had been a roundabout one. He had previously flown Boulton Paul Defiants, a variety of communications aircraft and, after recovering from a broken neck suffered in an accident while flying a Hawker Hurricane when he had only one hour on type, he briefly flew the Spitfire.

He was posted to the Mosquito as an intruder pilot in 1943 and immediately took to the aircraft, saying: "The Mosquito was one of the finest twin-engine aeroplanes that has ever been made. Apart from handling and aerobatic qualities which were almost as good as a single-engine fighter, she could

trot along at nearly 400mph when in a real hurry. Although constructed almost entirely of wood and plywood, I was soon to learn that this wonderful aeroplane would fly almost without any visible means of support. This, coupled with the fact that my navigator who, apart from being a good Bridge player, could also navigate and interpret the complicated 'Gee' box really well, ensured that we always managed to land on a friendly aerodrome."

During the build up to D-Day, one of the tasks given to 487 Squadron was to find and attack the 'V-1' sites that the Germans were busily constructing in France. Bovet-White described one such mission that had a dramatic outcome: "We were part of a flight of three Mosquitos winging their way to France one bright afternoon, in a nice tight

'vic' formation at 50ft. Leaving the south coast of England we dropped down to 20ft over the Channel, cruising along at a happy 289mph.

"Soon the coast of France loomed up in front of us, so full bore up to 3000ft, weaving gently to avoid the 'flak', and back down again at 400mph to 50ft over the fields of France, heading for our target.

"Five minutes later we saw a long convoy of German lorries moving slowly along a road at right angles to our course. Almost immediately, the flight commander's cannons and machine guns opened fire. I could see that most of his fire was going over the top of the lorries, so down went the nose of my Mosquito a little and, with thumb pressed hard on the firing button, much havoc and disintegration was caused

Crews of 487 Sqn briefing in a huddle prior to flying a mission. Their Mosquito FB VIs are loaded with a 250lb bomb under each wing.

Tight formation of three 'bombed-up' 487 Sqn Mosquito FB VIs (MM417 'EG-T' in the foreground with 'EG-V' and 'EG-D' beyond).

among the German convoy as the deadly hail of bullets and cannon shells found their target, and then –'crunch'!

"The Perspex cockpit cover shattered, the starboard engine ran very rough and a quick glance showed masses of wire thrashing about, flaying the starboard wing, which was considerably torn and had the wing tip missing. At one and the same time, back came the control column to gain height as quickly as possible and I stopped the starboard engine and feathered the propeller. My worst suspicions were now confirmed, we had hit some French telephone wires no more than 20ft above the ground. We had certainly managed to sever telephonic communications in that part of France!

"Fortunately, the Rolls-Royce Merlin engine on the port side was still singing a joyous song of power, but the Mosquito was vibrating quite a bit, with jagged pieces of the starboard wing flapping in a most un-aerofoil-like fashion. Using full throttle on the single engine we were just making 170mph and once, when the speed dropped to 160, we almost fell out of the sky. Obviously we only had 10mph above the new, unorthodox stalling speed of the reshaped Mosquito.

"As we approached the French coast heading for home as best we could, the German light 'flak' started. We let the two 500lb, 11-seconds-delay bombs go with a satisfactory 'wump, wump', but these did not seem to discourage the German 'flak'

gunners very much. So down went the Mosquito's nose again and, weaving rapidly, at 220mph, we dived for the English Channel. Occasionally, there would be a noise like hailstones on a tin roof, but mostly the 'flak' was blazing on one side or the other and quite soon it ceased. Then we had the serious business of getting back to England and down in one piece.

"Beachy Head was the nearest bit of England and Friston, a Spitfire aerodrome, was very close by. So, steering a steady course and climbing all we could, which was in fact only about 50ft a minute, we vibrated our way to England. The port engine was taking a beating, running at full bore, and the oil and water temperature were rising higher and higher, but at long last beautiful Beachy Head came into view.

"Obviously, the landing would have to be made at no less than 160mph, some 50mph faster than normal, and we were going to cover a lot of the grass area at Friston before stopping, but I decided to give it a try. As we made a circuit I let the wheels down, but the flaps refused to lower. Settling down to 165mph, I lined up with the grass strip.

"We were certainly moving, and as we touched down it seemed obvious that we were quickly going to run straight off the end at Friston and fall 175ft off the cliffs into the sea, despite all the brakes could do. So, off with the fuel tap and up with the undercarriage lever; the tattered Mosquito sank on to her belly and scuffed to an untidy halt. My navigator and I jumped out of the 'Mossie' as quickly as possible and then we realised that there was still 200 yards to go to the cliff edge. However, a quick look at the noble old lady showed that she would never have flown again anyway. The fuselage and tailplane were riddled with holes, the starboard wing was torn in dozens of places and one wondered how she had managed to stay in the sky at all.

"At the hilarious party in the mess that evening they told us that we had also brought back 150ft of French telephone wire with us."

(Derek Bovet-White was later awarded the DFC. He passed away in 1996, aged 83) ■

Mosquito FB VI MM401 'SB-J' of 464 Sqn with wing damage similar to that experienced by Derek Bovet-White. This aircraft, flown by Squadron Leader A G Oxlade (pilot) and Flight Lieutenant D M Shanks (navigator), was hit by anti-aircraft fire while attacking a flying-bomb site in the Pas de Calais on February 21, 1944. The port engine was shattered, and the port undercarriage and most of the outer starboard wing was blown off. Despite the damage, the crew flew MM401 back and crash-landed safely at Friston, where Bovet-White landed his badly damaged 'Mossie'.

# Tactical reconnaissance and the Air Spotting Pool

The provision of photographic reconnaissance images to the Allied commanders was obviously of vital importance for their planning and decision making processes. The RAF's strategically-orientated photographic reconnaissance (PR) was conducted by the specially-modified Spitfire and Mosquito PR aircraft of 106 (Photographic Reconnaissance) Group based at RAF Benson, which was, for historical reasons, part of Coastal Command. Meanwhile, tactical reconnaissance ('Tac Recce') in the European theatre was the business of 2 TAF's Reconnaissance Wings (34, 35 and 39 (RCAF) Wings) with their five squadrons of Mustang Mk 1/1As, three squadrons of Spitfire PR XIs, and a squadron of Mosquito IX/XVIs.

Oblique recce photograph of German beach defences taken by a 2 TAF Tac Recce aircraft, clearly from very low level.

## 'TAC RECCE' PRIOR TO D-DAY

These Tac Recce units were particularly heavily tasked as D-Day approached. The number of reconnaissance requests increased exponentially as Army and Navy commanders sought low-angle, oblique photography to show the latest beach obstacles and defences, landing craft approach routes, the routes inland from the beaches, and the topography, shape and configuration of the terrain they were going to encounter. Closer to D-Day there was concern over the degree of flooding the Germans had been able to achieve and what effect this would have on movement inland, away from the beaches. The 2 TAF Mustangs and Spitfires flew hundreds of dangerous sorties, many of them at ultra-low-level, to ensure that the German defences and the Normandy hinterland held no secrets. In common with other aspects of the Allied air campaign prior to D-Day, to continue the deception campaign against the Germans, more photographic reconnaissance missions were tasked to the north and east of the Seine than in the actual invasion area.

## THE AIR SPOTTING POOL

One of the essential firepower elements of the D-Day assault was an intense and devastating naval bombardment, which commenced at 5am on June 6.

The task of spotting for the naval gunfire from the ships of the Allied Fleets against the invasion area on D-Day, required the 'pooling' of resources in a classic example of the combined operations that characterised much of Overlord. A special temporary formation, known as the 'Air Spotting Pool', was set up at the RN Air Station at Lee-on-Solent, with squadrons trained and tasked in ensuring the accuracy of the naval gunfire.

Unsurprisingly, four of the Air Spotting Pool's units were RN Fleet Air Arm Seafire III squadrons, well used to the task in hand. Two RAF Spitfire Mk.V Squadrons, 26 and 63, were also trained up and drafted into the pool to increase the number of spotters and to ensure continuous coverage during the bombardment period.

The RAF Tac Recce Mustang pilots were already trained for artillery spotting, and the Mustang 1/1As of 2, 414 and 268 Squadrons were also used for this important but dangerous task up to midday on June 6, before returning to their photo-recce and armed-recce roles.

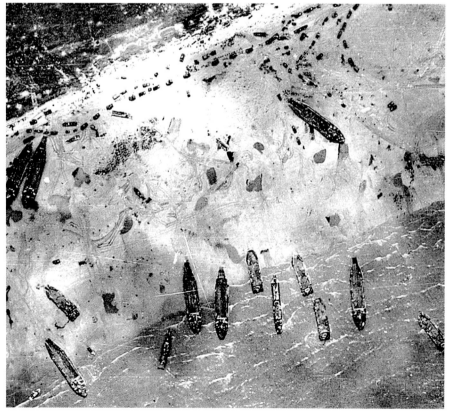

Recce photograph of Graye-sur-Mer invasion beach on D-Day taken by a 2 TAF Tac Recce Mustang.

Mustang Mk 1 in D-Day invasion stripes over a column of Allied Sherman tanks.

Mustang Mk 1s of 2 Sqn RAF.

## AFTER D-DAY

Once the invasion had occurred and the Battle of Normandy had commenced, the TAC Recce units became the eyes of the commanders at the front, providing continuous, extensive and rapid intelligence of enemy movements and of Allied successes.

The Tac Recce pilots had a photographic task to perform, to bring back images to be assessed by the expert photographic interpreters, but they were also trained to use 'eyeballs Mark 1' to gather intelligence. Anything of importance that they saw on their sorties, such as the location and details of tanks, artillery, anti-aircraft sites, vehicle parks, troop concentrations and any new construction, was recorded in a written report. Backing up the courageous work of the recce pilots were the equally important skills of the photographic interpreters who analysed the images and reported the resulting intelligence to commanders.

In common with most other 2 TAF units, the Tac Recce squadrons moved to forward operating bases in France as space became available from July onwards and then advanced with the ground forces.

## 'BEFORE AND AFTER'

Occasionally, the Tac Recce pilots were treated to a complete end-to-end cycle of their work – the 'before and after' views. Not many were as immediate as on the sortie flown by Flight Lieutenant Larry Seath in a Spitfire PR XI of 400 (RCAF) Squadron on July 6, 1944. Having completed his briefed task of taking vertical shots of bridges near Caen and at Saint-André-sur-Orne, he set course for the squadron's base at Odiham, just as Allied bombers commenced attacks on the bridges.

Seath returned to the target area and recorded the results of the attacks on the same sortie; the bridge at Saint-André-sur-Orne had been destroyed and those near

# Mustang 1/1A

Caen damaged. The original Allison-engine versions of the North American P-51 (officially not P-51s, but NA-73s and NA-83s) were designated Mustang 1 and 1A by the RAF. The Mustang had first entered service with the RAF in January 1942, making its combat debut in May that year with 26 Squadron, from Gatwick.

The single-speed, single-stage supercharger fitted to the Allison V-1710-39 engine of the Mustang 1/1A had been designed to produce maximum power output at a low altitude (the maximum rated output was 1220hp at 10,000ft). Above 15,000ft, however, the Mustang's performance reduced markedly. Rather than becoming a Fighter Command asset, therefore, it was initially allocated to Army Co-operation Command, where its excellent low-altitude performance and long range could be utilised effectively for tactical reconnaissance and ground attack duties.

## PERFORMANCE

When it entered service the Mustang 1 had the best low level performance of any RAF fighter; its maximum speed was quoted as 382mph at 13,700ft. Its low-drag airframe gave it a 30mph speed advantage over the Spitfire Mk.V at 5000ft and it was actually 35mph faster at 15,000ft, despite the British fighter's engine being the more powerful. The Mustang's combat range at low level was impressive too; it was able to cover 480 miles on its internal fuel of 180 US gallons, and could fly for 750 miles with two 75 US gallon drop tanks fitted.

## CAMERAS

The Tac Recce Mustang 1/1As were fitted with two F24 cameras; a vertical camera in

a quick detachable mount and an oblique camera mounted aft of the pilot's head, shooting through a hole cut in the left side of the canopy Perspex. The cameras were controlled by the pilot and were automatic in their operation.

## ARMAMENT

The Mustang 1 carried an armament of eight mixed machine guns: Two 0.5in (12.7mm) machine guns were mounted under the engine cowling firing through the propeller, and each wing housed two 0.303in (7.62mm) Browning machine guns and a single 0.5 gun, with the larger gun mounted between the .303s. The Mustang 1A was equipped with four 20mm Hispano cannons, two in each wing, with most of the long barrels of the cannons protruding well ahead of the wing leading edges.

## ARMED RECONNAISSANCE

From 1942 onwards, the emphasis for the Mustang Tac Recce squadrons, swung towards offensive operations and armed reconnaissance. Taking advantage of targets of opportunity the Mustangs attacked railway locomotives, canal barges, military motor transport vehicles and enemy aircraft on the ground. By 1944 the RAF Mustang Tac Recce squadrons were experts at these sort of operations.

Despite the generally 'bad press' that the Allison-engine Mustangs have received over the years, the RAF actually found the aircraft to be extremely useful in the Tac Recce and armed reconnaissance roles. The final RAF Mustang 1s were not struck off charge until 1945.

# Spitfire PR Mk.XI

Considered by many to be one of the finest photographic reconnaissance aircraft of the Second World War, the Spitfire PR Mk.XI entered service with 541 (PR) Squadron RAF in December 1942. This variant of the Spitfire, modified from the Mk.IX, provided an all-round improvement in performance over previous versions, with more powerful engines (Rolls-Royce Merlin Mk 61, 63, 63A or 70 were fitted to Mk.XIs) and with aerodynamic improvements such as a retractable tail-wheel and flush mounted cameras.

## PERFORMANCE

The most powerful of the engines fitted to the PR XI was the Merlin 63 which produced a remarkable 1710hp at 8500ft, giving a maximum level speed of well over 400mph. The PR Mk.XI was unarmed; in place of the Spitfire's normal gun armament it carried 66½ gallons of fuel in the leading edge of each wing. It also had an enlarged oil tank under the nose, to provide for the long duration PR missions, which changed the profile of the nose from the fighter variants of the Spitfire. Fitted with a slipper tank providing a total fuel load of 307 gallons, the PR XI's maximum range was 1650 miles.

## CAMERAS

The standard camera fit was two F24s (later, F52s) as split verticals plus, in some aircraft, an oblique F24. In the Tac Recce role the Spitfire PR XI could be fitted with two five-inch-lens F8 cameras in a blister under each wing, which had only minimal effect on its aerodynamics. These wing cameras pointed downwards, played out at an angle of 10° and were used to photograph targets from medium and low altitudes.

## RAF PR XI UNITS

In June 1944, the RAF had five squadrons of Spitfire PR Mk XIs on it strength. 541 and 542 Squadrons, based at Benson, Oxfordshire, were part of Coastal Command's 106 (PR) Group and were engaged in strategic PR duties. 400 (RCAF) Squadron based at Odiham, 4 Squadron at Gatwick and 16 Squadron at Northolt were 2 TAF's Spitfire PR XI Tac Recce units, whose work mostly took place at medium, low and ultra-low altitudes. ■

Spitfire PR Mk.XI PL775 'A', of 541 Squadron RAF.

Spitfire PR Mk.XI in its element.

Spitfire PR Mk.XIs at a forward airfield.

Spitfire PR Mk.XI PL965 'R' of Peter Teichman's Hangar 11 Collection – the only surviving airworthy PR Mk.XI.

# 268 Squadron Mustangs
## Directing the big guns

Allison-engine Mk 1A Mustangs were flown by 268 Squadron RAF as part of 35 (Recce) Wing, 84 Group, 2 TAF. By 1944, 268 Squadron was primarily a low-level photographic reconnaissance and 'Tac Recce' unit with a mixture of aircrew drawn from across the Commonwealth, including Australia, Canada and New Zealand, as well as British pilots.

### NAVAL GUNFIRE SPOTTING
Prior to D-Day, the 268 Sqn pilots were trained (along with other RAF Mustang units and two RAF Spitfire squadrons) for naval gunfire artillery spotting duties as part of the 'Air Spotting Pool'.

These sorties involved pairs of aircraft operating at relatively low level. The actual operating height depended on the cloud base, but was always low enough for the pilots to be in visual contact with the surface and with the naval gunner's targets, which also put them well within range of light enemy 'flak'. Once in position and having made radio contact with the ship they were spotting for, the Mustangs generally flew at high speed, with tight, high G turns, to keep the target in view.

The lead aircraft was the 'spotter' who called the fall of shells to the ship until the target was bracketed and then ordered "fire for effect" to engage and hopefully destroy the ground target, which would typically be enemy artillery or bunkers. The spotter's wingman was there to 'ride shotgun' and protect his back while the leader concentrated on map references and observing the shells landing.

There were occasions when this saved the formation from attack by enemy aircraft, but more often it was to provide warning of an impending attack by Allied fighters that became suspicious of the low-flying, circling pair, with a shape quite similar to Bf 109s, notwithstanding the black and white D-Day invasion stripes on the under-surfaces.

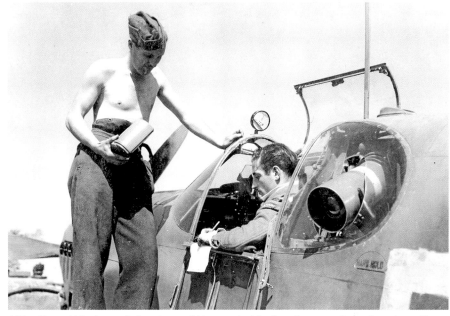

A 'Tac Recce' Mustang pilot makes out his report while the airman waits on the wing with the film canister in his hand. Note the sideways facing oblique F24 camera poking through the hole in the cockpit Perspex.

### THE EVE OF D-DAY
On the evening of June 5, 1944, Group Captain Peter Donkin DSO, the Wing Leader of 35 (Recce) Wing, called his Mustang pilots to a briefing. Donkin was, by this stage of the war, a very experienced Mustang 'Tac Recce' pilot and Wing Leader, who also happened to have the distinction of having been the very first Allied servicemen to be attacked by the Germans during the Second World War. He informed the pilots that the invasion would begin at midnight with the first waves of airborne forces and that the seaborne invasion would land at first light the following morning. All personnel were confined to camp and spent a listless night listening to the constant drone of paratroop aircraft, glider tugs and heavy bombers passing overhead on their way to France.

The news was not a total surprise to the pilots as the wing's Mustangs had been painted with black and white invasion stripes that day. The low level tactical reconnaissance squadrons had received a dispensation regarding the extent to which they would carry the invasion stripes. Most Allied aircraft were required to carry the black and white stripes fully encircling the fuselage and wings of the aircraft. The 'Tac Recce' Mustangs, though, in order not to compromise the effectiveness of their camouflage when operating at low level, were only required to wear the invasion stripes on the under surfaces of the rear fuselage and under both wings where they would be most visible to Allied naval forces and ground troops beneath them.

### D-DAY
The Mustang pilots were up early on June 6, breakfast was from 3.30am and detailed briefings for the naval gunfire spotting sorties were then given by Captain Parish and Captain Wilson RN. The first pair of 268 Squadron aircraft took off from their base at Gatwick at 4.55am for naval gunfire spotting missions, two more pairs took off five minutes later and a further five pairs were airborne by 6am. The remaining Mustangs were flown to Lee-on-Solent from where operations would continue with other units of the 'Air Spotting Pool'.

### 'AIR SPOTTING POOL' DUTIES
Initially, the Mustangs were tasked exclusively with naval gunfire spotting for British Home Fleet ships operating in support of the landing forces. As the day wore on they were also requested to conduct

The RN battleship HMS *Warspite* firing its big guns. It was reputedly the first Allied warship to open fire against the German coastal defences on D-Day.

tactical reconnaissance of the beaches and the area beyond, bringing back some of the first and finest images of the invasion beaches. Most of the Mustang pilots experienced intense and accurate, heavy and light 'flak' over the invasion area, much of it from Allied ships beneath them, despite the aircraft's invasion stripes on their undersides. The squadron's one recorded loss for D-Day was Mustang Mk 1A FD495 'R' (the 268 Squadron aircraft wore no squadron code letters only their individual aircraft letter). This aircraft, flown by Flt Lt Eric Woodward, failed to return from a naval gunfire observation tasking over the invasion area and may have been a casualty of Allied naval anti-aircraft fire. Eric Woodward has no known grave and his name is recorded on the Runnymede Memorial.

All of the squadron's pilots brought back with them their own images of the invasion, both photographic and locked away in their memories. Each had their own 'front row seat' view as the landings took place beneath them. Most had vivid memories of the impact of naval gunfire that they had directed on to the invasion beaches just before the landing took place, and on to remaining pockets of resistance afterwards.

Others remembered the effects of the German defences, with landing craft destroyed and crippled, and of the waves of Allied aircraft prowling over the Invasion fleet awaiting some reaction from the Luftwaffe. More than one pair of the squadron's Mustangs had to avoid the attentions of the masses of Allied fighters over the beachhead, their lack of invasion recognition stripes on their upper surfaces requiring closer inspection and confirmation of their friendly status. Most of the squadron's pilots flew twice in the day on sorties lasting around two and a half hours.

## IMPRESSIONS OF D-DAY

The commanding officer of 268 Squadron, Squadron Leader A S Mann DFC, flew a sortie over the beachhead area, taking off at 9.25am, to direct naval gunfire on to two targets – German coastal defence batteries in large concrete bunker emplacements – which were both hit.

This was his recollection of the momentous day: "D-Day was upon us quite suddenly. Early naval gunfire direction sorties were briefed at Lee-on-Solent, and we flew there at 'first light'. Bill Tuele, a Canadian, was my number two, and after the main briefing we were taken through the detail of our individual shoots by very convincing naval experts who also made it clear that we should make our sea crossing at 4000ft, not the usual wave-top height, because the ships were going to be 'trigger-happy' and would take exception to any aircraft approaching at sea level!

"Once we were airborne, we set off to the south, and there it was – a fine view of tremendous activity. Ships, ships, ships and small craft as far as the eye could see in any direction, their wakes pointed southwards. Many thousands at the start of the greatest sea-borne invasion in the history of the world. It was the sensation of a lifetime!

"There were one or two 'puffs' on track to our rendezvous, but nothing of concern. We found our ships, made contact, and set about the morning's work. Two coastal gun emplacements near Trouville were the targets allocated to my section. After a couple of good sighting shots our guns were on number one target, and the first salvo straddled it; others followed. The second emplacement got similar treatment. Big guns really are the best and the Navy were certainly on form! My happy calls of congratulations were returned in calm and measured tone with a single word of thanks and we were back off to Lee-on-Solent, airborne for two and a half hours. After a satisfactory debriefing, a short rest and a sandwich we were back to Gatwick in 20 minutes. Most of the squadron had a 'look in' on this day; we had been waiting for a long time. Now the first hurdle was behind us and everything seemed to be going well on the ground. D-Day was a success for the squadron, but marred by the loss of a Mustang with a most experienced and valued member of the team."

Australian Flying Officer Basil Rachinger RAAF flew two missions with 268 Sqn during the day in Mustang 1A FD476 'B', both as No 2 to Flight Lieutenant Maurice Lissner. On the first they took off at 5am for a naval shoot and on the second they were retasked in the air for a 'Tac Recce', as the planned target had already been neutralised. Rachinger's diary for June 6 gives an interesting first-hand insight into the day's action:

"Controlled the bombardment of enemy coastal defences by *Montcalm* (a French cruiser with nine 6in guns) just prior to the initial landings at Port en Bassin (at 2000ft, one hour 20 minutes over the target). Had a box seat view of the whole proceedings which looked remarkably under control – also not a Hun in the sky – bags of 'flak' and lots of our own boys though. Quite impressive watching utter hell let loose on both sides: 'Ack ack', coastal guns, rockets galore, aerial bombing, naval bombardment and thousands of ships across the Channel as far as the eye could see.

"Shell holes, water spouts, smoke, flames, smoke screens and debris added impressiveness to the general proceedings. A destroyer sunk, a battleship hit, a landing craft vanished leaving a dirty mark in the water, Spitfire in a death dive, E boats in Bassin blazing furiously, town razed to ground level, aircraft burning on the ground. We flew the second sortie from Lee-on-Solent at 9am (55 minutes over the invasion area). Hun coastal resistance ceased, barges now on a regular shuttle service to and from the beach. Did a Tac R trying to find targets for more Naval Bombardment but without success. Flew five hours between 5am and 11am when we returned to base – happy but very tired."

## TURN-ROUND

As the Mustangs landed at Lee-on-Solent they were refuelled, rearmed and had any problems that had arisen during the morning sorties rectified. The pilots debriefed with the army liaison officers and the intelligence officers, while grabbing a cup of tea, a quick cigarette and perhaps a hot bacon sandwich. There would be a quick briefing from the Intelligence Officers on the next sortie, maybe a quick word with the CO or the flight commander, some flight planning with the maps and charts, calculating the headings, the distances, the time at a given airspeed between each point,

Recce photograph of the invasion beach at Anselles taken by a 268 Sqn Mustang Mk 1A on D-Day.

areas to avoid, and then it was back to the aircraft and on the way for the next sortie. Just after lunch time, a BBC Radio recording team arrived and recorded interviews with selected pilots, capturing their impressions of the events they had seen during the day.

## 'TAC RECCE' MISSIONS
In the afternoon 268 Squadron was retasked with tactical reconnaissance in the areas behind the invasion beaches, looking for German reinforcements being moved into the area, with the naval gunfire spotting task being continued by other RAF and Fleet Air Arm units flying Spitfires and Seafires. The squadron's aircraft brought back the required information, including photographs showing the extent of the Allied advance and lack of movement from any German reinforcements trying to move towards the beachhead. As the Mustangs landed from recce sorties the cameras were stripped of their exposed film magazines, reloaded with fresh ones, refuelled and rearmed if necessary. The pilots were debriefed by the intelligence officers on what they had seen and then they scoured the fresh, wet prints straight from the mobile film processing unit, to pick out possible targets for future sorties and point out features of interest.

## D-DAY+1
On June 7, D-Day+1, 11 pairs of 268 Squadron Mustangs were despatched during the day for 'Tac Recce' sorties. The primary purpose of all these sorties was to check for the movement of any German reinforcements towards the beachhead area. There was no significant enemy movement sighted during the sorties conducted in the morning, while those in the afternoon and early evening saw a higher level of ground activity and also an appearance by four possible Bf-109s on one sortie. The German anti-aircraft fire during the afternoon sorties was also much more active, with heavy 'flak' being received from a number of locations.

One notable sortie for the day was that by Basil Rachinger in FD506 'A' with Flying Officer Frank Normoyle RAAF in FD544 'V' as his wingman. They took off from Gatwick at noon to conduct a 'Tac Recce' covering Trouville – Lisieux – Evreux – Bernay – Trouville. They were separated over the coast due to thick cloud cover, but Rachinger went on alone and on the way shot up five trucks loaded with German troops; he also reconnoitred Evreux airfield seeing no enemy aircraft present there.

He noted the details of the sortie in his diary at the time: "I got airborne with Frank Normoyle as my No 2 at midday. Crossed out of England at Selsey Bill instead of the usual Beachy Head exit and made landfall at Trouville across the Seine estuary from Le Havre. Cloud was ten tenths with a base of between 1500 and 3000ft, so we had to stooge under it. Frank lost me just after crossing into France so I went on alone.

Found trains galore at Lisieux which I photographed – town burning – on to Evreux where I found five truck-loads of Hun troops who sure scattered pronto when I turned four cannon on to them.

"I knocked over quite a few of them and peppered the trucks, I wish Frank could have been there to add fire support. Proceeded on to Bernay, then back to Trouville without further incident, except some meagre 'flak' from Bernay. Sky was full of fighters, but luckily they were ours. Met Frank back at base."

## SUBSEQUENT DAYS
The following few days saw the squadron flying sorties at the highest rate possible, in order to bring back information on the movements of German reinforcements trying to get through to the beachhead.

Many times the squadron aircraft returned with photographs that led to the despatch of rocket firing Typhoons or bombers to disrupt the Germans' reinforcement efforts. A number of aircraft returned to base showing the scars of clashes with the German defences, the Luftwaffe at this stage starting to make its reappearance over the battlefront, but the greatest threat still remaining that from enemy flak. The squadron's Mustangs also added to the Germans' woes, letting loose with their four 20mm cannon where appropriate, especially against German troop and supply transports. ■

Mustang 1A of 35 (Recce) Group at low level over occupied France.

# Night Fighters

The defence of the UK homeland against German night-time raids was, by the time of D-Day, the responsibility of the RAF's Air Defence of Great Britain (ADGB) and its dedicated night fighter squadrons, now mostly equipped with de Havilland Mosquitos, although some Bristol Beaufighters remained in service in June 1944.

In the spring of 1944, 29, 264, 409 (RCAF), 410 (RCAF), 488 (RCAF) and 604 (AuxAF) Squadrons, equipped either with Mosquito night fighter (NF) Mk.XII or XIIIs, formed 85 (Base) Group, within 2 TAF, for the purpose of providing night fighter cover leading up to, and in the wake of, D-Day, for the invasion forces. These aircraft would operate not in direct defence of the UK, but as offensive night intruders over occupied Europe, hunting down Luftwaffe aircraft which threatened Allied bombers or, later, the surface forces at night.

## NIGHT INTRUDERS

The RAF had begun night intruder operations in May 1942, with non-radar-equipped medium bombers and fighter bombers attacking German night fighter airfields. From mid-1943 radar-equipped night-fighter Beaufighters were engaged in offensive intruder operations in support of Bomber Command. In November 1943, 100 (Bomber Support) Group was formed to continue these operations, with Mosquito night fighters gradually replacing the 'Beaus'; the group also provided electronic radar counter measures support to the Bomber Command operations. These night-fighter intruders not only had the benefit of airborne intercept (AI) radars but were also fitted with equipment that allowed them to home on to the emissions from the German night fighters' radars. Luftwaffe night fighter losses to the RAF night intruders steadily mounted and eventually a so-called 'Moskitopanik' was induced among German night fighter squadrons, with just about every unexplained loss being blamed on the RAF night-intruder Mosquitos.

## MASTERY OF THE NIGHT SKY

During the build-up to D-Day there were very few nights when the enemy operated over the areas patrolled by the 2 TAF night fighters and few conclusive actions occurred. Even German reconnaissance aircraft usually failed to penetrate the defences beyond mid-Channel. With the RAF mounting standing patrols by day and night, Allied mastery of the sky over the English Channel was now complete. Although the air supremacy that existed everywhere by day could not be claimed to be as comprehensive by night, as witnessed by the significant losses still being experienced by Bomber Command, the total air supremacy over the UK and its approaches proved to be of incalculable value to the Allied armies and navies, which were able to complete their preparations for the D-Day assault virtually unmolested.

## D-DAY

On the night of June 5-6, 1944, the 2 TAF night fighter Mosquito NF XIIIs conducted defensive night patrols over the invasion areas. A standing airborne 'pool' of six Mosquito night fighters was maintained off Cherbourg, with the aircraft being constantly relieved so that continuous cover over the beaches could be maintained.

Mosquito NF XIII of 604 Sqn ready to taxi for a night mission from B51/Lille-Vendeville in late 1944.

View into the cockpit of Mosquito NF Mk.XIII HK382 'RO-T' of 29 Sqn at Hunsdon in 1944.

AI Mk VIII indicator, with the visor removed, as seen from the navigator's seat of a Mosquito NF Mk.XIII. The receiver unit (bottom) was hinged so as to fold back into the space beneath the indicator unit in order to render access and egress from the cockpit door.

One of the ADGB night fighter Mosquito squadrons, 418 (RCAF) Squadron, was tasked to perform a secondary role on the night of June 5-6, acting as 'flak bait' and drawing searchlights and 'flak' away from the more vulnerable paratrooper and glider dropping transport aircraft. So successful were they, that two of the Mosquitos were actually hit by 'flak', one so badly that it crash-landed near its base at Holmsley South, near Bournemouth, and burned out. Its crew escaped with their lives.

## BEYOND D-DAY
The Mosquito night fighters maintained cover over the beachhead from dusk to dawn from D-Day to D-Day +37. By the end of June 1944, the combined efforts of the six Mosquito night fighter squadrons of 85 (Base) Group had resulted in 76 enemy aircraft destroyed, plus five probably destroyed. In July these six Mosquito squadrons downed a further 55 enemy aircraft and also claimed two 'probables'.

From mid-June, with the Germans launching ever increasing numbers of V-1 flying bombs, many of the night fighter Mosquitos participated in 'anti-diver' night patrols against them, with considerable success. As Allied ground forces overran the V-1 launch sites, the night fighters were able to return to operations over the continent, finding the night air now full of aircraft. However, most were Allied aircraft, and many interceptions ended

with the identification of the target as a 'friendly'. Some though, resulted in the destruction of yet another Luftwaffe aircraft.

As other Allied aircraft, particularly the fighter-bombers, moved on from the landing grounds in France with the advancing Allied ground forces, the 2 TAF night fighter units were able to move to the airfields they had vacated.

The first to do so was 409 (RCAF) Squadron, which deployed forward on August 24. Subsequently, the 2 TAF night fighter Mosquitos advanced with the Allied forces and continued to provide the vital element of air superiority when darkness fell.

## MOSQUITO NF XIII
The first unit to receive the NF XIII Mosquitos was 85 Squadron at the end of February 1943. By D-Day the six 2 TAF night fighter intruders squadrons were all equipped with the Mosquito NF XIII.

The NF XIII was the production equivalent of those Mosquito NF XIIs which had been modified to carry the centimetric AI Mk.VIII radar in a solid 'thimble' nose radome in place of the earlier versions' static aerial systems. This arrangement necessitated the removal of the nose-mounted 0.303 machine guns, leaving the armament as the four 20mm Hispano cannons under the forward fuselage. Later aircraft had the so-called 'universal' or 'bull-nose' radome fitted.

The NF XIII benefited from having the strengthened wing of the Mosquito FB VI, which allowed it to carry underwing fuel drop tanks which increased its range to 1800 miles. Powered by two 1460hp Rolls-Royce Merlin 21 or 23 engines, the NF XIII had a top speed of 370mph giving it a considerable speed advantage over most of the German night fighters and bombers that were its prey.

The NF XIII's AI Mk.VIII was a centimetric radar, operating in the 10cm waveband and employing a dish-based scanning system in place of the AI Mk.IVs static-aerial system. The British invention of the cavity magnetron by the Telecommunications Research Establishment (TRE) provided the necessary leap forward in microwave technology that led to the centimetric radar. The AI Mk.VIII's radar dish was 28in in diameter and rotated at 200rpm, at the same time tilting up and down, and from left to right, thus tracing a spiral scan ahead of the aircraft at up to 45°. A new type of indicator display was developed for the AI Mk.VIII, providing the radar operator with all the information he required on one screen.

The very first victim of a Mosquito NF XIII was a German Me 410 night fighter, shot down on November 8, 1943, by HK367 of 488 Sqn. Subsequently, the NFXII proved to be a very capable night fighter and intruder, it was well-liked by its crews and met with considerable success. ∎

# 'Nighthawks'
## 409 Squadron (RCAF)

Having been formed as a night fighter squadron in June 1941, 409 'Nighthawk' Squadron (RCAF) was, by D-Day, part of 2 TAF's 85 Group and was equipped with the Mosquito NF XIII. In mid-May 1944, the squadron moved to West Malling, near Maidstone, Kent, in preparation for the impending invasion of Europe. In May the ban on night fighters chasing 'bandits' across the Channel (imposed because of the need to keep the AI VIII radar secret from the enemy) was lifted and the crews were also issued with French money and maps. Night intruder operations were on and clearly there was more action to come.

### D-DAY

On June 5, the squadron personnel were briefed by the station commander that the next day would be D-Day. That night, Flying Officer 'Red' Pearce with his navigator, Flying Officer G W Moores (RAF), scored the squadron's first victory in over a year when they attacked and probably destroyed a German bomber over the English coast.

On the evening of D-Day, June 6-7, working with mobile GCI (Ground Control Intercept) fighter control units that had gone ashore with the assault forces, 409 Squadron flew its first sorties over the beachhead. Patrols on the first three nights after the invasion were uneventful; it appeared that, apart from a few scattered raids, the Luftwaffe was late getting into the fray.

On June 9, Squadron Leader R S Jephson, the 'B' Flight commander, got the squadron's first kill over France. Jephson and his navigator, Flying Officer C D Sibbett, were flying on a beachhead patrol when the controller vectored them after a 'bogey'. Sibbett's AI radar soon registered a 'blip' and the navigator brought his pilot on to the tail of a Ju 188. Following standard night fighting procedure, Jephson closed in, identified his target, and then opened fire. His first burst set the enemy's starboard engine on fire, the second started a blaze in the port engine, on the third burst the Ju 188's fuselage disintegrated and the enemy aircraft fell from the sky, exploding as it hit the ground about 30 or 40 miles south-east of Le Havre.

### THREE IN ONE NIGHT

The next night, 409 Squadron experienced the satisfaction of shooting down three enemy aircraft in one night. Flying Officers C J Preece and W H Beaumont distinguished themselves on this occasion by destroying two Ju 188s. Preece knocked down his first victim with a fine piece of deflecting shooting, scoring three times with three bursts. Continuing their patrol the crew were vectored after another 'bogey' about three-quarters of an hour later. Beaumont got a contact on his AI showing the target aircraft to be 2500 yards ahead and he directed Preece onto it. At 1000 yards the pilot gained visual contact with the target and, at 800 yards he was able to identify it as another Ju-188.

Closing to 250 yards, Preece fired a one-second burst. The enemy aircraft exploded so violently that Preece had to pull the Mosquito up sharply, to avoid a wing which broke off the

Junkers aircraft. The third kill that night went to Flying Officers R L Fullerton and P Castellan. Fullerton had a little difficulty getting on to the tail of his target. Finally, after overshooting and re-setting four times, the crew got an AI contact at a range of two miles and this time the interception was straightforward. Two bursts from the Mosquito's four 20mm cannons sent the German aircraft spiralling earthwards with the starboard engine on fire.

To add to the night's achievements Squadron Leader 'Johnny' Hatch, the 'A' Flight commander, returned with one engine unserviceable and shut down, making a perfect single-engine landing at West Malling.

Mosquito NF XIII, with the 'thimble' nose radome for the AI Mk.VIII and underwing drop tanks, at Hunsdon in 1944.

Mosquito NF XIII (this is actually HK382 'RO-T', a 29 Sqn aircraft).

## JUNE 1944

On June 19, the 'Nighthawks' moved to join 410 (RCAF) Squadron at Hunsdon, Hertfordshire, from where they continued their night-time hunting. In the 25 day period from D-Day to June 30, 409 Squadron saw more action than during the previous three years of its night fighting operations.

It flew a total of 227 night sorties, destroyed 11 enemy aircraft, probably destroyed two, and damaged five. It operated over the Normandy beachhead every night except one, June 26, when patrols that had taken off had to be recalled due to deteriorating weather. During the month one of the squadron's Mosquitos was shot down over France and the crew taken prisoner of war. Another aircraft's crew were killed when their aircraft hit high tension wires on returning from a patrol. Two other aircraft were written off in crashes, although the crews escaped injury.

## 'ANTI-DIVER' PATROLS

From the middle of June the squadron began to fly one or two patrols nightly against the V-1 flying bombs which were being launched against England by the Germans. Flying Officers Preece and Beaumont were the first to destroy one of the 'doodlebugs' on the night of June 18; a second fell to Squadron Leader Jephson's guns on June 20.

During the first part of July the 'Nighthawks' were employed almost exclusively on night 'anti-diver' patrols against the V-1s. When the squadron returned to regular night fighting duties over Normandy in mid-July the number of these flying bombs launched against England was reducing as their launch sites were overrun, although it was October before the V-1 attacks ceased completely.

## JULY 1944

In July 1944, 409 Squadron destroyed eight enemy aircraft and damaged another. Six of these were German Ju 88 night fighters. Up until this time 409 had seen little of these aircraft, for it was the German's policy to use them mainly for home defence. As the tide of battle rolled towards Germany,

engagements between the intruder Mosquitos and the Ju 88 night fighters became more frequent. By the end of hostilities 409 Squadron had destroyed 20 Ju 88s, probably destroyed two more and damaged another.

One victory over a Ju 88 on July 26 cost the squadron one of its most experienced crews, Squadron Leader Jephson and his navigator Flying Officer Roberts. They engaged the enemy aircraft over Caen and a burst from Jephson's guns caused it to explode so violently that the Mosquito was damaged by the blast and the debris, and both engines stopped. Jephson reported via R/T that he and Roberts were going to bale out, but on discovering that his navigator was injured and unable to move, Jephson courageously decided to stay with the aircraft, informing the GCI controller that he was going to attempt a crash landing. This was an extremely hazardous undertaking in the dark and, tragically, both of the crew were killed in the subsequent crash.

On August 6, the squadron suffered another fatality when Wing Commander M W Beveridge DFC, the 409 Squadron CO, was killed when his aircraft (MM587) was shot down by a Ju 88 hunting in formation with a Fw 190. Miraculously, his navigator survived a very low-level bale-out, after getting stuck in the escape hatch and being pushed out by his pilot.

Four nights later Squadron leader 'Johnny' Hatch and his navigator, Flight Lieutenant J Eames (RAF), turned the tables on one of these Fw 190/Ju 88 combinations. As they came within visual range of the two aircraft the Fw 190 turned off to starboard; Hatch followed it, knowing full well that the Ju 88 would be positioning on his tail.

Before that could happen though, a two second burst of cannon fire from the Mosquito sent the Fw 190 spiralling earthwards in flames. Hatch turned sharply, looking for the Ju 88, but it had melted away into the night sky and all further contacts turned out to be friendly bombers. A week later Hatch and Eames marked up a double victory, shooting down a Ju 88 after a running fight and then blasting another Ju 88 out of the sky.

## INTO FRANCE

On August 24, the 'Nighthawks' had the distinction of being the first night fighter unit to operate from European soil when the squadron moved to Carpiquet in France. Two weeks later the squadron moved on to St Andre and at the end of September it left that badly battered airfield for Le Culot. The 'Nighthawks' continued to make night kills and also took more casualties, but by the end of the war in Europe the unit had accounted for more than 60 enemy aircraft.■

A Mosquito NF XIII ready for take-off for a night patrol.

# Coastal Command
## Protecting the Flanks

Coastal Command B-17 Fortress Mk.IIA of 220 Sqn patrolling over the Atlantic Ocean.

Leigh Light under the wing of an ASW Liberator.

In the months preceding D-Day, there were signs that the Germans were reducing the number of U-boats operating in the Atlantic, presumably to conserve their submarine forces for the forthcoming invasion. They also started to move some of their Norwegian-based boats into the Atlantic and thence southwards to the English Channel and to the French West Coast ports to reinforce the U-boat flotillas in the Bay of Biscay.

The Allies recognised this and fully realised the threat that could be presented to the D-Day invasion fleets by these U-boats. In addition, the Kreigsmarine had considerable numbers of small warships – fast motor torpedo boats, known as E-boats, and the T-boats, which resembled small destroyers – plus conventional destroyers, midget submarines and unmanned radio-controlled explosive motorboats. If these German vessels and submarines got in among the convoys in the English Channel on D-Day or in the following weeks, as the convoys steamed back and forth across the Channel to resupply the invasion forces, it could be extremely costly and could even threaten the success of the invasion.

The task of preventing this and of guarding the flanks of the invasion fleets fell almost entirely to RAF Coastal Command with some additional assistance from the US Navy's Consolidated Liberator maritime squadrons, which came under the operational control of 19 Group, Coastal Command.

Coastal Command B-24 Liberator GR Mk.V: Equipped with radar, loaded with depth charges and fitted with stub launch rails for rockets, this was one of the German U-boats crews' most feared opponents.

## ANTI-SUBMARINE WARFARE (ASW)

By 1944, Coastal Command was a formidable force. It now possessed some 24 UK-based, ASW squadrons equipped with long-range Consolidated B-24 Liberators, Boeing B-17 Fortresses, Handley Page Halifaxes and some Vickers Wellington land-based maritime patrol and attack aircraft, together with Short Sunderland and Consolidated PB-Y Catalina flying boats. These anti-submarine aircraft were employed in escorting convoys and hunting U-boats in the Atlantic, the Bay of Biscay and the Western Approaches.

From January to the end of May 1944, Coastal Command aircraft sighted and attacked over 100 U-boats; 24 of which were sunk outright, while others were seriously damaged. The tide of war was turning against the German submariners.

An outstanding part of the operations prior to D-Day was Coastal Command's May offensive in the sea areas between Norway, Shetland and Iceland, against the U-boats attempting to redeploy from Norwegian havens to reinforce the Biscay flotillas. The first sighting and attack against one of these U-boats was made on May 16, appropriately by a Norwegian crew flying with the RAF in Coastal Command. During the next fortnight, 12 more U-boats were depth-charged from the air; six of them were sunk and some of the others were forced back to port in Norway.

U-boat hunting at night, when they were most likely to be on the surface, was aided by a number of technological advancements including radar, magnetic anomaly detectors and the Leigh Light. This was a powerful carbon arc searchlight fitted to a number of Coastal Command's aircraft to illuminate German U-boats on the surface at night. The 'nacelle' version fitted under the starboard wing of the Coastal Command

Coastal Command 404 Sqn Beaufighters armed with rockets at Davidstow Moor, Cornwall, June 1944.

Liberators, for example, was a 20in searchlight mounted in a nacelle of 32in diameter slung from the bomb lugs under the wing and producing a maximum beam intensity of 90 million candles.

## ANTI-SHIPPING STRIKE/ATTACK

In June 1944 Coastal Command also had under its control nine squadrons of anti-shipping, strike/attack, fighter-bombers, mostly Bristol Beaufighters. In a sign of things to come, one squadron, 248 Squadron at Portreath, had already re-equipped with the de Havilland Mosquito in the anti-shipping role. (Coastal Command also included a number of Royal Navy Fleet Air Arm squadrons flying antiquated Fairey Swordfish and also Grumman Avengers torpedo bombers). These aircraft would be responsible for protecting the flanks of the invasion fleets from German surface raiders, as well as attacking convoys attempting to re-supply the German forces.

The Coastal Command Strike Wings fought in some of the bitterest and bloodiest engagements of the war, all at low level and at close quarters. They suffered heavy losses, in the same proportion as

Bomber Command, but they inflicted even greater damage on the enemy in relation to their own losses. During the Second World War, the British public was only vaguely aware of the dramatic and ferocious events involving the Coastal Command Strike Wings and their attacks on enemy shipping.

At the time, anti-shipping attacks came under the strictest secrecy, with only brief details being released to the press and the BBC. This secrecy was in place, not least, because of the success of the Government Code and Cipher School at Bletchley Park in decrypting the 'Hydra' code used by the enemy convoys (after acquiring cipher material from the captured U-boat U110 on May 8, 1942).

This intelligence provided accurate and timely information on the movement of German coastal convoys, allowing planned strikes by Coastal Command.

By 1944 the anti-shipping-strike units had honed their tactics against the heavily-armed vessels that were their targets. The concept of operations was to employ closely-coordinated mass formation attacks. Anti-'flak' aircraft, armed with cannons, bombs, or rockets, saturated the heavily

German Navy Schnellboot S-17.

armed shipping with multiple-direction diving attacks. This allowed the torpedo-carrying 'Torbeaus' to carry out their ultra-low-level run-in to their release point through a reduced 'flak' barrage. Engagements between the Beaufighters of the Strike Wings and German surface vessels must be classed as some of the most dangerous and ferocious encounters of the entire war. The sky would be full of shells, bullets and missiles travelling in all directions, with the opponents in full view of each other. Inevitably, casualties were extremely heavy on both sides.

## OPERATION CORK – ASW AFTER D-DAY

The Allied D-Day assault was unopposed by German naval forces, not least because total surprise had been achieved. In subsequent days and weeks, however, the enemy attempted to interdict Allied shipping, but came up against Coastal Command's aircraft in the process. The anti-U-boat operation by Coastal Command was named Operation CORK and comprised continuous day and night air patrols between southern Ireland, the Cornish Peninsula and Brest Peninsula with the aim of preventing U-boats from breaking into the Channel and coastal waters around the South of England.

The plan was that a Coastal Command ASW aircraft would search with its radar every part of the CORK area, from southern Ireland to the mouth of the Loire, 20,000 square miles, every 30 minutes, day and night for an indefinite period. Thirty minutes was chosen because a U-boat was believed to use, in a crash dive, about as much battery energy as could be charged into the batteries in 30 minutes on the surface. If a U-boat had to crash dive every 30 minutes it would show no net gain from charging its batteries while on the surface between dives. If it ever arrived in the fighting-zone it would be with its crew exhausted, little compressed air available to surface and its batteries low on reserves.

Three patrol 'belts' were laid across the western end of the English Channel: two

between the coasts of Cornwall and Brittany, and a third from west of the Scillies to Ushant. From D-Day onwards, for a period of six weeks, twenty-four hours a day, Coastal Command aircraft patrolled these belts on the 'endless chain' principle. After dark the Leigh light carrying aircraft took over.

On D-Day there were 36 U-boats in Bay of Biscay ports. The submarines began moving out on the evening of June 6, but Coastal Command presented a solid wall of air power to the enemy. The submarines were harried almost from the hour they sailed, though at a cost to the aircraft hounding them. The U-boats carried heavy 'flak' defences and, in the first 24 hours after sailing, they shot down four low-flying anti-submarine aircraft, including a Wellington of No 407 Squadron, with the deaths of the six crew members on board. Two Liberators were also lost. In the same period, however, U-955 was sunk and five more U-boats were so damaged they had to return to port.

As the operations progressed so the enemy losses mounted and approximately 24 U-boats were lost between D-Day and the end of June. Total losses to Coastal Command in the month of June were 10 aircraft and 80 airmen. Overall, during these operations, aircraft of Coastal Command flew 2197 ASW sorties in the Channel and Western Approaches; 72 enemy submarines were sighted and 40 were attacked.

## ANTI-SHIPPING STRIKES D-DAY ONWARDS

In the last weeks before D-Day the Beaufighters flew patrols along the enemy coast in search of E-boats and other light naval craft that were operating from bases between Ijmuiden and Cherbourg. Such patrols marked the first stage of operations designed to ensure that the Allied invasion fleets would not be molested by surface craft during their passage to Normandy from ports in southern England.

The main operations were planned to begin on the eve of D-Day, when squadrons of Coastal Command and the Fleet Air Arm would co-operate with surface vessels of the

Allied navies in a wide and complicated pattern of patrols which, it was hoped, would seal both the eastern and western entrances to the Channel.

An example of this activity was the anti-shipping strike force of 10 Mosquitos of 248 Squadron from Portreath along with 31 Beaufighters of 144 and 404 Squadrons from Davidstow Moor, which took off at 6.45pm on June 6, 1944. At 8.15pm the formation spotted a U-boat, but it crash dived. About 40 minutes later, the formation sighted three Seetier Class enemy destroyers on a northerly course at 15 knots. The Mosquitos climbed to give

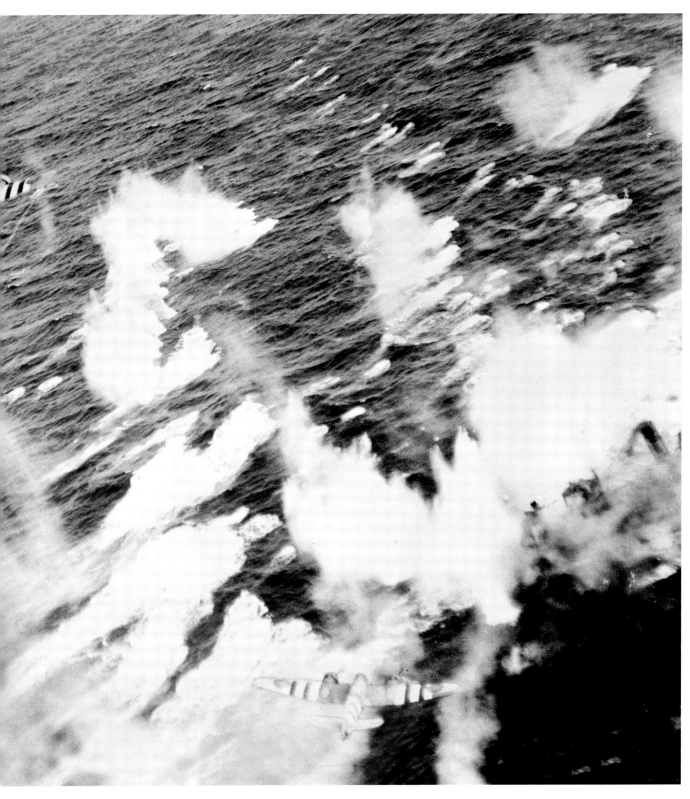

cover and the Beaufighters attacked with Rocket Projectiles (RP) and cannon fire out of the sun. Strikes were observed on the middle of the first ship which caused an explosion and fire; the ship stopped.

The rear vessel received numerous underwater RP hits and sank. The other was hit by RPs, stopped and was left smoking. One Beaufighter was lost to the ships' anti-aircraft fire. On their return to base, the formation saw a Ju 188 shadowing six Allied destroyers. Two of the 248 Squadron Mosquitos attacked. Hits were observed on the cockpit of the Ju 188, and the starboard engine caught

fire. The enemy aircraft rolled on its back and spun steeply into the sea shedding pieces of fuselage.

The overwhelming Allied air and naval power entirely prevented daylight surface attacks on convoys proceeding across the English Channel. They also limited the success of nocturnal attacks. In the first week after D-Day, German E-boats managed to sink only three small freighters, two LST (Landing Ship Tank) transports and a half-dozen small craft; as the enemy surface vessels were returning to their bases at dawn, they were harried by the Coastal Command strike/attack aircraft.

The Coastal Command anti-shipping and strike squadrons flew 1672 reconnaissance and 315 strike sorties during the weeks following D-Day.

## THE RESULTS

At the conclusion of three months of maritime operations, from D-Day onwards, the German naval units and merchant shipping in Western Europe had been hammered unmercifully and the Kreigsmarine had been unable to interfere with the Allied invasion fleets and convoys, largely due to Coastal Command's operations against it. ∎

'Protecting the Flanks of the Invasion'. Six Bristol Beaufighters from 236 Squadron, part of RAF Coastal Command's North Coates Strike Wing, attacking Kriegsmarine E-boats (Schnellboots) near the French coast in June 1944. Hit-and-run raids by these fast German torpedo boats could have posed a significant threat to Allied shipping supporting the D-Day invasion and subsequently resupplying the Allied forces on the Continent. This picture depicts a typical early morning operation to hunt for them. New Zealand Squadron Leader 'Bill' Tacon has led the attack with cannon and 25lb rocket projectiles in Beaufighter TF X NE746 'MB-Q', sustaining some damage to the aircraft in what the squadron's operations record book records as "intense and accurate" return fire. Artwork: Gary Eason

# "Sighted Two Subs, Sank Same"

At 10.14pm on June 7, 1944, Flying Officer Kenneth Owen Moore (RCAF), known as 'Kayo' to his friends, lifted his heavy, anti-submarine Consolidated B-24 Liberator GR Mk.V, coded 'XB-G' off the runway at St Eval, near Newquay, Cornwall. Twenty-one-year-old 'Kayo' Moore was the captain of a crew of nine other airmen (six of them Canadians) who were setting off on a long Operation CORK patrol. They were playing their part in closing the English Channel's south western approaches to German U-boats from the Bay of Biscay and, thereby, protecting the flanks of the Allied invasion shipping steaming back and forth between England and Normandy.

By now Moore had some 30 operations under his belt and had already been credited with crippling a U-boat in action in March 1944. The long-range, 224 Squadron Liberator he was flying could carry a weapon load of 5000lb and had a ferry range of 3300 miles. Carrying a normal munitions load of depth charges, the typical sortie duration for a Coastal Command Liberator on an Operation CORK sortie was 13½ hours. With an air-to-surface radar fitted and the huge Leigh Light under the starboard wing, the aircraft had a genuine and effective night-hunting capability. The weather in the early hours of June 8 was ideal for 'sub' hunting. It was a warm night, the stormy weather of D-Day had dissipated, the sky was full of stars and the moon was bright, laying a silver beam across the calm sea.

Flying Officer 'Kayo' Moore DSO RCAF in the cockpit of a B-24 Liberator.

## ATTACK AGAINST U-441

Suddenly, at 2.11am, the voice of the radar operator, Warrant Officer William Foster, jolted the whole crew to action stations: "Contact dead ahead, range 12 miles." The crew's extensive training and regular practice produced an immediate, calm and well-drilled response. Moore took the big four-engine bomber down to 200ft over the sea and homed in on the radar contact. With two miles to go, he told Foster to switch the radar off in case the submarine had detection equipment. As they reached the position identified on radar, Moore spotted a U-boat off to one side, riding on the surface, clearly illuminated in the moonlight. Swinging round in a gentle turn and letting down to only 50ft he began the attack run from the submarine's beam. The submarine's crew had been caught by surprise and as the sailors ran towards their large calibre 'flak' guns, the Liberator's front gunner opened up on them, hitting some.

The big aircraft flashed over the conning tower of the submarine, and the bomb-aimer, Warrant Officer Johnston 'Jock' McDowell, peering through the low-level Mk III bomb sight, pressed down on the release button.

Six depth charges straddled the U-boat perfectly, three on each side of it. Seconds later the rear gunner yelled: "Oh God, we've blown her clean out of the water." By the time Moore had hauled the Liberator back round, all that he could see was the water still heaving from the explosions, patches of black oil and some dark objects, which were probably bodies, floating among the slicks.

His subsequent report grimly noted: "U-boat was observed to lift out of the sea and disintegrate and was then hidden from view as plumes rose up to full height." U-441 had been sunk with the loss of all 51 sailors on board, the day after her crew had shot down a sub-hunting Vickers Wellington with the deaths of the six RAF crewmen.

B-24 Liberator GR Mk.V, BZ877, '2-Q' of 86 Sqn, the type flown by Moore and his crew on June 8, 1944, and which sank two U-boats on one sortie.

U-441 returning to port in Brest in happier times for her crew. All 51 lost their lives when the U-boat was sunk on June 8, 1944.

A German U-boat crew frantically abandoning their submarine, which is down at the stern and moments from sinking.

'Kayo' Moore (right) with his arm round the shoulders of his bomb aimer 'Jock' McDowell, in front of their Liberator.

## ATTACK AGAINST U-331

Liberator 'XB-G' resumed the patrol and 30 minutes later, the highly improbable occurred. At a range of six miles, just off the coast of Ushant, France, a second radar contact was obtained. At a range of two and a half miles the crew spotted another U-boat on the surface, illuminated in the moonlight, but in a position unsuitable for an attack. Moore muscled the Liberator round in a steep turn, descending to 50ft to attack from the submarine's starboard beam. This second attack was almost a repeat of the first, except that there was 'flak' from the U-boat in an exchange of fire with the Liberator's gunners. The aircraft's depth charges straddled the submarine, two on one side and four on the other.

This time however, the U-boat seemed only to drop a little at the stern and list slightly to starboard. Then mid-upper gunner Don Griese shouted: "She's going down," and as Moore banked round he saw the U-boat's bow sticking up almost vertically out of the water. Then it slid down into the sea stern first and was gone. On the next pass over the spot, the Liberator's Leigh Light illuminated three inflatable dinghies crowded with sailors, floating amid a cluster of debris on a thick black oil slick. This U-boat was U-331; four of the submarine's crew died but the other 47 survived.

## AFTERMATH

Following this second attack and victory, Moore told his wireless operator to send a laconic message to base, which simply read: "Sighted two subs, sank same." This was the war's only double submarine kill by a single aircraft during one patrol. For his gallantry and skill, Moore was awarded the Distinguished Service Order (DSO) effective from August 22, 1944; a United States Silver Star also followed. For their part in the attacks, radar operator, Warrant Officer William Foster, and bomb aimer, 'Jock' McDowell, received the DFC, while the flight engineer, Sergeant J Hammer, was awarded a DFM.

The RAF and RCAF public relations officers and the Press were ecstatic at the achievement of Moore and his crew; they were almost equally delighted to learn that the crew always flew with a good luck mascot, a stuffed teddy bear named 'Dinty', which was dressed in a miniature battle dress, with Canada shoulder flashes, an observer brevet and patent leather flying boots! ∎

Some other members of Moore's 224 Sqn crew with 'Dinty' the mascot. From left they are Fg Off Gibb (navigator), Fg Off Ketcheson (second pilot), WOs Davison, Foster, Greise and Werbeski (all WOpAGs).

# BE PART OF THE HEART

## THEY STAND READY TO FACE DANGER AND UNCERTAINTY EVERY DAY. WILL YOU GIVE THEM THE SECURITY OF OUR SUPPORT?

For over 100 years, every serving member of the Royal Air Force has been ready to protect those you cherish most. Now, you can do the same for them.

After looking after your loved ones, would you consider leaving a gift in your Will to the RAF Benevolent Fund? To be part of the heart of the RAF Family by giving its people the support they need, when they need it. Everything from confidential counselling to mobility aids as well as support for injuries, illness and bereavement.

## TO RECEIVE YOUR FREE GUIDE TO LEAVING A GIFT IN YOUR WILL, CALL 0800 042 1111 OR VISIT RAFBF.ORG/GIFT

SCAN ME WITH YOUR CAMERA